KNOWING THE PAST,
FACING THE FUTURE

Edited by
Sheila Carr-Stewart

Knowing the Past, Facing the Future

INDIGENOUS EDUCATION IN CANADA

PURICH
BOOKS

Purich Books, an imprint of UBC Press
2029 West Mall
Vancouver, BC, V6T 1Z2
www.purichbooks.ca

Printed in Canada on FSC-certified ancient-forest-free paper (100% post-consumer recycled) that is processed chlorine- and acid-free.

Library and Archives Canada Cataloguing in Publication

Title: Knowing the past, facing the future : Indigenous education in Canada / edited by Sheila Carr-Stewart.

Names: Carr-Stewart, Sheila, editor.

Description: Includes bibliographical references and index.

Identifiers: Canadiana (print) 20190166428 | Canadiana (ebook) 20190166444 | ISBN 9780774880343 (hardcover) | ISBN 9780774880350 (softcover) | ISBN 9780774880367 (PDF) | ISBN 9780774880374 (EPUB) | ISBN 9780774880381 (Kindle)

Subjects: LCSH: Indigenous peoples – Education – Canada. | LCSH: Indigenous peoples – Education – Canada – History. | LCSH: Off-reservation boarding schools – Canada. | LCSH: Off-reservation boarding schools – Canada – History. | LCSH: Education and state – Canada. | LCSH: Education and state – Canada – History. | CSH: Native peoples – Education – Canada. | CSH: Native peoples – Education – Canada – History. | CSH: Native peoples – Canada – Residential schools. | CSH: Native peoples – Canada – Residential schools – History.

Classification: LCC E96.2 .K66 2019 | DDC 371.829/97071—dc23

Canadä

UBC Press gratefully acknowledges the financial support for our publishing program of the Government of Canada (through the Canada Book Fund), the Canada Council for the Arts, and the British Columbia Arts Council.

**Honouring
the Blue Quills Native Education Council,
1970–71**

Stanley Redcrow

Ralph Blackman

Theresa Gadwa

Horace Jackson

Donald Janvier

Alice Makokis

Louis McGilvery

Edith Memnook

Eugene Monias

Laurence Mountain

Lawrence Quinney

Margaret Quinney

Emma Steinhauer

Isabelle Steinhauer

CONTENTS

KNOWING THE PAST, FACING THE FUTURE

INTRODUCTION

Sheila Carr-Stewart

> The future of our people looks truly bleak. [We need to]
> reclaim our right to direct the education of our children.
>
> – Harold Cardinal, *The Unjust Society*, 1969

The late Harold Cardinal, in *The Unjust Society: The Tragedy of Canada's Indians*, sought to bring to the forefront the "shameful chronicle of the white man's disinterest ... trampling of Indian rights ... and cultural genocide." This history, he argued, had "atrophied our culture and robbed us of simple human dignity."[1] Cardinal was reacting, in part, to the Liberal government's 1969 *Statement of the Government of Canada on Indian Policy*, also known as the White Paper, which proposed to abolish the Indian Act, close the Department of Indian Affairs, and transfer all responsibility and programs for "Indians" to the provinces.[2] Treaties negotiated and signed by the Crown and First Nations peoples would be abolished because, the federal government argued, they did not benefit First Nations people: "A plain reading of the words used in the treaties reveal the limited and minimal promises which were included in them."[3] The government stated that the treaties' ability to meet "the economic, educational, health and welfare needs of the Indian people has always been limited and will continue to decline. The services that have been provided go far beyond what could have been foreseen by those who signed the treaties."[4] The goal of future policy would be elimination of "Indian status" and assimilation.

Opposition to the White Paper brought First Nations people across the country together in a united front. Leaders argued that the government was simply absolving itself of historical promises and responsibilities, including the treaty right to education, which were enshrined in specific treaties and legislation, including the Indian Act. The Indian Chiefs of Alberta presented their own paper, *Citizens Plus*, often referred to as the Red Paper, to the prime minister in Ottawa in June 1970. *Citizens Plus* in turn led the National Indian Brotherhood to produce *Indian Control of Indian Education* in 1972.[5] The policy paper was the work of Chiefs and Band Councils from across Canada. It sought to change the existing education system and "to give [Indigenous] children the knowledge to understand and be proud of themselves and the knowledge to understand the world around them."[6] The education system as it existed then had been formally established at the time of Confederation, when the federal government, through the 1867 BNA Act, became responsible for the education of Indigenous peoples: Status Indians and some Métis would attend schools on reserves; non-Status Indians and some Métis would attend provincial schools. In response to resistance to the White Paper from First Nations, the federal government withdrew it and accepted *Indian Control of Indian Education* in principle. Canada committed to transferring control of education to Band Councils, which would work in partnership with the federal government.[7]

These promises were made decades ago, yet the provision of a quality education for Indigenous people remains an ongoing struggle. Despite its promise, the federal government failed to initiate new legislation relating to First Nations schools, and on-reserve schools suffer in comparison to their provincial counterparts. The Indian Act barely contains two pages dedicated to education, and there are no formal policies on administration, standards, school building requirements, curriculum, student support, teacher well-being, or

Sheila Carr-Stewart

the involvement of parents, guardians, and communities. Nor is there adequate funding. The funds being provided do not support curriculum development, professional development, leadership training, or counselling.[8] Teachers in First Nations schools are paid less than their provincial counterparts. The result has been a well-documented education gap between Indigenous students and non-Indigenous students in terms of graduation rates and entry into the labour market.

In response, some First Nations have opted out of the Indian Act. In 1998, the Mi'kmaq in Nova Scotia created their own educational system through legislation passed by both the provincial and federal governments. By all measures, it is an excellent system.[9] In 2016, twelve First Nations in Manitoba formed a school division, which has an expanded jurisdiction and receives additional funding from the federal government. In 2018, the four First Nations of Maskwacis joined their eleven schools together into a Cree-based school board governed by the Maskwacis Education Commission. It is funded by the Alberta and Canadian governments. From the Atlantic Ocean to the Prairies, First Nations are taking control of education for their children and communities.

Yet the work is only beginning, as became clear when the Truth and Reconciliation Commission of Canada (TRC) presented its final report in 2015, calling on governments, educational and religious institutions, civil society groups, and ordinary Canadians to take action to overcome the legacy of residential and industrial schools – the government-sponsored boarding schools that began to appear in 1880 with the goal of assimilating Indigenous children to Euro-Canadian culture by separating them from their parents and communities.[10] Because of the TRC, Canadians are becoming more aware of their country's long-term lack of commitment to First Nations education and of the history of broken promises and misguided experiments that has led to the current state of affairs. They are now more aware of how residential schools affected the 150,000 Indigenous people who attended them and the families of the more than 3,200 children who died in them.[11] They are now more aware of the intergenerational trauma caused by the schools and how it has contributed to the current marginalization of Indigenous people.

The TRC issued ninety-four calls to action to advance reconciliation. Items 6 to 12 relate to education and include the following:

8. We call upon the government to eliminate the discrepancy in federal education funding for First Nations children being educated on reserves and those First Nations children being educated off reserves.

10. We call on the federal government to draft new Aboriginal education legislation with the full participation and informed consent of Aboriginal peoples.[12]

The TRC also called for commitments to improve curricula and the success rates of Indigenous students, to protect the right to teach and learn Indigenous languages, and to enable parents to enjoy the same responsibilities and level of accountability as parents in public school systems.[13] Item 11 called on the "federal government to provide adequate funding to end the backlog of First Nations students seeking a postsecondary education."[14] Item 12 called on "the federal, provincial, territorial, and Aboriginal governments to develop culturally appropriate early childhood education programs for Aboriginal families."[15]

Following the release of the commission's final report, Prime Minister Justin Trudeau stated: "We need nothing less than a total renewal of the relationship between Canada and Indigenous peoples ... We will renew and respect that relationship."[16] Thus, nearly a century and a half after Confederation and the introduction of the Indian Act, Canadians are being called upon to address the lack of commitment to Indigenous education across the country and, ultimately, the genocide inflicted on Indigenous people through more than a century of Western educational policies and practices. In response to this call, *Knowing the Past, Facing the Future* traces the arc of Indigenous education since Confederation and draws a road map of the obstacles that need to be removed before the challenge of reconciliation can be met. Part 1, "First Promises and Colonial Practices," explores the colonial landscape of education, including the treaty right to education and the establishment of day, residential, and industrial schools. Part 2, "Racism, Trauma, and Survivance," addresses the legacy of the schools, experienced by today's generation of Indigenous peoples in the form of intergenerational trauma and internalized racism but also in the form of persistence, survival, and revitalization. Part 3, "Truth, Reconciliation, and Decolonization," explores contemporary issues in curriculum development, assessment, leadership, and governance and the possibilities and problems associated with incorporating traditional knowledge and Indigenous teaching and healing practices into school courses and programs.

First Promises and Colonial Practices

Long before Europeans arrived to colonize North America, Indigenous peoples lived and prospered and had their own approaches to education. As self-determining nations, each with their own language, culture, and governance and leadership systems, they adapted to changing environments and "evolved and grew within the spiritual traditions given to them by the Creator."[17] As Cree scholar Verna Kirkness has written, Indigenous education was "an education in which the community was the classroom, its members were the teachers, and each adult was responsible to ensure that each child learned how to live a good life."[18] Children met and overcame the challenges of living off the land, and the environment, in the words of Evelyn Steinhauer, "imposed a discipline that produced resilient, proud, and self-reliant people."[19] As explained by Chief John Snow of the Stoney First Nation, education was interwoven into life, with each member passing on valuable knowledge through the spoken word.[20]

Indigenous knowledge and systems of education were simply ignored when European governments, in their quest for territorial expansion, began to colonize North America. When the French began to explore and settle territory along the St. Lawrence in the early sixteenth century, missionaries played an integral role in colonialism as Catholic priests and nuns sought to convert Indigenous peoples to the Christian faith and to "civilize" them through schools structured on European models.[21] After the British conquered New France in 1760, Protestant missionaries were slow to arrive, but in the early nineteenth century they began to settle in Indigenous communities, where they too sought to Christianize Indigenous people and to change their "manners and sentiments."[22] By the time of Confederation, the Catholic and Protestant churches were engaged in a competition for souls that stretched across the nation and included fifty Western schools for Indigenous students. The majority of church-run schools were funded exclusively by the churches, which paid minimal, if any, salaries to teacher-missionaries. Although the missionaries often learned Indigenous languages in order to communicate with potential converts, they did not recognize Indigenous forms of education and taught within the Western system of education.[23]

Along with missions, treaties were an integral part of the colonization process, and the conventions for treaty making in Canada go all the way back to the Covenant Chain of the early seventeenth century. The first era of treaty making ended with the Conquest, when the King of England, George III, issued the Royal Proclamation of 1763, which laid out the principles of treaty making between Indigenous people and the British Crown. The proclamation stated explicitly that Indigenous people reserved all lands not ceded or purchased by them. Although the Royal Proclamation created a constitutional framework for the negotiation of treaties, Indigenous peoples and the Crown approached the treaties differently.[24] Representatives of the Crown sought clear access to the land and the elimination of all Indigenous claims. First Nations, by contrast, wished to share their land with the newcomers. While treaty commissioners spoke English and had been educated in Christian, Western schools, Chiefs and Counsellors spoke Indigenous languages and had been educated in holistic education systems that had served their people from the beginning of time. At the treaty meetings, the two groups met for days, sometimes weeks. When they separated, the treaty commissioners returned to Ottawa, where they prepared the written treaty document, which was then sent to each Chief. By contrast, First Nations Elders or oral recorders kept the words of the treaties alive in their communities, and the nation's understanding of the treaty was passed along orally from generation to generation until the present day.[25]

When Canada entered into Confederation in 1867, the BNA Act gave responsibility for education to the provinces, but the federal government was responsible for "Indians, and Lands reserved for the Indians."[26] The Indian Act, a consolidation of previous legislation passed by Parliament in 1876, became the main legal instrument through which the federal government administered "Indian" status, local First Nations government, and the management of reserve land and monies. The act also outlined the federal government's obligations, including education, to First Nations.

The new nation of Canada, which only included Nova Scotia, New Brunswick, Quebec, and Ontario at the time of Confederation, expanded quickly as Sir John A. Macdonald pursued his vision of a country that stretched from sea to sea. The federal government purchased Rupert's Land from the Hudson's Bay Company, and the territory became Manitoba and the North-West Territories in 1870. In 1871, British Columbia joined Confederation on the promise of a transcontinental railway, and Prince Edward Island was added in 1873. Before it could build the railway and fill the Prairies with settlers, however, the federal government was required to enter into treaties with the Indigenous peoples who occupied the territories. Between 1871 and 1921, it negotiated a series of eleven treaties, known as the Numbered Treaties, and each one included a statement relating to the provision of schools, which was discussed in detail by Chiefs, Headmen, and the treaty commissioners at the meetings. Chiefs and Headmen had an understanding of Western education based on decades of interaction with explorers, entrepreneurs, missionaries, representatives of the Crown, and early settlers.

As the first of my contributions to this volume shows, Indigenous people knew what they wanted when it came to schools. Chapter 1, "One School for Every Reserve: Chief Thunderchild's Defence of Treaty Rights and Resistance to Separate Schools, 1880–1925," explores how one of the Cree Chiefs in the Treaty 6 area of present-day Saskatchewan defended his vision for a community school that would support both an Indigenous and Western education. Treaty 6, which was signed in 1876, states that "Her Majesty agrees to maintain schools for instruction in such reserves hereby made, as to her Government of the Dominion of Canada may seem advisable, whenever the Indians of the reserve shall desire it."[27] Each of the Numbered Treaties promised First Nations a Western education, one that would not affect their own language and culture but would instead provide a second level of instruction in addition to what they learned from Elders and parents. However, as the evolution of schools at the Thunderchild Reserve shows, the federal government had no desire to administer or pay for education as a treaty right. For the most part, it ignored the Numbered Treaties and instead governed according to the Indian Act, which restricted the role of Chiefs and Councillors in the education of their people and left Indigenous education in the hands of religious organizations, which continued to compete for souls and for meagre federal government funds, often on the same reserve. Although the federal government failed to keep its promise to build and maintain schools, policy-makers made sure that the schools built by churches followed the same rules, norms, and processes as provincial schools and, in Saskatchewan, that meant supporting denominational or separate schools. (In Canada, education is defined as a provincial responsibility. Saskatchewan, Alberta, and Ontario have publicly funded provincial schools that are either Roman Catholic or Protestant.) Although Chief Thunderchild wanted one community school for his nation and cared little whether it was Catholic or Protestant so long as

Sheila Carr-Stewart

it provided a Western education to his people so they could participate in the new economy, he instead got two poorly funded denominational schools that not only sought to Christianize and Westernize children, eliminating the children's mother tongue and culture in the process, but also created divisions in the community. The day schools established at the Thunderchild Reserve ultimately failed. This failure, which occurred in First Nations communities across the country, was blamed on First Nations people rather than on inadequate funding and the government's failure to meet treaty promises. The failure of day schools set the stage for mandatory attendance at residential and industrial schools in the 1880s.

The Indian Act gave the Department of Indian Affairs authority to arrest and fine parents for not sending their children to schools, and it gave the governor-in-council the authority to create residential and industrial schools. In Chapter 2, "Placing a School at the Tail of a Plough: The European Roots of Indian Industrial Schools in Canada," Larry Prochner traces the idea for residential and industrial schools back to their roots: Philipp Emanuel von Fellenberg's farm school for the poor at Hofwyl, near Berne, Switzerland. At the school, teacher and pupils lived together as a family, and the underlying premise was class-based: the rich would attend grammar schools while the poor would work the land to develop the mind. Egerton Ryerson visited Hofwyl before he made his report on schools in Upper Canada in 1847, which led to the opening of a few industrial schools in Ontario.

As Prochner outlines, however, the idea of industrial schools was revived in the 1870s when Nicholas Flood Davin made his *Report on Industrial Schools for Indians and Half-Breeds* in 1879. Davin had been appointed by the government to investigate American schools, also influenced by Hofwyl. In addition, the federal government's interest in the schools stemmed from its failure to support reserve farming. Rather than providing agricultural training for First Nations, the government sought to isolate children in institutions where they would learn manual labour. The turn to residential and industrial schools in the 1880s reflected a policy shift from assimilation to segregation.[28] The first two Indian industrial schools in western Canada – the Church of England's Battleford Industrial School and the Roman Catholic Qu'Appelle Industrial School – opened in the early 1880s. Within a decade, there were more than twenty industrial schools in the West. But the schools deviated from Fellenberg's original model and were quickly seen as a failure because of the "appalling quality of education ... harsh treatment of children by staff, and ... inadequate food and living conditions."[29] They also cost the federal government too much money.

In response, Sir Clifford Sifton, the superintendent of Indian affairs, decided to support cheaper, church-run boarding schools located on or close to reserves. In my second contribution to this volume, Chapter 3, "The Heavy Debt of Our Missions: Failed Treaty Promises and Anglican Schools in Blackfoot Territory, 1892–1902," I draw on mission reports from the Diocese of Calgary to show how these shifts in federal policy affected the provision of educational services in the Treaty 7 area. The churches were left with "the burden of educating Indian" children with limited federal funding. All of the schools established in Treaty 7 territory were initially day schools; however, over time all the denominations established boarding or residential schools. The federal government usually only paid half the cost of school construction, leaving the remainder for the churches and First Nations communities, a clear violation of the Crown's treaty obligation to provide schools and teachers. To make up the difference, churches relied on donations and grants from their adherents in Canada and Europe.

The end result was a system in which Indigenous children were forced to attend poorly financed schools run by missionaries who were paid less than their counterparts in provincial schools and who could barely afford to clothe and feed and maintain the health of their students. Children often spent ten years in residential school, where they were given new clothes and names, separated from their parents and often their siblings, forbidden to speak anything but English, and

Sheila Carr-Stewart

spent a great part of the day performing manual labour or religious observances. Resistance was met with excessive punishment and physical abuse. If they were fortunate enough to survive the regular outbreaks of disease that plagued the schools, children returned to the reserve stripped of traditional knowledge and with skills they couldn't put to use. By 1930, the residential school system included around eight schools, most of them in western Canada and the territories. It wasn't until the 1940s, that both the churches and the government accepted that the schools were ineffective. Following the Second World War, the Senate and the House of Commons appointed a committee to look at the Indian Act, including education. In 1951, the churches were removed from administrating First Nations schools, and all teachers in them were subsequently hired by the federal government. However, they continued to be paid less than their provincial counterparts. Faced with resistance from Indigenous communities at the time of the White Paper, the Department of Indian Affairs took over the system in 1969 and decided to phase out the schools. Some stayed open, however, under the control of Indigenous bands. The last closed in 1996.

Racism, Trauma, and Survivance

In a speech made on May 28, 2015, Supreme Court Chief Justice Beverley McLachlin stated that Canada had attempted to commit "cultural genocide" on Indigenous peoples and that it was "the worst stain on Canada's human rights record." Sir John A. Macdonald's goal at the time of Confederation had been to "take the Indian out of the children," which was, "in the buzz word of the day, assimilation; in the language of the twenty-first century, cultural genocide."[30]

In his contribution to this volume, Chapter 4, "If You Say I Am Indian, What Will You Do? History and Self-Identification at Humanity's Intersection," Jonathan Anuik ties the past to the present by exploring how the federal government's Indian policy and the Indian Act, by defining who and what an "Indian" is, struck at the very heart of Indigenous identity. For instance, when the law was changed so that "Indian" children had to attend residential schools in 1920, the government determined eligibility by looking at whom it had registered as Status Indians under the Indian Act. When these "Indian" children entered the schools, instructors assumed they were dirty, lacked knowledge of science, and were irreligious; they assumed that they, not the children's parents, could best prepare them for the future. Staff, Anuik argues, "conflated being 'Indian' with being damaged by their communities, and they sought to heal wounds inflicted by what were considered to be irreligious and illiterate parents." They instead inflicted new wounds. To overcome this legacy, Anuik stresses that teachers need to be aware of the importance and history (or lack of it) of self-identification. The assignment of labels by governments, schools, and teachers, he shows, continues to affect how students are treated in the classroom and how they think about their own abilities. By showing how he addressed the issue of outside labelling in his own classroom, Anuik offers educators a tool to build learning environments that accurately represent the peoples whom they educate.

In Chapter 5, "Laying the Foundations for Success: Recognizing Manifestations of Racism in First Nations Education," Noella Steinhauer likewise connects the past to the present by showing how historical disparities between provincial and First Nations schools are reflected in negative attitudes towards "rez" schools among some First Nations students and families. Much like substance abuse or violence, these attitudes, she reveals, are manifestations of internalized racism, which includes feelings of "shame for being associated with a population of people who were relegated to reserve communities, where all aspects of their lives were legislated by the government." The first step on the path to success, she argues, is overcoming internalized racism (an individual problem) by viewing it instead as appropriated racial oppression (a sociocultural problem). In order to do this, Steinhauer, along with other contributors to this volume, sees the need for educators to carve out what Willie Ermine refers to as ethical spaces, places where dialogue that respects different worldviews can take place.[31]

Sheila Carr-Stewart

In Chapter 6, "Iskotew and Crow: (Re)igniting Narratives of Indigenous Survivance and Honouring Trauma Wisdom in the Classroom," Karlee Fellner draws on the story of Iskotew and her experience working as a psychology intern with Indigenous children in schools to show that overcoming the past also depends on creating new counternarratives of survivance, resilience, and resurgence. She illustrates how educators can draw on Indigenous ways of knowing, being, and doing, particularly storytelling, to move classrooms and communities from the dominating system, which is rooted and steeped in colonial narratives and labels of deficit and pathology, towards Indigenous approaches that honour trauma wisdom. From an interconnected Indigenous perspective, trauma is not an indication of a pathology; rather, symptoms and behaviours may indicate that an ancestor is trying to communicate a message about how balance, wellness, and healing are needed in a given environment.

Truth, Reconciliation, and Decolonization

While the chapters in Part 2 emphasize the need for educators to understand how the past continues to resonate in the present, influencing everything from how Indigenous students are labelled to how they view First Nations schools, the chapters in Part 3 open a dialogue on how Indigenous peoples and educators can "move beyond memories of the past to begin a journey towards a curriculum based on a shared future." In Chapter 7, "Curriculum after the Truth and Reconciliation Commission: A Conversation between Two Educators on the Future of Indigenous Education," Harry Lafond, a Cree educator and politician, and Darryl Hunter, a white educator, engage in a conversation that identifies potential paths and pitfalls for curriculum over the next few decades. Noting that discussions of curriculum have moved away from trying to figure out how to adapt the current system to meet the needs of Indigenous students, they join others in arguing that Indigenous students need to go out on the land with parents, teachers, and Elders, that they need to experience immersive classrooms so that they can truly understand their cultural values. Decolonizing the current system in order to focus on Indigenous culture, content, worldviews, and belief systems, they warn, will require educators to unearth and explore assumptions and to move beyond the Western paradigm, which focuses almost exclusively on the textbook. Seeing education as a spiral progression, Lafond argues that a school curriculum that respects and honours Indigenous people should be developed at the local level in consultation with Elders, and it should begin with a strong sense of place and connection to the land, moving outward from that "point as youth mature emotionally, spiritually, physiologically, and intellectually in stages." Whereas history is about representing the past, "curriculum is about representing spirit, emotion, thought, and behaviour for the future."

In Chapter 8, "Indigenous and Western Worldviews: Fostering Ethical Space in the Classroom," Jane Preston argues that one of the first steps towards building a curriculum based on a shared future is understanding each other's worldviews, the "lens through which one perceives and interprets life." Because our core values and norms are embedded within us and frequently prevent us from understanding others, in order to improve and renew education, we need to create ethical spaces "where different views, cultures, and life experiences are recognized equally within a mutually respected, balanced team of diverse people."[32] Within the educational world, Preston says, teachers and administrators need to recognize the underlying assumptions of the Indigenous and Western worldviews, which she outlines in a general way, to stimulate greater respect for cultural diversity at all levels of the system, from ministerial teams and school boards to parent-teacher associations and student sports teams. Only then will people accept that for Indigenous people the learning process is the experience of life itself. It is hands on and experiential; it promotes independence, self-reliance, observation, discovery, and respect for nature; and it can't be confined to the classroom.

Community-based initiatives and the Truth and Reconciliation Commission of Canada are already fostering change. In Chapter 9,

"Supporting Equitable Learning Outcomes for Indigenous Students: Lessons from Saskatchewan," Michael Cottrell and Rosalind Hardie relate the lessons learned from key initiatives in the province to close the so-called educational gap between Indigenous and non-Indigenous students. They argue that the term *educational gap* should be viewed as a label that causes more harm than good. It should be seen instead as evidence of an educational debt owed to Indigenous people after more than a century of broken treaty promises. Following the recommendations of the Joint Task Force on Improving Education and Employment Outcomes for First Nations and Métis Peoples, they break down the steps that need to be taken on three fronts: fostering dignified mutual relationships in ethical spaces, reducing poverty and the prevalence of racism, and recognizing First Nations and Métis cultures and languages.

In Chapter 10, "Hybrid Encounters: First Peoples Principles of Learning and Teachers' Constructions of Indigenous Education and Educators," Brooke Madden draws on interviews and observations of early career teachers in Vancouver to show the benefits and drawbacks of trying to include Indigenous content and approaches to learning in the classroom. In this case, the teachers were applying the "First Peoples Principles of Learning," published in British Columbia by the First Nations Education Steering Committee, in the classroom. Although the teachers felt that the principles helped them to embed Indigenous knowledge and worldviews in the curriculum in authentic, meaningful ways, Madden found they overrelied on the document as a support for and authority on Indigenous education. Rather than drawing on the knowledge of local First Nations, they interpreted the perspectives from within the Western paradigm, resulting in pan-Indian or Eurocentric projections of Indigenous knowledge and worldviews in the classroom.

Finally, in Chapter 11, "The Alberta Métis Education Council: Realizing Self-Determination in Education," Yvonne Poitras Pratt and Solange Lalonde bring the volume full circle by showing how the federal government's and courts' ability to define who is Aboriginal or Indian has affected the educational experiences of the Métis, who were "recruited into and excluded from residential schooling on an irregular and erratic basis." The Métis, they argue, have been prevented from speaking with a collective voice, and they outline the steps that have been taken by the Alberta Métis Education Council to assert that voice, and the Métis right to self-determination, in educational programming. Viewing *the United Nations Declaration on the Rights of Indigenous Peoples* and the TRC as guiding frameworks, they advise us to view the places where Indigenous and non-Indigenous knowledge traditions meet not as problem areas but as places of hope and possibility where a truly inclusive model of education can be built.

⋚∣⋛

Since 1867, Canada has supported or been involved in a number of studies and reports that have focused on Indigenous education. At times these reports have created a stir, but the educational landscape of this country has changed very little from colonial times. Western paradigms still reign in the classroom, and self-determination in the realm of education continues to be an unfulfilled dream for many Indigenous people. The report of the Truth and Reconciliation Commission of Canada and initiatives by Indigenous communities suggest that we are poised at a historic moment of change. *Knowing the Past, Facing the Future* identifies the issues that Indigenous people have faced over the past century and a half, and it indicates the steps that need to be taken before the challenge of reconciliation can be met. At a time when decolonizing Canada's education system remains a struggle, the contributors to this volume reveal the possibilities and potential pitfalls associated with incorporating traditional knowledge and Indigenous teaching and healing practices into school courses and programs. Most importantly, the issue of funding is a thread that runs throughout this volume and the history of Indigenous education to the present day. The federal government needs to heed the TRC's call to initiate new legislation on Indigenous education. Some communities, such as the First Nations schools in Nova Scotia have opted out of the Indian Act and for twenty years have administered quality schools that turn out successful students. Their example, and the case studies explored in this volume, show that the best education systems for Indigenous peoples will be connected to the land and created from the ground up rather than cobbled together from the remnants of a colonial system that was never committed to maintaining the treaty right to education or putting Indigenous peoples on the path to success.

Notes

1 Harold Cardinal, *The Unjust Society: The Tragedy of Canada's Indians* (Edmonton: Hurtig, 1969), 1–2.

2 Government of Canada, *Statement of the Government of Canada on Indian Policy (The White Paper, 1969)*, http://aadnc-aandc.gc.ca/eng/1100100010189/ 1100100010191. In this volume, *Indigenous* is used unless specific reference is being made to Government of Canada legal categories, defined by section 35 of the Constitution Act, 1982, in which *Aboriginal peoples* refers to the "Indian, Inuit, and Métis peoples of Canada." In this and in historical contexts, "Indian" is and was used to refer to legally defined identities set out in the Indian Act by the Government of Canada, such as "Status Indian" and "non-Status Indian." The term *Indian* is now considered outdated and offensive. *First Nations* is used to describe Indigenous peoples who are not Métis or Inuit.

3 Ibid., 6.

4 Ibid., 7.

5 National Indian Brotherhood, *Indian Control of Indian Education* (Ottawa: National Indian Brotherhood, 1972).

6 Ibid., 1.

7 Jean Chrétien, letter to George Manuel, President, National Indian Brotherhood, February 2, 1973.

8 Sheila Carr-Stewart, Jim Marshall, and Larry Steeves, "Inequality of Educational Financial Resources: A Case Study of First Nations and Provincial Educational Funding in Saskatchewan," *McGill Journal of Education* 46, 3 (2011): 363–77.

9 Marie Battiste, *Decolonizing Education: Nourishing the Learning Spirit* (Saskatoon: Purich, 2012).

10 Ibid.

11 Truth and Reconciliation Commission of Canada (TRC), *Final Report of the Truth and Reconciliation Commission of Canada*, vol. 1, *Summary: Honouring the Truth, Reconciling for the Future* (Toronto: Lorimer, 2015).

12 TRC, *Truth and Reconciliation Commission of Canada: Calls to Action*, 2012, http://nctr.ca/assets/reports/Calls_to_Action_English2.pdf.

13 TRC, *Final Report*, 320–21.

14 Ibid., 321.

15 Ibid.

16 "Trudeau Promises Full Federal Action on Final TRC Report," *National Observer*, December 15, 2015.

17 Harold Cardinal and Walter Hildebrandt, *Treaty Elders of Saskatchewan: Our Dream Is That Our Peoples Will One Day Be Clearly Recognized as Nations* (Calgary: University of Calgary Press, 2000), 3.

18 Verna Kirkness, "Aboriginal Education in Canada: A Retrospective and a Prospective," in *Approaches to Aboriginal Education in Canada*, ed. Frances Widdowson and Albert Howard (Edmonton: Government of Alberta/ Brush Education, 2013), 8.

19 Evelyn Steinhauer, "Parental School Choice in First Nations Communities: Is There Really a Choice?" (PhD diss., University of Alberta, 2007), 38.

20 Chief John Snow, *These Mountains Are Our Sacred Places: The Story of the Stoney People* (Toronto: Samuel Stevens, 1977), 6.

21 John S. Milloy, *A National Crime: The Canadian Government and the Residential School System, 1879–1986* (Winnipeg: University of Manitoba Press, 1999), 13.

22 Ibid.

23 See J.R. Miller, *Shingwauk's Vision: A History of Native Residential Schools* (Toronto: University of Toronto Press, 1996); and Robert Carney, "Aboriginal Residential Schools before Confederation: The Early Experience," *Historical Studies: Canadian Catholic Historical Association* 61 (1995): 13–40.

24 Roger Maaka and Augie Fleras, *The Politics of Indigeneity: Challenging the State in Canada and Aotearoa* (Wellington: University of Otago Press, 2005).

25 For more on the treaty process, see James Miller, *Compact, Contract, Covenant: Aboriginal Treaty-Making in Canada* (Toronto: University of Toronto Press, 2009) and Michael Asch, *On Being Here to Stay: Treaties and Aboriginal Rights in Canada* (Toronto: University of Toronto Press, 2014)

26 British North America Act, 1867 (UK), 30 & 31 Vict., c. 3.

27 Department of Indian Affairs and Northern Development (DIAND), *Copy of Treaty 6 between Her Majesty the Queen and the Plain and Wood Cree Indians and Other Tribes of Indians at Fort Canton, Fort Pitt, and Battle River with Adhesions*, DIAND publication QS-0574-000-EE-A-1 (Ottawa: Queen's Printer, 1964), 3.

28 See Nicolas Flood Davin, *Report on Industrial Schools for Indians and Half-Breeds* (Ottawa, 1879), https://archive.org/details/cihm_03651; and Sarah Carter, *Lost Harvests: Prairie Indian Reserve Farmers and Government Policy* (Montreal/Kingston: McGill-Queen's University Press, 1990).

29 TRC, *Canada's Residential Schools: The History, Part 1 – Origins to 1939* (Montreal/Kingston: McGill-Queen's University Press, 2015), 453–54.

30 "Chief Justice Says Canada Attempted 'Cultural Genocide' on Aboriginals," *Globe and Mail,* May 28, 2015.

31 Willie Ermine, "The Ethical Space of Engagement," *Indigenous Law Journal* 6, 1 (2007): 193–203.

32 Ibid., 193.

PART 1

FIRST PROMISES AND COLONIAL PRACTICES

1

"ONE SCHOOL FOR EVERY RESERVE"

Chief Thunderchild's Defence of Treaty Rights and Resistance to Separate Schools, 1880–1925

Sheila Carr-Stewart

At the time of Confederation, the vast majority of Canada's settlers were either Catholic or Protestant, and the right to have their children educated in a denominational school of their choice was a significant issue during the Confederation debates, as it is now. The British North America Act, which created the Dominion of Canada in 1867, recognized the right to denominational education. Section 93 stated, "Nothing in any such Law shall prejudicially affect any right of Privilege with respect to Denominational Schools which any class of Persons have by Law." In the following decade, between 1871 and 1877, Indigenous peoples and Crown representatives met to negotiate Treaties 1 through 7. First Nations people agreed to share their land with the newcomers in exchange for a variety of treaty rights, including the provision of schools on reserves whenever requested by a First Nation.[1] Chiefs and Headmen wanted their people to have the opportunity to pursue a Western education while maintaining their own culture, language, and spirituality: Western education would be in addition to Indigenous educational practices.

Treaty discussions and the treaties themselves (written in Ottawa) made no reference to denominational schooling, and adherence to Christianity was limited, at best, among First Nations in the 1870s. But the BNA Act also made the federal government responsible for "all matters related to Indians, and Lands reserved for Indians."[2]

Canada therefore imposed its constitutional commitment to denominational schooling on First Nations people through its educational policy initiatives and the Indian Act, the statute through which the federal government administered Indian status and management of reserve lands after 1876. The Plains Cree Chief Thunderchild, also known as Peyasiw-Awasis, actively resisted the imposition of a Roman Catholic school on his reserve in the North-West Territories (present-day Saskatchewan) and demanded one day school for one community, as had been guaranteed within Treaty 6. Chief Thunderchild's resistance is emblematic of the educational, social, and economic goals of First Nations and the broken promises of the federal government at the time of the Numbered Treaties. He wanted one school for his people and cared little about denominational rights. Department of Indian Affairs records show that his people got caught up instead in competition between the Roman Catholic and Anglican Churches. As the churches competed for new schools and new adherents, they fractured reserve communities into opposing factions, often with the promise of food and other resources, a development that occurred throughout Canada. These divisions ultimately set the stage for the success of off-reserve residential schools and the demise of Thunderchild's dream for strong, community-controlled schools, a dream being pursued today among First Nations throughout Canada.

"Our Lands Were Sold and We Did Not Like It"

On April 13, 1871, William J. Christie, the chief factor for the Saskatchewan District of the Hudson's Bay Company, wrote to inform the lieutenant-governor of the North-West Territories, Sir Adams G. Archibald, that three Cree Chiefs of the Saskatchewan District travelled to Fort Edmonton to meet with him. The Chiefs had said, "Our lands were sold and we did not like it."[3] They asserted, "We don't want to sell our lands ... no one has a right to sell them."[4] The purpose of their visit to Christie was to find out "the intention of the Canadian Government in relation to them."[5] Furthermore, they

Sheila Carr-Stewart

wanted Lieutenant-Governor Archibald, whom they recognized as the Queen's representative, to enter into treaty with them. They demanded "cattle, tools, agricultural implements, and assistance" to help them settle the land and support themselves in the new economy.[6] Within the context of a changing economic landscape, the demise of the buffalo, and the end of the fur trade, in which they had been active participants, the Cree Chiefs recognized the need to participate in the growing farming economy being established in their traditional territories.[7]

Christie, cognizant of the "rapidly increasing population of miners and other white people" moving into Cree territory, advised the Cree Chiefs that commissioners would be sent "to treat with them" according to the "liberal policy" of the government of Canada. He assured them of "fair promises for the future."[8] Christie relayed a promise and approach that dated back to Britain's Royal Proclamation of 1763, which "recognized the right of Indians to unceded lands in their possession, protected the Indians' interest in those lands and provided that rights in the land can be ceded only to the Crown."[9] Britain's Indian policy recognized that First Nations people lived on their traditional land and that "interest in those lands belonged" to them; "only the Crown could buy or accept Aboriginal lands."[10] Christie was fully aware, as were the Cree Chiefs, that during the year prior to his meeting with the Cree Chiefs, Canada had purchased the Hudson's Bay Company's charter to Rupert's Land – territory that stretched 3.95 million square kilometres (1.5 million square miles) south and west of Hudson Bay and that included the Cree's traditional territory.[11] Within the context of British Indian policy, Canada was required to enter into treaty with the original inhabitants of the land prior to opening up the land for settlement and development.[12]

The Cree Chiefs concluded their 1871 meeting with Christie by asking him to invite Lieutenant-General Archibald to "come and see us and to speak with us."[13] As a follow-up to the meeting, Christie, in a letter to Archibald, urged that it is "of most vital importance to the future of the country and the interest of Canada" that a treaty be entered into with the Plains Cree.[14] The Cree would wait five years before the Crown was ready to enter into treaty with them.

Treaty 6: Reciprocity, Equality, and Trust

Canada, on behalf of the Crown, negotiated Treaties 1 through 5 between 1871 and 1875. In 1875, the Reverend George McDougall, who "had been a resident as a missionary amongst these [Cree] Indians for upwards of fourteen years, and who possessed great influence over them," was hired by the governor "to convey ... to the Indians ... that Commissioners would be sent this summer, to negotiate a treaty with them, as had already been done with their brethren further east."[15] Alexander Morris, James McKay, and William J. Christie were appointed as treaty commissioners, and they travelled to Fort Carlton (and later Fort Pitt and Battle River) to treat with the Cree in August 1876. Morris informed the Cree gathered there that he and his fellow commissioners "were the Queen's Councilors" and that, as her servants, they were there "to speak from her to you."[16] After considerable discussion and "counterproposals," representatives of both parties reached a verbal agreement.[17] A written treaty document was subsequently produced by the Crown's representatives. Over the next months and years, other Cree bands adhered to Treaty 6, and First Nations in Saskatchewan and Alberta maintained that the treaty relationship with the Crown was "based on the principles of reciprocity, equality, and trust."[18]

Both parties to Treaty 6 incurred treaty obligations: the Cree agreed to share their land with the newcomers and, in exchange, the Crown agreed to pay allowances, which the Cree could "count upon and receive from Her Majesty's bounty and benevolence."[19] Treaty 6 set aside lands for each band "that desires ... a home of their own" (land that was "reserved ... as long as the Indians wish"), and it clearly stated that "no one can take their homes."[20] Treaty 6 recognized the Chiefs and Headmen as "servants of the Queen" who were responsible "for keeping order amongst their people."[21] In recognition of their roles, the Chief and Councillors were given "suitable uniform[s]

Sheila Carr-Stewart

indicating their office," and each Chief received a medal and a "flag to put over his lodge to show that he is a Chief."[22] Treaty 6 identified a variety of services and goods promised to the Cree people by the Crown, including a health chest to be kept on reserves, farming equipment and instruction, and annual treaty payments of $5.00 per person. The Crown's obligations regarding education were twofold: to instruct children and teach adults to be "self-supporting."[23] In regard to schools, Treaty 6 stated: "Her Majesty agrees to maintain schools for instruction in such reserves hereby made, as to her Government of the Dominion of Canada may seem advisable, whenever the Indians of the reserve shall desire it."[24]

The Indian Act, 1876

The same year that Treaty 6 was negotiated on the Prairies, Parliament in Ottawa, unbeknownst to the Cree, passed the Indian Act.[25] The statute applied "to any band of Indians in any of the said provinces or territories."[26] The act gave power to the superintendent general of Indian affairs (the minister) to govern "the said affairs, and control and management of the reserves, lands, moneys and property of Indians in Canada" and all other matters related to reserves and those who resided on them.[27] Furthermore, the act "laid out a complete blueprint for nearly every aspect of reserve life ... [and was] explicit in prescribing how reserve lands could be managed ... what social and cultural practices ... could be carried out ... how [First Nations people] should be educated and what form their political institutions should take."[28] In *Enough to Keep Them Alive*," scholar Hugh Shewell argues that the Indian Act placed "emphasis ... on subjugating Indians and preparing them for assimilation into the Canadian society and nationhood."[29] Between 1876 and 1927, the Indian Act was amended twenty-four times, each time articulating and widening the power of the superintendent general of Indian affairs. By extension, these amendments widened the role of Indian agents, the government's representatives on reserves, in the day-to-day life of First Nations people.

Conversely, the Indian Act increasingly limited the authority of Chiefs and Councillors. The act defined the role of the Chief and Council in the education of community members, stating that they could "frame, subject to confirmation by the Governor in Council, rules and regulations" related to "the construction and repair of school houses, council houses and other Indian public buildings."[30] In 1880, the act was amended further to enable the Chief and Council to frame rules and regulations pertaining to the "religious denomination of the teacher" hired to teach in schools located on the reserve.[31] The act stated that the teacher "always ... shall be of the same denomination as the majority of the band" but that the Catholic or Protestant minority could have a separate school with the approval of and under the regulations of the governor-in-council.[32] The clause, Shewell argues, reflected the government's "determination to make the Indians into imitation Europeans and to eradicate the old Indian values through education [and] religion."[33] Further amendments in 1894 vested the superintendent with the power to make all regulations pertaining to education,

> in addition to any other provisions deemed expedient. [He] may provide for the arrest and conveyance to school, and detention there, of truant children and of children who are prevented by their parents or guardians from attending; and such regulations may provide for the punishment, upon summary conviction, by fine or imprisonment, or both, of parent and guardians, or persons having the charge of children, who fail, refuse or neglect to cause such children to attend school.[34]

The governor-in-council was also given the authority to "establish an industrial school or a boarding school for Indians, or [to] declare any existing Indian school to be such industrial school or boarding school."[35] Solidifying the federal government's control, the 1894 amendments ensured the "committal by justices or Indian agents of children of Indian blood under the age of sixteen years, to such industrial school or boarding school, there to be kept, cared for and educated for a period not extending beyond the time at which such children shall reach the age of eighteen years."[36]

In contrast to the all-encompassing power of the superintendent general of Indian affairs, the involvement of Chiefs and Councils was restricted in 1920 to inspections: "The Chief and council of any band that has children in a school shall have the right to inspect such school at such reasonable times as may be agreed upon by the Indian agent and the principal of the school."[37] The Indian Act changed little until it was revised in 1951. Even then, the sections and clauses pertaining to education have survived, with only minor revisions and additions, to the present day.

Schools in the North-West Territories

Treaties 1 through 6, made between 1871 and 1876, required the federal government to "provide schools and teachers for the Indians when they settled on their reserves."[38] However, it was slow to meet this obligation because of financial considerations, and it did so unevenly.[39] In 1881, the Department of Indian Affairs adopted regulations whereby teachers in the North-West Territories would be remunerated at an annual rate that was not to exceed $504; in schools supported by a church, however, the department's annual contribution to a teacher's salary would be limited to $300 per year.[40] Across the Prairies, schools were established and operated predominately by Roman Catholic and Protestant church societies, and in 1885 the Department of Indian Affairs reported that 4,789 Indian pupils were attending school across Canada; 1,823 of them were in Manitoba and the North-West Territories.[41]

The quality of education on reserves and the federal government's reluctance to fund schools became an issue immediately. In 1883, the Indian commissioner, Edgar Dewdney, recommended to the prime minister a "carrot-and-stick philosophy" to improve education on reserves.[42] He recommended that the number of students required for the establishment of a school be reduced from twenty-five to twenty and that the students be a mix "between six and fourteen years of age." He also recommended that teachers' salaries be increased to $500 annually, that public school inspectors visit reserve schools, that parents who send their children to school be rewarded with midday meals and clothing, and that $200 rather than $100 be spent on the construction of schoolhouses.[43] The prime minister agreed in principle with Dewdney's proposal but noted that the existing federal "annual expenditure on education in the North-West Territories was $4,780 while the proposed scheme would cost a total of $16,165."[44]

Recommendations for increased expenditures on First Nations education were not implemented. Canada continued to rely on religious denominations to supplement the standard teacher's salary of $300 per annum. In a reference to the schools in the Battleford Agency in the newly formed province of Saskatchewan, the Indian agent noted:

> The teachers of all these schools have been receiving a uniform salary of $300.00 per annum, from the department, supplemented in two instances by an allowance of $60 for extra services, to which has usually been added by the Church of England $100 per annum ... in a few instances the salary has been more than earned through the untiring and unselfish efforts of the teachers; and it is gratifying to all interested in this work that by a recent departure the salaries of the day school teachers are not to continue uniform, but the more deserving are to receive recognition according to merit.[45]

Although the new policy was promising, increased salary for merit was rarely awarded. Only two awards for merit were award in the Treaty 6 area, and they were allocated as financial prizes for the management of schools. In 1885, Rev. J. Hines, the teacher at Assessippi, received $100 as first prize for the management of a school, while $60 was awarded to J.A. Youmans.[46] With these exceptions, teachers in First Nations schools continued to receive the standard salary. In his

Sheila Carr-Stewart

yearly report for 1896, the deputy superintendent general of Indian affairs, Hayter Reed, recognized that it was difficult to attract good teachers because of "the salaries the department has been in the habit of paying."[47] More than a decade later, he reported that day schools were frequently closed because of an "inability to secure teachers," particularly those "with certificates."[48] Reed argued that it was advisable to attract teachers who are "possessed of patience and energy and have a knowledge of farming."[49]

By offering teacher salaries below those paid in provincial schools, the federal government guaranteed that it would be difficult to recruit teachers for reserve schools. The Department of Indian Affairs noted that "only in exceptional cases is it possible to procure duly qualified teachers, owing to the meagerness of the remuneration."[50] Canada's reliance on the churches to provide and support teachers for reserve schools led Indian Affairs to note that an "informal union between church and state ... exists, and all Canadian Indian schools are conducted upon a joint agreement between the Government and the denominations as to finances and system."[51] Focused on expenditures rather than on educational outcomes, the federal government held a minimalist attitude towards the provision of education for First Nations people and desired "a proper return for the large outlay of funds" on First Nations education.[52] In 1902, it was noted that "the majority of pupils do not reach even the third standard during their school life."[53]

Over the next decade, the number and type of schools in Manitoba, Saskatchewan, and Alberta expanded to include day, boarding, and industrial schools, and the federal government's expenditures expanded along with them.[54] In 1913, Duncan C. Scott issued instructions to Indian agents, noting that "educational advantages are provided for the Indians in day, boarding and industrial schools" and that agents "should give earnest attention to the administration of the schools, and efforts should be made to increase efficiency."[55] Little attention was focused on student achievement. Rarely did Indian agents or school inspectors see any benefits of day schools.

With a focus on cost effectiveness rather than on educational attainment or the students' and communities' needs, day schools were frequently faulted for a variety of reasons. Lack of student attendance at day schools was consistently highlighted by members of the Department of Indian Affairs. The superintendent general did acknowledge, though, that the "scattered settlement upon Reserves, renders it most difficult to obtain the attendance of children at day schools, and that in winter, owing to lack of clothing, and the distances between their homes and the schools," it was difficult for children to walk the considerable distance to the school.[56] Others recognized that the "health of the Indians has had much to do with the irregularity of attendance."[57] Some Indian agents simply stated that parents did not "wish to see their children educated."[58] W.J. Chisholm, inspector of Indian agencies, argued that the lack of student attendance was the result of parents who did "not appear to recognize any authority or influence in this matter. There is utter indifference among them as to the benefits to be derived from the school."[59] Chisholm also commented, "I have found that day schools with few exceptions [are] suitably furnished with desks, stoves, pails, washbasins, towels, brooms, and so forth, and properly equipped with maps, black-boards, slates, books, and other stationery; all of which the government supplies; but in a few instances there has been a neglect in connection with fences, repairs, and the supply of fuel, which are provided by the bands."[60]

Chief Thunderchild: A Voice of Self-Determination

The Indian agent, with seemingly unbound power over all aspects of reserve life and the people, controlled the delivery and format of Western education and often excluded the community's input and desires. Chief Thunderchild questioned that control and championed his peoples' treaty right to education. Chief Thunderchild was born in 1849 and died in 1927. His life spanned from a time when the Plains

Cree controlled their territory and the buffalo chase to the Numbered Treaties and what he referred to as life "fenced into reserves" in central Saskatchewan under the unrelenting control of the Indian Act.[61] Chief Thunderchild led a band of thirty families. He had a "profound respect for the values" of his community and an "instinctive feeling" and a "deep concern for his people."[62] He was respected "for his wisdom and generosity and for his concern for the elderly, children, and those least able to look out for themselves."[63] A proud Cree, Chief Thunderchild toiled to ensure the unity of his people and, as a leader, encouraged them to "use love, and work out your own future. Do what is right."[64] He urged his people to share with one another, whether it be food or land.[65] The spirit of loyalty to the tribe was, for Chief Thunderchild, one of the finest qualities life bred into the Indian character.[66] The young men in his band were "loyal and truthful men," and Chief Thunderchild believed that "if a nation does not do what is right according to its own understanding, its power is worthless."[67]

Chief Thunderchild was not a part of the Cree delegation that journeyed to Fort Edmonton in 1871 to meet with Chief Factor Christie, but, like other Cree leaders, he was aware of the treaty negotiations between the Crown and other First Nations that had taken place east of their traditional lands and that culminated in Treaties 1 through 5. Chief Thunderchild attended the Treaty 6 negotiations at Fort Pitt in 1876 and "spoke eloquently" on behalf of his people. He "told those assembled for the treaty negotiations that he did not want to be cooped up on a reserve and that he, along with his followers, wanted to roam the prairies, following the buffalo as they always had. He urged the Cree not to abandon their ancient and proud heritage of freedom, self-reliance, and strong sense of identity."[68]

Refusing to sign the treaty at Fort Pitt in 1876, Chief Thunderchild asked, "What is five dollars a head for this land?"[69] For the next three years, he and his band pursued their traditional lifestyle, taught the young the ways of their people, and traversed the western prairie as they hunted for food. In search of the few remaining buffalo herds,

Chief Thunderchild and his band travelled in vain to hunt buffalo in Montana. Then, facing starvation, they returned to Treaty 6 territory. Indian Commissioner Dewdney was determined, however, "to use hunger to crush any nontreaty opposition."[70] He chose to give food rations only to those who took treaty. Their traditional sustenance from the buffalo no longer viable, Thunderchild's band adhered to Treaty 6 at Sounding Lake in August 1879. As his people accepted treaty, Chief Thunderchild stated, "I'm giving up my land, the animals that grow, the fish that are in the lakes, giving it all up to you. I trust that you will be able to provide me with the same thing as God has provided me in giving me this land."[71]

Chief Thunderchild's leadership of the band was confirmed by the Government of Canada.[72] Despite his initial reluctance to agree to Treaty 6, Chief Thunderchild wanted his people "to accept the necessity of change and to adapt to it without losing their identity as Indians."[73] He and his followers settled on their reserve lands in 1880. The lands were located west of Battleford in the Battleford Agency and were known as the Thunderchild Reserve. The reserve was described as having "advantages with regard to soil and wood. It has also the additional advantage of hay lands on the north side of the river."[74] A decade after adhering to the treaty, the Indian agent noted that "everything indicates progress on this reserve ... with the whole extent of the land under crop" and "the houses recently erected being neat structures, having wooden floors besides windows, and the dwellings generally on the reserve may be described as being comfortable."[75]

As settlers established farms and businesses around the reserve, Chief Thunderchild recognized that his people needed new skills; he recognized the necessity for change and that he wanted his people to live in "two worlds." Cognizant of the Crown's treaty obligation to maintain a school on the reserve "whenever the Indians of the reserve shall desire it," Chief Thunderchild insisted on "one school ... for every reserve."[76] Chief Thunderchild's demand for adherence to the Numbered Treaties and the provision of one school per community brought him into conflict with the government, which relied not on the Numbered Treaties but on the Indian Act as a mechanism to fulfill its responsibilities.

With Canada's commitment to the Numbered Treaties in abeyance (the federal government simply ignored them until the 1980s), educational services for First Nations people was limited to the parameters set by the Indian Act. Furthermore, Canada chose sections of the BNA Act that identified education as a provincial responsibility as a policy backdrop for First Nations education. It applied a specific section of the BNA Act that referred to denominational schools in the four founding provinces to First Nations children. It stated: "Nothing in any such Law shall prejudicially affect any right of Privilege with respect to Denominational Schools which any class of Persons have by Law in the Province at Union."[77] While Chiefs and Headmen, particularly across the West, wanted their people to have the opportunity to pursue a Western education, they did not associate it with Catholicism or Protestantism. Treaty discussions had simply focused on schools being built on reserves. Canada chose to impose the constitutional commitment to denominational schooling, which was important to Canadians in general, on First Nations peoples. Canada also looked to Ontario's education system and curriculum requirements as guidelines for First Nations schools.

Thunderchild Day School

Chief Thunderchild agreed that he would let the first missionary who visited the reserve build a school.[78] With the permission of Chief and Council, the Church Missionary Society (CMS) – an arm of the Anglican Church of England – established a day school in a house on the reserve. Thunderchild Day School opened, under the auspices of the CMS, in October 1885, and in its first year it attracted twenty-nine pupils, with an average daily attendance of eighteen. It was one of five Protestant schools in the Battleford Agency and one of a growing number of day and boarding schools, both Protestant and Roman Catholic, established in the North-West Territories. Members of the Thunderchild Nation maintained the school building and grounds and provided the fuel to heat the building.

In 1888, Indian agent P.J. Williams reported that all schools in the Battleford Agency had been "supplied with comfortable desks and seats, and a cupboard and table where all slates, and books can be put away when the school closes."[79] The furniture was made at Battleford Industrial School, which had opened in 1883.[80] One year later, however, the Indian agent noted that the Thunderchild Day School building was "entirely unfit for school purposes, condemned and new one recommended."[81] When the agent returned in 1894, the previously condemned "building had been willowed and plastered on the outside."[82] A year later, the agent noted that "the building [was] in good repair and school material plentiful." The following year, the school grounds included a fence and a small garden.[83]

The school's curriculum was dictated by the Department of Indian Affairs, and teacher training did not seem to be a requirement: all teachers were associated with the CMS, which supplemented their salaries. The first teacher was John Hope, "a native" and "a most painstaking and faithful teacher [whose] work is producing the best results."[84] Hope taught at the school for three years before moving to Sweet Grass Reserve in June 1888. In 1886, during the school's first year of operation, the school had the following enrollments: reading and spelling (23), writing (14), arithmetic (15), music and singing (20), and drawing (29).[85] When an Indian agent inspected the school in 1888, he noted that Hope graded the students "too high" and reported that of the eleven students who were present at the time of his inspection, only three were in Standard 2 while the remainder were in Standard 1. Only a few students knew "more than the alphabet."[86]

The curriculum at the time was graded from Standard 1 through 6 and covered a variety of subjects.[87] The English curriculum for Standard 1 required the recognition of simple sounds and words, the copying of words, and the ability to make sentences. Standard 6 required a "general knowledge" class and, for English, analysis of simple sentences, orthography, and oral and written composition.[88] In addition to English and general knowledge, classes included arithmetic, geography, ethics, recitation, and history.[89] The curriculum also included what were referred to as "industries" – gardening, making baskets, and knitting socks and mitts – which were later called "domestic science" and "household economy." School gardens were considered an "impetus" to education.[90]

After Hope left, the teachers included a Mr. C.T. Desmarais, who taught from 1894 to 1896 and was identified as "a good teacher," and Mr. M.B. Edwards, who taught in 1903 and was "held in high esteem by the Indians."[91] In 1894, the Indian agent recorded that the school had thirteen students in Standard 1, two in Standard 2, and three in Standard 3.[92] During an inspection the following year, he noted that Chief Thunderchild had been "present and took quite an interest in the [exam] proceedings during the ... inspection of the school."[93] Chief Thunderchild visited the school on other occasions, and the agent noted that two of the Chief's children attended the school.[94] By 1896, the school had a total enrollment of twenty-two pupils: sixteen in Standard 1, four in Standard 2, one in Standard 3, and one in Standard 4.[95] Although Mr. Edwards was held in high esteem, the agent noted that his replacement, Mr. G.F. Gibbs, held "excellent qualifications [but] has no influence whatever with the Indians, and without it he can have little success."[96] In 1907, Solomon Buller, "a recently discharged pupil of the Battleford Industrial School," became a teacher at the school. In his first year of teaching, the agent noted that his "scholarship is sufficient, but he lacks the special training necessary for this work, and like many inexperienced youths appears also to lack a sense of responsibility in regard to the discharge of his duties." Visiting Buller's classroom a month after this note, the agent noted "some slight evidences of an effort on the part of the teacher to improve the methods of instruction employed, and I suggested briefly some useful exercises by which the ordinary routine of the day could be varied with pleasure to the pupils as well as great advantage."[97]

Chief Thunderchild's Struggle for One Community School

For the people of Thunderchild Reserve, education was important but "the religion of the white man [was of] very little interest."[98] Thunderchild Day School nonetheless became a site where ongoing competition between the Roman Catholic and Protestant churches played out in the context of Euro-Canadian demands for denominational education. Throughout negotiation of the Numbered Treaties, First Nations people had been "assured ... that the treaty would not lead to any forced interference with their mode of life."[99] Chief Thunderchild was particularly concerned with maintaining Cree culture and spirituality and a cohesive community, as his people had done prior to entering into treaty. He believed that a single school on the reserve would keep the community together and, at the same time, assist both adults and children to learn new skills and participate in the new economy. He had allowed the Church of England to establish a day school on the reserve because it had been the first to ask, but the Chief and Council made it clear that "they did not want a second" school established on their reserve.[100]

On July 12, 1889, however, Hayter Reed, who was then Indian commissioner for the North-West Territories, wrote to the Roman Catholic bishop, Vital-Justin Grandin: "One of your missionaries at Battleford, has commenced the erection of a church on Thunderchild's Reserve, and as it is reported to me, against the open opposition of the majority of the band, and without the sanction of the Superintendent General, it is feared this may lead to some trouble." The following year, the Indian agent for Battleford, P. Williams, reported to the Indian commissioner that on May 7, 1880, he had attended a meeting on the Thunderchild Reserve at the request of the Chief. The meeting took place in the day school, and those in attendance included the farm instructor, the interpreter, Williams's teamster, and all "of the male population of the Reserve." When Williams asked the purpose of the meeting, he was informed by Chief Thunderchild that "Father Couchin had taken possession of a house on the Reserve and was putting it in shape to teach school." Williams subsequently asked Father Couchin to "desist further action until the Department was consulted and their sanction obtained." He also promised to overcome opposition to a second school.[101] Williams reported that "several of the Indians present said it would be good to have two schools because then they would be likely to get more tea and tobacco than if there was only one, but would not promise to send their children to a separate school."[102] At the conclusion of the meeting, the Chief and Council asked Williams "to protect their rights, stating that they understood that the Reserve was for the Indians and unless they wished it no one should be allowed to infringe on their property."[103] At a subsequent meeting with Reed, Chief Thunderchild informed him that he understood that in other First Nations communities, "wherever more than one denomination had been allowed on a Reserve, division of interests and dissensions among the Band had been observed to ensue."[104]

At the time, the teacher at the day school was the Reverend Donald D. MacDonald, a Church of England missionary. Father Couchin objected to Catholic children attending a school where Protestant religious instruction was being given. In response, MacDonald chose not to "read the Scriptures or give any religious instruction whatever, preferring to live in peace with all parties and confin[ing] himself to teaching religion on Sunday." Despite the Thunderchild Nation's demand that its treaty rights be protected, and even though the Protestant teacher had shown goodwill, the prime minister, John A. Macdonald, assured Archbishop Taché of the Diocese of St. Boniface that

> under no pretext are any of the Government officials to insist on the Indians sending their children to a school where their religious faith will be imperiled or not respected ... and that Catholic Missionaries shall be at liberty to exercise their ecclesiastical functions wherever there are Catholics or infidels and that the Department will see that the missionaries are in no way interfered with ... It is the aim of the Department to allow both Protestant and Catholic Missionaries

as much freedom in the exercise of their calling among the Indians as possible.

Reed, however, noted that, in dealing with church and school matters, "it must be borne in mind that while an Agent might be favourable to carrying out the wishes of a Missionary, the Indians might object, and as, under the privileges granted to them by the Treaty, the Department is bound to recognize their wishes in all matters appertaining to their Reserves." In reference to the situation at the Thunderchild Reserve, Indian Affairs noted that "the proposal is contrary to the wishes of the Chief and majority of the Band, and therefore it cannot be seen that the Department would be doing right, or that it would have any authority to authorize the establishment of another Church or School on the Reserve without the consent of the Indians."[105]

Nevertheless, it was argued that the Indian Act guaranteed a second school for "the minority" and that the "Treaty on the subject of Schools reads – And further, Her Majesty agrees to maintain Schools for instruction in such Reserves hereby made, as to her Government of the Dominion of Canada may seem advisable, whenever the Indians of the Reserve shall desire it."[106] Continuing to demand the establishment of a Roman Catholic school on the Thunderchild Reserve, the Bishop of St. Albert wrote that he "did not feel at ease ... with the persecution ... with regard to the Roman Catholics of Thunderchild's Reserve. You may rest assured in advance that I shall not cease to protest against such way, and that I shall only yield to force. I am grieved that the Government being made aware of this persecution should have approved it [and] is not stopping it at once."[107]

By December 1890, Father Couchin's efforts to establish a Catholic school on the Thunderchild Reserve were causing discord in the community. Food – a commodity scarce on the Prairies at the time – was being used to tempt new adherents to Catholicism. Agent Williams noted that "the priest fed them better than the Department did."[108] Williams, aware of growing strife in the community, wrote that if Father Couchin "persists in having a school in the Reserve, I fear there will be trouble as the Chief and his followers were deter-mined to resist it by force."[109]

Competition between the Roman Catholic and Protestant churches marred relations in the community. MacDonald wrote to Reed that

> the Indians were living at peace with one another and all seemed to work ... til the present Roman Priest Rev. Mr. Couchin arrived, and shortly after his arrival discord seemed to enlarge itself among the Indians till it has gone so far that the Reserve seems to hold two distinct classes of people who are daily at variance with one another, thereby causing their chief and the Indian Department, as well as ourselves, a great amount of trouble.[110]

MacDonald added that "Chief Thunderchild tries all he can to unite his Indians, but is unable to manage it, as the Priest tries all he can to keep the Indians from conforming to the wishes of their Chief."[111] MacDonald likened the priest's actions to when the "papists ... estab-lished a second school on Sweet Grass Reserve when only one school was wanted ... We [CMS] left because there were only a few children on the Reserve to warrant one school."[112]

Williams wrote a letter to Commissioner Reed in which he en-closed the "application from the Rev. Couchin applying for a Catholic school on Thunderchild Reserve giving the names of nearly all the male population of the Reserve as his supporters and who he states are clamoring for a Catholic school." In his reply, Reed wrote, "I know for a fact that not one of these Indians are asking for a school. The Chief and the majority of the names attached to the application asked me last summer to prevent the Priest from building or having a school on the Reserve, they said one school was all they wanted." In his letter, Williams had noted his personal distaste for Father Couchin: "There is no difficulty to get the children to go to the Protestant school or to the Catholic school if they had one, but the whole trouble is with the Priest ... I do not want this Priest on the Reserve."[113]

Father Couchin's superior then wrote to Reed that he was "grieved that the Government being made aware of this persecution (of Roman Catholics' right to denominational schooling) should approve [Thunderchild's wish to have only one school on his reserve] ... I shall not cease to protest against such ways, and ... I shall only yield to force."[114] In 1891, without the knowledge and consent of the Chief and Council, the Department of Indian Affairs granted the Roman Catholic Church permission to establish a school on Thunderchild Reserve. The priest held classes in a building that had previously served as a house for Thunderchild band members. On April 2, the Indian agent informed Reed that the "Chief and his followers have torn down [the] separate school lately erected on Thunder Child's Reserve"; the agent, in return, was told to "to use your utmost endeavors to bring about Peace between the two parties on Thunderchild's reserve and aid in erection of a second school building."[115] A second Roman Catholic school was erected and subsequently destroyed.

The Bishop of St. Albert wrote to Reed: "It appears that the too famous Thunderchild has, for the second time, destroyed the Catholic school ... on his reserve ... without any other reason than to show his opposition to the Catholic school ... I shall not fail against any other obstacle, to see that justice is done and requested that Thunderchild be prosecuted."[116] In response, Reed noted, "With regard to punishing him for what he has done, I may inform your Lordship for several reasons I am unable to agree to the wisdom of pursuing such a course."[117] Reed stated further:

> Without in any way desiring to minimize the gravity of the offence, I must point out that Chief Thunderchild was convinced from his understanding of the Treaty stipulations, that he was vindicating his rights, in resisting the establishment of a school on his Reserve without his consent ... He contended that no land could, under Treaty situations, be taken or occupied in the Reserve for such purpose, without permission of the Band.

Sheila Carr-Stewart

Reed informed the bishop that Thunderchild, "in pulling down the school building," had done so "with his flag flying and his [treaty] medal worn in the Queen's name." Furthermore, Thunderchild had "repudiated the charge of prejudice against the Roman Catholic Church as such, and declared that his people had attached themselves to the Episcopalian Church for the one reason that it was the first to interest itself in them since their advent to the Reserve. This being so, he, although a Pagan, considered that the first comers had the better claim."[118]

At a meeting between the commissioner and members of the Thunderchild Reserve, Reed informed the gathering that "the Chief had assured me that he had acted in no spirit of lawlessness, but in defense of his rights, as he understood them."[119] Reed subsequently noted that "while he took no vote on the matter ... there were very few of the Band not present at the meeting ... [and those who] were in favor of the Roman Catholic school ... were in the minority."[120] However, faced with unrelenting pressure by the Catholic Church, the ever-present authority of the superintendent of Indian Affairs, the government's need to protect denominational education rights, and growing division among his people, Chief Thunderchild acquiesced to the construction of a Roman Catholic school at the west end of the reserve. Reed stated that "the Indians would help with the reconstruction ... while students from the [Battleford] Industrial School would finish off the building as soon as possible."[121]

Catholic and Protestant denominational schooling had been imposed on First Nations people. The failure of Thunderchild's struggle to maintain his treaty right to have only one school in his community demonstrated not only the power of the federal government over the daily lives of his people but also its power to create discord in Indigenous communities. The distribution of food and other promises by the clergy divided the community and had a considerable effect on school attendance. As the struggle to impose denominational schooling waged, and when the Roman Catholic Church opened a residential school near the reserve in 1901, attendance at the Anglican-run Thunderchild Day School plummeted: in 1906, there were only six students enrolled.[122] The school closed on June 30, 1909. Although the Roman Catholic Church attracted more students, it likewise operated for a limited time, from 1891 to 1897: its enrollment decreased from a high of twenty-five students in 1891, to fifteen in 1894, and only eight in 1896.[123]

⋜⏐⋝

The efforts of Chief Thunderchild and his people to maintain one day school on their reserve, as promised by Treaty 6, were secondary to Canada's constitutional guarantee of denominational schooling for settler children. Gradually, across the North-West Territories, on-reserve day schools, whether established by Roman Catholic or Protestant organizations, closed as Canada, following the example of the United States, implemented an educational policy focused on boarding schools (later referred to as residential schools). At the time of Commissioner Reed's visit to the Thunderchild Reserve, "many opposed ... sending their children to Industrial school."[124] But the community's concerns were once again ignored. Mandatory attendance at residential schools ensured that First Nations children would be educated within denominational schools, without consideration of their parents' wishes. As Gregory Cajete argues, the schools "literally educate[d] Indian people out of cultural existence."[125]

Government preference for boarding schools was based on the ideology that they were "unquestionably doing better work than the day schools, as the pupils ... separated a great distance from their parents, do not follow them in their wild pursuits, nor are they left for any length of time subject entirely to home influence."[126] Indian Affairs argued that "in the residential schools, there is opportunity for a broader education than in the day schools. Particular attention is given to the class-room work, and in addition, the girls are taught domestic science, sewing, etc., while the boys receive instruction in farming, care of stock, and in many schools, some useful trade."[127]

When the Thunderchild (St. Henri) Indian Residential School opened a short distance from the Thunderchild Reserve in 1901, it quickly became the destination school for all children from the Thunderchild Nation and other surrounding reserves. Compulsory attendance of all physically fit children between the ages of seven and fifteen, which came into effect with amendments to the Indian Act in 1886, was enforced by Indian agents and the North-West Mounted Police and resulted in residential schools being filled to the limit of their capacity.[128] Attendance at Thunderchild Indian Residential School increased from twelve students in 1901, to twenty in 1910, to forty-eight in 1920.[129] The Indian commissioner noted that the Roman Catholic and Protestant churches contributed "largely" to maintaining boarding schools, and he expressed the opinion that the Department of Indian Affairs, "by aiding them, will, at the same expense as at present ... achieve very much better educational results than" in day schools.[130]

Residential schools were founded in and operated through a church-state partnership, and the government was the senior partner.[131] The government provided the core funding, set the standards of care, supervised the administration of the schools, and controlled the children, who were considered wards of the department.[132] Residential schooling educated First Nations children in Western ways and "transformed Aboriginal boys and girls into useful Christian Canadian men and women."[133]

The all-encompassing power of the Indian Act enabled Canada to impose its own goals on First Nations people and their communities. While the act recognized the Chief as the head of a First Nation, to Canada, the Chief was little more than a figurehead within the context of the act. Canada's decision was final in all matters related to First Nations peoples, including the focus and purpose of education. Chief Thunderchild championed the right of his band members to live in two worlds. He wanted the opportunity for his people to maintain their own culture, languages, and spirituality and to attend a Western school in their community. He trusted in the Crown's treaty promises that Western education would provide "fair promises for the future."[134] He wanted a community-based education in which his people would "strengthen [their] languages and cultures, build upon the strong foundations of ancestral heritage and culture,"[135] and succeed in the Western educational system. A balanced education was not to be. As historian John S. Milloy explains, "traditional Indian government was dismissed and replaced by the Indian-agent-controlled models of white government" and schools.[136] Chief Thunderchild's belief in the sovereignty of his people and their treaty rights was, at best, "shouldered aside and replaced by new institutions allowing unchallengeable departmental control."[137] Chief Thunderchild died in 1927, but his demand for a strong, quality, community-based school echoes throughout Canada today. It is a vision that is not likely to become a reality until the federal government provides First Nations with funding that supports culturally appropriate education, language training for students and parents, community educational leadership, and a commitment to First Nations educational growth.

Notes

1 Alexander Morris, *The Treaties of Canada with the Indians of Manitoba and the North-West Territories: Including the Negotiations on Which They Were Based, and Other Information Relating Thereto* (Calgary: Fifth House, 1991).

2 Peter A. Cumming and Neil H. Mickenberg, eds., *Native Rights in Canada* (Toronto: The Indian-Eskimo Association of Canada, 1998), 55.

3 Ibid., 170.

4 Ibid.

5 Ibid., 169.

6 Ibid., 171.

7 Arthur J. Ray, *Indians in the Fur Trade* (Toronto: University of Toronto Press, 1998); and Robert J. Talbot, *Negotiating the Numbered Treaties: An Intellectual and Political Biography of Alexander Morris* (Saskatoon: Purich, 2009).

8 Morris, *Treaties of Canada*, 168, 169.

9 Thomas Isaac, *Aboriginal Title* (Saskatoon: Native Law Centre, 2006), 4.

10 Thomas Isaac and Kristyn Annis, *Treaty Rights in the Historic Treaties of Canada* (Saskatoon: Native Law Centre, University of Saskatchewan, 2010), 48.

Sheila Carr-Stewart

11 Peter C. Newman, *Company of Adventurers: How the Hudson Bay Empire Determined the Destiny of a Continent,* vol. 1 (Markham, ON: Penguin, 1985), 87.

12 Isaac and Annis, *Treaty Rights,* 55.

13 Morris, *Treaties of Canada,* 171.

14 Ibid., 170.

15 Ibid., 172.

16 Ibid., 199.

17 Ibid., 178.

18 Talbot, *Negotiating,* 62.

19 Department of Indian Affairs (DIA), annual report, 1964, 2.

20 Morris, *Treaties of Canada,* 204–5.

21 Ibid., 206.

22 Ibid., 207.

23 Ibid., 196.

24 Department of Indian Affairs and Northern Development (DIAND), *Copy of Treaty 6 between Her Majesty the Queen and the Plain and Wood Cree Indians and Other Tribes of Indians at Fort Canton, Fort Pitt, and Battle River with Adhesions,* DIAND publication QS-0574-000-EE-A-1 (Ottawa: Queen's Printer, 1964), 3.

25 Ibid.

26 An Act to Amend and Consolidate the Laws Respecting Indians, S.C. 1876, c. 18, s. 88 (hereafter Indian Act).

27 Ibid., s. 2.

28 Alain Cunningham, *Canadian Indian Policy and Development Planning Theory* (New York: Garland, 1999), 35–36.

29 Hugh Shewell, *"Enough to Keep Them Alive": Indian Welfare in Canada, 1873–1965* (Toronto: University of Toronto Press, 2004), 13.

30 Indian Act, 1876, s. 63(6).

31 Indian Act, 1880.

32 Indian Act, 1880, s. 74(1).

33 Shewell, *"Enough to Keep Them Alive,"* 14.

34 Indian Act, 1894, s. 137(2).

35 Ibid., s. 138.

36 Ibid., s. 138(2).

37 Indian Act, 1920, s. 9(5).

38 Brian Titley, *The Frontier World of Edgar Dewdney* (Vancouver: UBC Press, 1999), 56.

39 Ibid.

40 Ibid.

41 DIA, annual report, 1885, 190.

42 Titley, *The Frontier World,* 56.

43 Ibid.

44 Ibid., 57.

45 DIA, annual report, 1909, 351.

46 Ibid., 1885, 175.

47 Ibid., 1896, xxxvii.

48 Ibid., 1919, 31–32.

49 Library and Archives Canada (LAC), Department of Indian Affairs, RG 10, vol. 3647, 8128/10490.

50 DIA, annual report, 1907, 413.

51 Ibid., 1921, 8.

52 Ibid., 1895, xxi.

53 Ibid., 1902, 378.

54 Ibid., 1885, 175; 1914, 113. In 1885, the cost to Canada for teachers' salaries within the North-West Territories was $4,841.94 plus a total of $10 for school books, $22.50 for four maps, and $1,614 for biscuits for students in the day schools. In 1914, within Saskatchewan alone, the federal government expended $35,358.14 on teacher and staff salaries in day schools, $65,068.64 in boarding schools, and $36,603 for staff at industrial schools.

55 DIA, annual report, 1913, 8.

56 LAC, RG 10, vol. 3647, file 8128/41174.

57 DIA, annual report, 1903, 464.

58 Ibid., 1902, 190.

59 Ibid., 1904, 442.

60 Ibid., 1902, 378.

61 Edward Ahenakew, *Voices of the Plains Cree*, ed. Ruth M. Buck (Regina: Canadian Plains Research Center, 1995), 50.

62 Ibid., xx, 2.

63 Jack Funk, *Outside the Women Cried: The Story of the Surrender by Chief Thunderchild's Band of Their Reserve Near Delmas, Saskatchewan, 1908*, rev. ed. (New York: iUniverse, 2007), 9.

64 Ahenakew, *Voices of the Plains Cree*, 64.

65 Ibid., 55.

66 Ibid., 60.

67 Ibid., 46, 47.

68 Funk, *Outside the Women Cried*, 9.

69 Ibid., 10.

70 Blair Stonechild and Bill Waiser, *Loyal Till Death: Indians and the North-West Rebellion* (Markham, ON: Fifth House, 2010), 39.

71 Archie King, "After 100 Years Thunderchild Remembers," *Saskatchewan Indian* 9, 6 (1979): 12.

72 Ahenakew, *Voices of the Plains Cree*, 3.

73 Ibid.

74 DIA, annual report, 1886, 128.
75 Ibid., 1888, lxii.
76 DIAND, *Copy of Treaty 6*, 3; and Ahenakew, *Voices of the Plains Cree*, xiv.
77 British North America Act, 1867 (UK), 30 & 31 Vict., c. 3, s. 93(2).
78 Ahenakew, *Voices of the Plains Cree*, xiv.
79 DIA, annual report, 1888, 86.
80 Ibid., 1889, 92.
81 Ibid.
82 Ibid., 1894, 172.
83 Ibid., 1895, 301; 1896, 371.
84 Ibid., 1887, 92.
85 Ibid., 1886, 128.
86 Ibid., 1889, 92.
87 See, for example, DIA, "Programme of Studies for Indian Schools," 1896, in DIA, annual report, 1896.
88 Ibid., 1896, 1.
89 Ibid., 1886, 128.
90 Ibid., 1895, 301; 1894, 172; and 1914, 115.
91 Ibid., 1903, 464.
92 Ibid., 1894, 172.
93 Ibid., 1895, 301.
94 Ibid., 1896, 371.
95 Ibid.
96 Ibid., 1905, 414.
97 Ibid., 1907, 351–52.
98 Ibid., 1898, 129.
99 DIA, annual report, 1899, xxxvi.
100 LAC, Record of Indian Affairs, RG 10, vol. 3817, file 57562/78605.
101 Ibid.
102 Ibid.
103 Ibid.
104 Ibid.
105 Ibid.
106 Ibid.
107 Ibid., file 57562/68599.
108 Ibid., file 57562/68547.
109 Ibid.
110 Ibid., file 57562/74361.
111 Ibid.
112 Ibid.
113 Ibid., file 57562/68547.
114 Ibid., file 57562/68599.

115 Ibid., file 57562/76750.

116 Ibid., file 57562/77255.

117 Ibid., file 57562/78605.

118 Ibid.

119 Ibid.

120 Ibid.

121 Ibid.

122 DIA, annual reports, 1886–1906. There were twenty-four students in 1891, twenty-two in 1896 (eleven boys and eleven girls), ten in 1901 (seven boys and three girls), and six in 1906 (all boys).

123 DIA, annual reports, 1891–97.

124 LAC, RG 10, vol. 3817, file 57562/78605

125 Gregory Cajete, *Look to the Mountain: An Ecology of Indigenous Education* (Skyland, NC: Kivaki Press, 1994), 22.

126 DIA, annual report, 1902, 190.

127 Ibid., 1918, 23.

128 Indian Act, 1886, s. 137(2); DIA, annual report, 1918, 13.

129 DIA, annual reports, 1901–20.

130 LAC, RG 10, vol. 3647, file 8128/41174.

131 John S. Milloy, *A National Crime: The Canadian Government and the Residential School System, 1879 to 1986* (Winnipeg: University of Manitoba Press, 2017), xxxvii.

132 Ibid.

133 Ibid., xxxvi.

134 Morris, *Treaties of Canada*, 16.

135 Marie Battiste and Jean Barman, eds., *First Nations Education in Canada: The Circle Unfolds* (Vancouver: UBC Press, 1995), xi.

136 John S. Milloy, "The Early Indian Acts: Development Strategy and Constitutional Change," in *As Long as the Sun Shines and Water Flows: A Reader in Canadian Native Studies*, ed. Ian A.L. Getty and Antoine S. Lussier (Vancouver: UBC Press, 1983), 57.

137 Ibid., 61.

2

PLACING A SCHOOL
AT THE TAIL OF A PLOUGH

The European Roots of Indian Industrial
Schools in Canada

Larry Prochner

In Canada, Indigenous peoples' right to education is confirmed in treaties. Treaty 1, concluded in 1871, states: "Her Majesty agrees to maintain a school on each reserve hereby made, whenever the Indians of the reserve should desire it."[1] As the Truth and Reconciliation Commission of Canada and numerous studies have shown, however, the government failed to meet its obligations. Instead, it provided inadequate schools based on principles of efficiency and economy.[2] The turn to Indian industrial schools in the 1880s is a key example of this failure.[3]

Histories of Indigenous education in Canada focus on church-run and government-sponsored residential schools, many of which were industrial schools, which provided work training and a basic education in a residential facility.[4] In 1998, when Scott Trevithick reviewed the state of Canadian research on residential schools, seventy studies had been published since the 1960s, and he pointed to the need for greater breadth and depth in the treatment of topics such as gender, school staff, and church involvement in the schools.[5] Over the past two decades, the literature has grown immensely, with publications on a wider array of topics[6] and a growing number of first-person accounts.[7] In recent years, the Truth and Reconciliation Commission, which created a record of residential schools as part of its mandate, has encouraged more historical research.

Although a lot has been written about Indian industrial schools, very little has been written about their European roots, particularly the model that inspired them: Philipp Emanuel von Fellenberg's farm school at Hofwyl, his estate near Berne, Switzerland.[8] Fellenberg was a colleague of Johann Pestalozzi, famed for organizing schools for the poor, for his experience-based methods, and for his approach to education, in which teacher and pupils lived as a family. Fellenberg integrated Pestalozzi's ideas with experiments in agricultural science at his own school for the poor and in the other schools that made up his educational colony, also called Hofwyl. The Truth and Reconciliation Commission highlighted Fellenberg's ideas in its history of residential school education. In Canada, Egerton Ryerson, the superintendent of education for Upper Canada, prepared a report on schools in 1847. The commission noted: "The educational model [Ryerson] proposed was based on the Hofwyl School for the Poor, near Berne, Switzerland."[9] A number of other studies have traced the model for Indian industrial schools to Hofwyl,[10] yet the Swiss institution has never been described in detail.[11] Here, I detail Fellenberg's idea of work as education for poor children, which was Hofwyl's great appeal for Ryerson, who also served as a consultant to the Department of Indian Affairs on industrial schools. For Fellenberg, "work on the land not only improved physique but also developed the mind."[12] Or, as British social reformer and parliamentarian Henry Brougham expressed the idea, Fellenberg developed a method for "placing a school at the tail of a plough."[13] In Canada, Ryerson, inspired by Fellenberg and others, recommended the creation of Indian industrial schools. The boarding schools would be modelled on the family, with the teacher as "parent," and would preserve class distinctions by focusing on work as education. But the industrial schools that were established in the 1880s deviated from his recommendations and Fellenberg's model in ways that ultimately led to their failure and generations of trauma. The federal government had failed to support reserve agriculture, a treaty obligation, but blamed reserve residents for the failure in order to justify sending their children to industrial schools that were church-run and poorly financed. In negotiating treaties, First Nations representatives sought provisions for education "that would enable them not only to survive the loss of their traditional lifestyle but also to participate fully in the new economy."[14] The government's provision of industrial schools deviated completely from Indigenous peoples' wishes and desires for education.

Industrial School Experiments, 1830s to 1850s

The colonial government's interest in industrial schools for Indigenous children occurred in the 1830s as pressure for land for European settlement both strained relations between the Canadian government and Indigenous peoples in Upper Canada and stimulated new interest in education as a mechanism of empire. Lieutenant-Governor Francis Bond Head, with the support of colonial secretary Lord Glenig, forced Indigenous land surrenders in Upper Canada and advocated for a segregationist policy of removing the region's Indigenous peoples to Manitoulin Island. After Bond Head left his post, government policy concerning Indigenous people shifted back to assimilation, termed "civilization," as described in the 1845 *Report on the Affairs of the Indians in Canada*, requested by the governor general, Sir Charles Bagot. The Bagot Report recommended a key role for manual education in the civilization process.[15] The report's commissioners drew from interviews with Indian Department staff and with missionaries, including Indigenous Methodist missionary Rev. Peter Jones, to conclude that

> education [of Indigenous youth] must consist not merely of the training of the mind, but of a weaning from the habits and feelings of their ancestors, and the acquirements of the language, arts and customs of civilized life. Besides the ordinary routine of a primary School, the young men should be instructed in husbandry, gardening, the management of stock, and simple mechanical trades; the girls in

domestic economy, the charge of a household and dairy, the use of a needle, etc.; and both sexes should be familiarised with the mode of transacting business among the whites. It is by means of Industrial or Manual Labour Schools, in which the above branches of instruction are taught, that a material and extensive change among the Indians of the rising generation may be hoped for.[16]

The preference for residential schools instead of day schools was clearly more than an educational matter: it signalled a shift in policy aimed at managing relationships with Indigenous people through their children.

In his speech before the assembly of Ojibwe leaders in Orillia in 1845, gathered to discuss the matter of boarding schools, Thomas G. Anderson, the visiting superintendent of Indian affairs, stated:

> It has ... been determined, that your children shall be sent to Schools, where they will forget their Indian habits, and be instructed in all the necessary arts of civilized life, and become one with your white brethren. In these Schools they will be well taken care of, be comfortably dressed, kept clean, and get plenty to eat. The adults will not be forced from their present locations. They may remove, or remain, as they please; but their children must go.[17]

Even before this time, industrial schools for Indigenous children had been established in Upper Canada. In 1830, the New England Company opened the Mohawk Institute, which functioned as a boarding school with a manual education program from 1834.[18] The institute was a prototype for subsequent schools.[19] It operated as a boarding facility with a focus on children; it combined work training with religious education; and it provided instruction in English only. The model was not widely spread, however. In the 1830s, the few schools available for Indigenous children were mainly organized as day schools.

Larry Prochner

Egerton Ryerson: From Mission Teacher to Policy Leader

The superintendent of education for Upper Canada, Egerton Ryerson, provided the "scientific" rationale for Indian industrial schools in his expert report in 1847, thereby backing up the Bagot Report's recommendations. Ryerson had had direct experience with a similar educational plan on a smaller scale twenty years earlier. He began his career as a missionary to the Ojibwe peoples at a Methodist farm colony at the Credit River in Upper Canada in the 1820s.[20] The Methodists' activities were guided by Christianization of Indigenous peoples as a first principle, followed by a plan for their civilization (i.e., assimilation). Civilization strategies included teaching reading, writing, and geography in an infant school and industrial education in which children and adults learned carpentry and other trades, along with European agricultural methods, through their work.[21]

In later years, Ryerson was a newspaper editor and became involved in political debates, both in the church and in relation to the colonial government. He continued his career as an "educational missionary" in his role as superintendent of education from 1844 to 1876.[22] In 1846, he wrote a *Report on a System of Public Elementary Instruction for Upper Canada* as a framework for education reforms and a common school system.[23]

Ryerson referred directly to the schools at Hofwyl in his report, commenting on the importance Fellenberg placed on physical education: gymnastics, swimming, fencing, and other sports and games. Ryerson believed that physical education was best taught in industrial schools (for the poor) and grammar schools (academies for the elite) in which training was both thorough and prolonged.[24] Gymnastics was a featured activity for grammar school pupils at Fellenberg's school, as seen in Figure 2.1, which depicts children climbing upright poles to great heights, throwing javelins, and playing leapfrog and field hockey. The pupils' time on the playing field was used as a break from their studies and for physical and moral training. A visitor in

Figure 2.1 Elite students engaging in gymnastics at Hofwyl, Switzerland, 1840. | From Joseph Meyer, *Meyer's Universum* (Hildburghausen: Bibliographishen Institut, 1840).

the 1830s described their play: "Two or three run to the circular swing, another climbs the pole, while a party of the little ones jump on the horizontal tree, and commence a sport I have never seen before ... Some are off to the gardens."[25] It is important to highlight that the children in the illustration are all from Hofwyl's academy (grammar school) for wealthy pupils. For Fellenberg, the grammar school pupils' physical activity and recreation were classed as "manual education," whereas for pupils in the school for the poor, manual education involved work in the fields.[26]

Ryerson's interest in physical education fit his view of child development and education in which drill and discipline were linked with moral training, which he believed was more important for some children than training the intellect. As historian Alison Prentice explains, "sometimes [Ryerson] argued that the heart was more important than the mind and that the moral feelings ought to be cultivated rather

Larry Prochner

than the intellect. Certainly he believed this to be essential when intellectual development was already weak, as he claimed was often the case among North American Indians and among the labouring classes."[27]

Ryerson included two additional allusions to Hofwyl in his report. One was that Hofwyl's pupils were from different backgrounds, by which he meant that pupils in the academy were Protestant and Catholic.[28] This statement reflected his preference for nonsectarian schools. The other was to emphasize that poor pupils should be taught bookkeeping as preparation for farm management. Ryerson highlighted the Hofwyl superintendent's belief that "no part of the instruction of his agricultural [poor] pupils" was more important than "teaching them a thorough system of keeping farming accounts."[29] Even in the limited references to Hofwyl in Ryerson's report, a picture emerges of a distinct class-based education system. And though it was contrary to Ryerson's vision of common schools for all, a similar picture emerged in Upper Canada from the 1850s with the establishment of alternative schools for the elite.[30]

Shortly after Ryerson completed his report, the superintendent of Indian affairs, George Vardon, asked him for suggestions on developing Indian industrial schools. Ryerson drew on the example of Hofwyl in his four-and-a-half-page reply to Vardon.[31] He began by distinguishing industrial schools from manual labour schools. According to Ryerson, manual labour schools set instruction as the priority, with work "pursued only two or three hours a day, and more as a recreation than as employment."[32] He contrasted this model with industrial schools, which he preferred, where the aim was "the making of pupils industrious farmers, and [where] learning is provided for and pursued only so far as it will contribute to that end."[33] Ryerson stressed that Indian industrial schools should focus only on agriculture and not on other trades, such as carpentry or printmaking, which would add to the schools' cost and create staffing problems. Agricultural training would be supplemented by a "plain English education" that would include instruction in English language, arithmetic, geometry, geography, history, natural history, agricultural chemistry, writing, drawing, vocal music, bookkeeping (farmers' accounts), and religion.[34] The schools would be efficient (church run with a government grant-in-aid and minimal government oversight) and self-sustaining through pupils' labour. Ryerson drew on the example of the Hofwyl school to stress the importance of the school's staff and, above all, the leadership of its director:

> It follows as a necessary consequence that everything as to human agency in regard to the success of these schools, depends upon the character and qualifications of the superintendent and agents employed to conduct them. It was the piety and judgement and example of the late excellent Mr de Fellenberg, more than any code of rules, that rendered his agricultural school for the poor ... a blessing to hundreds of peasant youth, and a model of all similar establishments.[35]

Ryerson concluded that the Hofwyl school was "the *beau ideal* of what I would wish our Indian industrial schools to be."[36]

Despite government interest and Ryerson's report, only two industrial schools were established in the mid-nineteenth century. In about 1849, the day school at Alderville, Ontario, moved into an existing boarding school to become the Alnwick (Alderville) Industrial School, regarded as one of the first in Canada.[37] The Mount Elgin Institute opened at the Muncey mission in the same period. Yet, as historian Donald Smith has noted, neither school followed Ryerson's suggestions to restrict training to farming and to limit the school to boys (with girls remaining in day schools).[38] The expanded training strained the schools' finances, and a typhus outbreak killed four children at the Alnwick school. Within a decade, the colonial government and Indigenous parents regarded the schools as failed experiments.[39]

The Industrial School Ethos

Despite Ryerson's view that industrial and manual labour schools were distinct institutions, they were essentially the same: both were formed under a Christian work ethic. Manual labour schools evolved from workhouses in Europe, where the workhouse "philosophy" was based in the Calvinist idea that labour was a form of service to God. In this view, work had a moral value and served as a form of repentance and as a means for human improvement. Work was both redemptive for pupils and a way for parishes to relieve their burden of caring for the poor. While members of higher social ranks viewed the poor to be morally and spiritually deficient, they also believed their deficits could be corrected through manual labour, leading to a regeneration of society in which rich and poor each understood their place.

While the same idea was applied to all poor, individuals living outside society's margins – that is, those termed gypsies, travellers, or vagabonds because they did not live in permanent settlements – were a particular focus for workhouse schools. Local governments objected to these peoples' mobility; "the wandering poor" had been defined as a social problem since medieval times. As historian Tim Cresswell has observed, people who were mobile – "without a place" – "were ... nightmare figure[s] for a settled society."[40] This was true for their children, too, and the outcome of any planned intervention was strengthened if children could be separated from the influence of their parents, for example, into some sort of long-term residential facility.

Workhouses had developed with the "discovery" of rising numbers of poor in seventeenth-century Europe. In his "Essay on the Poor Law," published in 1697, English philosopher John Locke set out a plan for relieving society of the problem. His essay is notable for its harsh approach, including the treatment of children.[41] Locke's plan for children fit his environmentalist view of child development, in which sensation or reflection leads to growth of knowledge. His view foretold the "modern model" of the child, in which all children were seen as "capable of improvement through careful education" – that is to say, schooling could prepare all children to take their place as workers.[42]

According to Locke, the growing number of poor stemmed from a moral breakdown – a "relaxation of discipline and corruption of manners."[43] The poor were a burden on society, while at the same time there was a need for their useful work. Locke's scheme set out to re-establish discipline and reduce the cost of caring for the poor by having them contribute to their upkeep through their own work. The poor's participation in the scheme would be compulsory: vagrants would be punished in workhouses established for their forced employment in, for example, wool spinning.

Locke's plan especially targeted families with large numbers of children, whom he described as living like "begging drones."[44] Male family members aged fifteen to fifty would be forced into "hard labour" breaking stones.[45] Children aged three to fourteen would be placed into a "working school" during the day, spinning or knitting, so that their labour was not lost until they were older. He believed this ar-rangement would also benefit mothers by taking "the children off her hands," allowing women greater freedom to seek employment.[46] In addition, he believed the children would benefit from a religious education in the schools. In Locke's cost-benefit analysis, the chil-dren's labour would compensate in ten years for the cost of their care and education. It was therefore important to gather them into work-houses while they were young and to keep them there for as long as possible.

The scheme was manifest in workhouses in England, in which, by the late eighteenth century, half of all inmates were children, and in the Church of England missionary-run spinning schools in Scot-land and colonial Ireland from the early 1700s.[47] Spinning schools in Scotland, which were also called industrial schools, evolved within agricultural colonies.[48] One historian notes that they were "similar to the U.S. Bureau of Indian Affairs boarding schools with their manual labour programs that were introduced in the late nineteenth century."[49] Indeed, there was a parallel between the treatment of the poor in England and of Highlanders and the treatment of Indigenous people in the colonies.[50] Historian Nina Reid-Maroney explains that in col-onial Canada, as in Britain, moral, physical, and spiritual health were tied together: "The manual labour school became an evangelical concept weighted with the reformist vision of mind and body transformed through self-discipline."[51]

The nomenclature for children's institutions that combined work with basic religious training was varied: they were called manual labour schools, reformatories, or houses of reformation, refuge, or industry. Indeed, industrial schools were mostly indistinguishable from reform schools. Both met sociologist Irving Goffman's conditions for a total institution.[52] Admission was involuntary; they used coercive means to achieve compliance (though over time punishments would be psychological, using shaming or isolation rather than corporal punishment); and their aim was to reform children.

Visitors' Accounts of Hofwyl's Schools

A month after he had been appointed superintendent of education for Upper Canada in 1844, Egerton Ryerson embarked on a year-long European tour. Although his activities involved sightseeing and self-improvement – he lived in Paris for three months learning French – his main objective was to visit schools to learn about modern systems of European education. His fact gathering was the basis for his *Report on a System of Public Elementary Instruction for Upper Canada*. Educational borrowing from Europe was common in the nineteenth century; however, it was critical for Ryerson, who, because he "was not an innovator," needed to draw on "proven" foreign systems.[53] Ryerson was a borrower twice over in his report: his biographer notes that much of his report was cribbed from US educator Horace Mann's 1844 report for the Massachusetts Board of Education, which detailed Mann's own tour of Europe in 1843.[54]

Ryerson arrived at Hofwyl in October 1845 following travels through England, Holland, Belgium, France, and Italy. Along the way, he observed other schools for poor children: a Protestant school with eight hundred pupils in Holland, and another with eleven hundred pupils. Ryerson's time at Hofwyl was brief, no more than a day, and his description in his diary highlighted the scenery but provided no details about the school beyond the division of the schools by social classes: the gymnasium for the wealthy; the *Realschule* and intermediate school for pupils from the Swiss middle class; and the agricultural school, where he had his evening meal, for poor pupils. He wrote:

> Travelled through a mountainous and picturesque country to Papier-mühle; walked three miles to the celebrated school of M. de Fallenberg [sic]; had the whole system explained – gymnasium, real, intermediate, poor, and limited to the number of thirty; dined at the Agricultural School, – situated on a gentle hill, in the midst of the valley of Switzerland, surrounded by mountains, – I have been abundantly repaid in spending a whole day in surveying such an establishment.[55]

Fortunately, many visitors came to Hofwyl over the forty years of its operation, and more than one hundred of them published detailed accounts of what they observed.[56] Historian Philipp Gonon calls both Hofwyl and Pestalozzi's school at nearby Burdorf sites of pilgrimage for educators and destinations for travellers with a general interest in education.[57] An engraving of Hofwyl was published in the 1840 edition of Joseph Meyer's *Universum.* It depicts "Hofwil Castle," which was used for the academy and called "the big house" by English pupils.[58] The scene was enhanced by the artist with the addition of a third storey to the institute. Figure 2.2, from an 1839 publication, is likely a more realistic view; it features the castle on the left, with the barn and agricultural implements in the foreground showcasing activities for poor students.

Through reports in books and periodicals by educators and philanthropists such as William Woodridge and John Griscom, Hofwyl was well known in the United States and Canada from the 1820s.[59] The description that follows draws on a selection of mainly English-language reports from 1818 to the 1840s. Many accounts sound similar, and it is likely that the Hofwyl tour was fairly standardized over the

Figure 2.2 Barn and agricultural implements at Hofwyl: the playground for poor students. | Instituts d'Hofwyl, 1839, *Le Magasin Pittoresque*, 13.

years. For example, a number of the reports include detailed information on the school's schedule, suggesting that visitors were given a pamphlet during their visit. Fellenberg, who died the year before Ryerson's visit, met many visitors himself, using the tours to promote his school and to seek donations. Ryerson did not name his tour guide; however, it may have been Fellenberg's son, William von Fellenberg, who directed Hofwyl after his father's death. The Hofwyl schools closed in the next few years due to leadership problems, although some accounts attributed their closing to the civil war in Switzerland in 1847.[60]

Hofwyl began as a school for wealthy children in 1804; the industrial school was added in 1809.[61] By the late 1820s, it was a renowned "educational colony" with separate schools for rich and poor, a girls' school, a model farm, workshops for making agricultural equipment and clothing, a normal school for training teachers, and residences for pupils and teachers.[62] Three hundred staff and pupils lived at Hofwyl in the 1820s and '30s.

Hofwyl's founding coincided with a high interest in education for the poor in Europe and the beginnings of state school development. Education was seen as a way to manage the underclass, as with workhouse schools, inculcating values of work, teaching them subservience to the rich, and, more broadly, educating them as citizens loyal to the nation. It was also a practical way to build a skilled labour force in line with the new agricultural science. Fellenberg is known for his contributions to agriculture and education.[63]

Pupils in the school for the poor were initially conscripted. As Henry Brougham reported, they were "gathered from the highways and hedges."[64] He wrote: "The peasants in [Fellenberg's] neighborhood were at first rather shy of trusting their children for a new experiment; and being thus obliged to take his pupils where he could find them, many of the earliest were the sons of vagrants, and literally picked up on the highways."[65]

When Brougham visited Hofwyl in 1816, he saw thirty or forty children who had been rescued from their "degraded circumstances" in this way.[66] He wrote, "With hardly any exception they were sunk in the vicious and idle habits of their parents, a class of dissolute vagrants, resembling the worst kind of gipsies."[67] The school for poor children was formally known as the agricultural school, but it was commonly called the "farm school" and its pupils the "rural pupils."[68] Because it was under the direction of teacher Thomas Vehrli, the farm school was also known as Vehrli's school, and the pupils were "Vehrli's boys." The school claimed an incredible degree of success. In its first fifteen years, apparently only one pupil was expelled, which was attributed to the boy's "corrupt propensities."[69]

Boys were expected to live at the school for nine years, from age twelve to twenty-one, working the entire time on the farm and making it nearly self-sufficient. Indeed, the revenue from the farm's production allowed Fellenberg to keep the tuition lower for wealthy students in the academy. Visitors commonly remarked on the low cost of operating the Hofwyl farm school, and this was part of its appeal to Ryerson. John Griscom, an American Quaker who toured the school in 1818, wrote, "The produce of the labour of these boys, bears no inconsiderable proportion of the expense of their maintenance and instruction."[70] Brougham, too, was impressed by Fellenberg's ability to accomplish so much "with such slender means."[71] Food costs were kept low because meals were meagre and consisted of products from the farm: bread and an apple for breakfast, vegetables for dinner at noon, whey and boiled potatoes for supper, and meat once a week. Though the poor pupils received no wages, Fellenberg devised a system of small rewards of money once per year, recognizing pupils' skills in catching rats or gardening. Fellenberg held the money for the pupils in a savings bank and gave it to them when they left the school at age twenty-one.

For Fellenberg, the aim of education was to prepare pupils for their place in society. In his view, the rich and the poor should understand their relationship, which hinged on the poor's useful labour and the gratitude of the rich for the work of the poor. This reasoning informed his academy for wealthy pupils, called the Scientific Educational Institution for the Higher Social Classes.[72] Yet there was little direct contact between the two groups. When Lady Byron visited Hofwyl in 1828, she described the scene one afternoon: "The upper-class boys used the fencing room," while the "rural scholars" could be seen "breaking stones for the repair of roads."[73] The sons of Welsh industrialist Robert Owen, having attended the school a decade earlier, confirmed the separation of the academy and farm school pupils.[74] Owen's eldest son, Robert Dale Owen, wrote about it in his memoir: "We did not see much of the Vehrli-Knaben [Vehrli boys] as we called them."[75] And apart from seeing the wealthy pupils in their play outdoors, the academy was strictly off limits to visitors. The reason, Griscom believed, was that frequent interruptions would be "extremely troublesome."[76] Ryerson reported learning about the academy – he had "the whole system explained – gymnasium, real, intermediate, poor" – but the focus for visitors was the farm school.

The farm school's curriculum included geography, history, mineralogy, botany, reading, writing, and arithmetic, all of which were linked to nature and the boys' work and were similar to Ryerson's recommended school subjects for Indian industrial schools. Whereas rural pupils were educated in the vernacular (German), pupils at the academy learned Latin and Greek under the direction of about twenty teachers, allowing for an individual approach with the sixty students. Other subjects taught in the academy were history, natural philosophy, chemistry, mechanics, mathematics, drawing, and music, along with gymnastics, riding, and fencing.

The pedagogy and curriculum were different at the farm school. Rousseau's *Emile, or On Education* influenced Fellenberg's educational ideas. Brougham, commenting on the farm school, observed, "The education of the lower classes is principally negative. For it is nearly sufficient to set them good examples, and keep idleness and vice out of sight."[77] Brougham was restating Rousseau's idea of negative education, in which education is matched to a child's stage of development by preventing children's exposure to certain elements. For example, if, as in Rousseau's view, young children learn through self-activity, then they should be kept from having books. As Rousseau explained, they have no need for reading, because a child's "whole environment is the book from which he unconsciously enriches his memory, till his judgment is able to profit from it."[78] Rousseau called reading "the curse of childhood."[79] A ban on books was meant for children aged two to twelve, the stage Rousseau called "the age of nature." Brougham and other visitors commented on the near absence of books for the pupils, who were aged twelve and up, at the farm school. Brougham wrote: "The boys never see a newspaper, and scarcely a book; they are taught, *viva voce*, a few matters of fact, and rules of practical application. The rest of their education consists simply of inculcating habits of industry, frugality, veracity, docility, and mutual kindness."[80] Instruction rarely took place in the schoolroom. Instead, pupils were said to enjoy conversations with their teacher about botany and other such topics as they worked in the fields. However, a visitor at the school in the late 1830s noted that instruction for farm school pupils had become more formal over time; the pupils took their lessons with teachers in the intermediate school.[81] It is likely that Ryerson observed this type of arrangement rather than the incidental instruction of earlier times.

The farm school had a strong moral aspect, what Griscom called its "moral charm."[82] In Brougham's view, the teachers' kindly and fair treatment of pupils was planned "to win their affections" and teach them the value of work and its relation to their happiness.[83] This lesson was made easier by their isolation on the farm and their training by older, more experienced boys under the supervision of a teacher. As Brougham noted, "a constant and even minute superintendence, at every instant of their lives, forms of course a part of the system."[84] Indeed, their teacher lived in residence with the pupils in family-type groupings, patterned on a domestic arrangement, in which they shared labour, meals, and all other aspects of daily living. Griscom wrote that their teacher, Thomas Vehrli, "lives with them, sleeps, and works with them, dresses as they do, and makes himself their friend and companion, and their instructor."[85] While Vehrli was no longer at Hofwyl at the time of Ryerson's visit, a group of pupils still lived and worked with a single teacher.

The adults in charge took a parental role in both the academy and the farm school. Robert Dale Owen, who had been a pupil in the academy, recalled that Fellenberg asked them to call him *Pflege-vater* – foster father.[86] Brougham also noted that pupils considered Fellenberg to be their "adoptive father."[87] The intensity of pupils' relationship with their teacher is shown in the way farm school pupils were introduced into the colony. In 1832, a visitor observed twenty-five new rural pupils and their teacher in a cottage they had built in the forest near Hofwyl, in which they had lived over the winter. Through their isolation, the pupils were made to rely on their teacher in a way similar to Rousseau's Emile, who depended entirely on his tutor. The influence of Rousseau at Hofwyl was seen in the presence of Dafoe's *Robinson Crusoe* in the cottage's schoolroom, a book that Rousseau recommended to cultivate Emile's imagination.[88] The visitor was inspired to comment, "They are in the position of Crusoe on the island, and Hofwyl is their stranded vessel, from which they obtain the objects most necessary to them; they must look to their own resources for the rest."[89] And the pupils, like Emile, were meant to learn a fundamental lesson from Crusoe, "of transforming the raw materials of nature into a useful condition," which they experienced by building their cottage.[90] However, a more prosaic interpretation of the new pupils' induction through isolation was to ensure their constant supervision, and bonding with their fellows and their teacher, to reduce the chance they would leave the school. Boarding schools had certain requirements from a practical point of view. Fellenberg needed to maintain a minimum number of farm school pupils to make the colony self-sustaining.

The farm school's timetable reveals the extent of work done by pupils. Brougham, visiting in 1816, noted there were one-and-a-half to two hours of lessons per day, except for Sunday, when there were six hours of lessons. In contrast, from Monday to Saturday, the pupils worked nine to ten hours each day, a ratio of lessons to work of about one to three. Another visitor, Mr. Fennel, noted in 1828 that the morning lesson was optional: "If there be nothing particular to engage them in the fields, they are occupied with lessons till half past six, when they breakfast."[91] The hours of work and instruction remained the same across twenty years of visitor reports. Pupils were divided into work crews according to their age: "Some pick up stones, some weed, some thresh, some tend the plough, dig, sow, reap, as the work of the farm may require."[92] Their teacher worked alongside them, both as an overseer and for their instruction. The pupils' time was tightly managed until 7:00 p.m., at which time "they are then at liberty to work in their little gardens, or to improve themselves in the school-room."[93] One observer noted that their long work hours helped the pupils value the few hours they had for school work.[94]

The situation was reversed in the academy, where pupils were occupied in "sedentary employment" – that is, lessons – for six to eight hours of the day.[95] For pupils in the academy, lessons were their work.

Fennel wrote: "At Hofwyl, scholastic instruction is in the education of the rich, what manual labour is in that of the indigent."[96] Other activities in the academy included athletic endeavours, such as swimming, gymnastics, and treks in the Alps. Robert Dale Owen, a pupil at the school in 1818, recalled six-week expeditions in the summer, on two occasions walking three hundred kilometres from the school to Lake Maggiore in Italy and back.[97] As mentioned earlier, Ryerson was especially impressed with physical education in the academy at Hofwyl.

Some visitors were critical of the rural pupils' education at Hofwyl. They objected to the preponderance of agricultural training, which matched Fellenberg's aim "to fit the child for his particular position in society."[98] As one historian observed, the farm school pupils "were virtually indentured labourers engaged in cultivating 250 acres of arable land."[99] However, it was exactly this aspect of the farm school that most visitors, including Ryerson, admired.

Many schools were established on the Hofwyl model outside of Switzerland, as farm schools or academies, but the two types of schools were rarely integrated into a single colony as envisaged by Fellenberg. Lady Byron, who visited Hofwyl in 1828, established a Hofwyl-inspired school for poor children at Ealing in 1834. Pupils were provided with garden allotments to mimic the experience of farm work. One visitor remarked, "It seems to be an education well-fitted to make them industrious and happy, and ready to turn their hand to anything; boys especially qualified for new settlers in our colonies."[100] However, Lady Byron found that she needed to provide cash inducements to parents to ensure their children's regular attendance. And although Lady Byron did not want to call her institution an industrial school, owing to its meaning in England as a workhouse, by 1840 it was known as the Ealing Industrial School.[101] The name "Hofwyl" also became sufficiently known among the elite that it was used to recruit students to academies. One in Middlesex called "Hofwyl-House" advertised its "education on plans founded on the practice of Fellenberg, Pestalozzi, and others."[102] Another was established in the colony of New South Wales in the 1840s; it promised that pupils would be trained according to Fellenberg's plan "as far as circumstances will allow."[103]

Regardless of whether the schools were prep schools, industrial schools, or juvenile reformatories (which were also called farm schools or industrial schools), the principles of the Hofwyl model were the same: a "family" arrangement of pupils with the teacher in "parental" authority; education organized as a means to retain and strengthen distinctions of social class; and a focus on work as education, defined as labour for poor pupils and recreation and academic studies for the wealthy.[104]

Industrial School Revival, 1880s and '90s

The renewed start-up of industrial schools for Indigenous children in Canada in the 1880s, after the schools' failure in the 1850s, coincided with the opening of industrial schools as reformatories for Euro-Canadian youth.[105] Earlier schools, like the Protestant Industrial School that opened in Halifax in 1863, were based on the English workhouse model.[106] The later schools, such as the Victoria Industrial School for Boys established in 1889 in a rural area outside Toronto, more closely matched the Hofwyl idea. The Victoria school had "family-like" living arrangements in cottage-style dormitories, in which a male and female "officer" also resided, and a focus on work on the school's farm and in learning trades.[107] The schools were developed to contain and train a wide range of "neglected and dependent children," which in Ontario included "vagrants, beggars, destitute orphans, children growing up 'without salutary parental control and education'[108] and uncontrollable children whose parents asked that they be admitted."[109] Industrial schools for Indigenous children were similar in almost every respect to reformatories, although, ostensibly, they were schools, and the children were pupils, not inmates.

European settlement and the quest for land was the driver for the government's revival of Indian industrial schools in the 1880s. In addition, as described by historian Sarah Carter, the government's renewed interest stemmed directly from its failure to support reserve farming, which, like schools, was a treaty obligation.[110] The promised equipment, seed, livestock, and training were not forthcoming, and reserve farming was mostly unsuccessful. However, the government blamed Indigenous peoples for the lack of success, judging them unfit for farming and thereby of participating in the new settler economy. Attention turned from agricultural training for Indigenous adults to isolating children in institutions for learning via manual labour, reflecting a policy shift from assimilation of First Nations peoples into Canadian society to segregation. There was a similar trend towards segregation in the United States, as shown in policies of removal and the growth in numbers of boarding schools. In some instances, existing manual-labour boarding schools were reorganized as industrial schools or simply renamed as such; others were opened to Indigenous students, and some were newly built. In 1878, the first Indigenous students were enrolled at the Hampton Normal and Agricultural Institute in Virginia along with its African American students. In 1879, the Carlisle Indian Industrial School in Pennsylvania was established as the first off-reservation boarding school in the United States.

The Canadian government watched American developments, and in early 1879 the minister of the interior enlisted journalist and aspiring conservative politician Nicolas Flood Davin to visit Washington and prepare a report on Indigenous education.[111] Davin's investigation primarily involved meeting with US government officials and Indigenous leaders in Washington. However, he also visited a school – not Carlisle or Hampton, but the White Earth Boarding School in Minnesota. The school was one of several on the White Earth Reserve, which was created in 1867 as part of the US Indian Department's experiment in "agrarian assimilation."[112] Davin was impressed by what he learned, and he returned to Ottawa with the message that "the Indian Department at Washington have not much hope in regard to the adult Indians, but sanguine anticipations are cherished respecting the children regarding their training in industrial boarding schools."[113]

Davin's report drew on recommendations for the schools made by C.A. Ruffee, the Indian agent at the White Earth Agency. He wrote: "An Indian Reservation should have manual labour schools, or, in other words, boarding industrial schools; mills, both saw and grist; blacksmith and carpenter's shops ... [and] all the young men of a tribe or tribes, who desired it, should be taught some trade."[114] Ruffee, however, did not believe the White Earth school was anywhere near this "ideal," as he described in his report to the US commissioner of Indian affairs in 1879. He protested the lack of government support, including financial support, for industrial education at the school: "I respectfully suggest that greater importance should be attached to the industrial department, wherein the rudiments of farm and home labor should be taught; it will be of great practical utility."[115]

Davin's report did not reveal that he was aware of any limitations of industrial schools, nor did he seem aware of problems with the industrial schools that had failed in Canada or that continued in the existing schools in Ontario. He stressed their economy and efficiency, believing they would eventually be "self-supporting" through their farms.[116] The only caution he noted was that the US commissioner of Indian affairs "is not in favour of the contract system" (a system in which schools were operated by missions and funded by government on a per capita basis) "because the children at schools under contract do not, as a rule, get a sufficient quantity of food."[117] Nevertheless, Davin's report to the minister recommended that "wherever the missionaries have schools, those schools should be utilized by the Government, if possible; that is to say, a contract should be made with the religious body controlling the school to board and educate and train industrially a certain number of pupils."[118] The subcontracting system proved to be one cause of the schools' eventual breakdown.

The first two Indian industrial schools in western Canada opened in the early 1880s: the Church of England's Battleford Industrial School in 1883 and the Roman Catholic Qu'Appelle Industrial School in 1884. Within a decade, there were more than twenty industrial schools in the West. The schools quickly showed their weakness: they were expensive

Larry Prochner

to operate, yet they were severely underfunded under the per capita system instituted in 1893. In many instances, they were badly managed, staffed by poorly trained teachers, and provided minimal attention to children's basic needs. Indigenous parents protested by keeping their children at home, leading to increasingly coercive school attendance policies. Moreover, the schools failed to meet their aim to prepare Indigenous youth to be farmers: graduates returned to reservations with skills they were unable to put to use.

⋛⋚

What can we learn from Hofwyl's influence on industrial schools in Canada? While the Indian industrial schools clearly used work as the principal method of education, as did Hofwyl, they differed from Hofwyl in their organization as congregate institutions, a choice made based on their cheaper cost and greater control of pupils despite the risk they presented to children's well-being. In most other respects, the Canadian schools were similar to the Hofwyl model. Each aimed to fit pupils to their place in society through a process of resocialization.

There is a final, curious reference to Hofwyl in Canadian residential school history. In 1897, the Department of Indian Affairs reprinted Ryerson's report, a half-century after it had been submitted and more than a decade after Ryerson's death, in an appendix to a set of statistics on "Indian Schools in the Dominion."[119] It is this copy, which is available online at Library and Archives Canada, that is most frequently cited in the secondary literature. The superintendent of printing, perplexed by the request to reprint it, wrote to Clifford Sifton, the minister of the interior and superintendent general of Indian affairs, in 1897:

> I beg you to say that I cannot understand why you should confound this matter [Ryerson's 1847 report] with any copy of the Annual Report, as it has nothing to do with the [annual] report. It is true that there is a statement called "Statement of Indian Schools" published in the annual report, but the present statement [Ryerson's] is a particular

one made some years ago, and has no connection with the Report [on statistics].[120]

Ryerson's 1847 report was nevertheless published in the 1897 document. The likely explanation is that Indian Affairs intended to use it to justify industrial schools at a time when government regarded them as a failure.[121] Indeed, an Indian Affairs study of residential schools in 1897 confirmed the appalling quality of education at the schools, the harsh treatment of children by staff, and the inadequate food and living conditions.[122]

Sifton's plans for mass immigration to western Canada drove his education policies, which focused on cutting costs for the schools and containing Indians on reserves. His favoured approach was cheaper boarding schools located on or near reserves, which provided a basic education without costly industrial training.[123] The settling of the West by Europeans, including by my great-grandparents, Germans from southern Russia, relied on such policies. Indeed, my ancestors farmed in Assiniboia in the 1890s near Davin, named for their member of Parliament, Nicolas Flood Davin, in the heart of Treaty 4 territory. While the Hofwyl model was loosely followed in Canada, the origins of industrial schools and their successors were closer to home: a legacy of colonial policy and western expansion that gave little attention to the education or welfare of Indigenous children.

Notes

1 Indigenous and Northern Affairs Canada, "Treaties 1 and 2 between Her Majesty the Queen and the Chippewa and Cree Indians of Manitoba and Country Adjacent with Adhesions," https://www.aadnc-aandc.gc.ca/eng/1100100028664/1100100028665.

2 Brian Titley, *A Narrow Vision: Duncan Campbell Scott and the Administration of Indian Affairs in Canada* (Vancouver: UBC Press, 1986), 82.

3 The term *Indian industrial school* is used in this chapter because it was used historically. I also use the terms *Indigenous* and, less frequently, *Aboriginal* to refer to First Nations, Métis, Inuit, and Native American persons. Despite

controversy regarding the term *Indian,* because of a history of pejorative usage, I use it in certain contexts, when appropriate.

4 The terms *boarding school, industrial school,* and *residential school* were often used interchangeably during the late nineteenth and early twentieth centuries. By the 1920s, *residential school* was the common term for schools providing a common facility for living and learning: see David Wallace Adams, *Education for Extinction: American Indians and the Boarding School Experience, 1975–1928* (Lawrence: University of Kansas Press, 1995); Brenda J. Child, *Boarding School Seasons: American Indian Families, 1900–1940* (Lincoln: University of Nebraska Press, 1995); K. Tsianina Lomawaima and Teresa L. McCarty, *To Remain an Indian: Lessons in Democracy from a Century of Native American Education* (New York: Teachers College Press, 2006); James R. Miller, *Shingwauk's Vision: A History of Native Residential Schools* (Toronto: University of Toronto Press, 1996); John S. Milloy, *A National Crime: The Canadian Government and the Residential School System, 1879–1986* (Winnipeg: University of Manitoba Press, 1999); Magdalena Milosz, "'Don't Let Fear Take Over': The Space and Memory of Indian Residential Schools" (master's thesis, University of Waterloo, 2015); Derek G. Smith, "The 'Policy of Aggressive Assimilation' and Projects of Governance in Roman Catholic Industrial Schools for Native Peoples in Canada, 1870–95," *Anthropologica* 43 (2001): 253–71; Clifford E. Trafzer, Jean A. Keller, and Lorene Sisquoc, eds., *Boarding School Blues: Revisiting American Indian Education* (Lincoln: University of Nebraska Press, 2006); Robert P. Wells, *Wawahte: Indian Residential Schools* (Victoria, BC: FriesenPress, 2016); Andrew Woodford, *Indigenous Boarding Schools, Genocide, and Redress in Canada and the United States* (Lincoln: University of Nebraska Press, 2015); and Eric Taylor Woods, *A Cultural Sociology of Anglican Mission and the Indian Residential Schools in Canada: A Long Road to Apology* (London: Palgrave Macmillan, 2016).

5 Scott R. Trevithick, "Native Residential Schools in Canada: A Review of the Literature," *Canadian Journal of Native Studies* 18, 1 (1998): 49–86.

6 See, for instance, Sarah de Leeuw, "Artful Places: Creativity and Colonialism in British Columbia's Indian Residential Schools" (PhD diss., Queen's University, 2007); Anthony Di Mascio and Leigh Hortop-Di Mascio, "Residential Schooling in the Arctic: A Historical Case Study and Perspective," *Native Studies Review* 20, 2 (2011): 31–49; Allan Downey and Susan Neylan, "Raven Plays Ball: 'Indian Sports Days' within Indigenous and Colonial Spaces in Twentieth-Century Coastal British Columbia," *Canadian Journal of History* 50, 3 (2015): 442–68; and Ian Mosby, "Administering Colonial Science: Nutrition Research and Human Biomedical Experimentation in Aboriginal Communities and Residential Schools, 1942–1952," *Histoire sociale/Social History* 46, 91 (2013): 145–72.

7 See, for instance, Pauline Dempsey, "My Life in an Indian Residential School," *Alberta History* 59, 2 (2011): 22–27; Agnes Jack, *Behind Closed Doors: Stories from the Kamloops Indian Residential School,* rev. ed. (Penticton, BC: Theytus Books, 2006); and Joseph A. Merasty, *The Education of Augie Merasty: A Residential School Memoir* (Regina: University of Regina Press, 2015).

8 A school for the poor was one of several schools established by Fellenberg at his farm colony at Hofwyl. The colony, including its schools, is referred to as Hofwyl. Individual schools are referred to by their names.

9 Truth and Reconciliation Commission of Canada, *Canada's Residential Schools: The History, Part 1 – Origins to 1939* (Montreal/Kingston: McGill-Queen's University Press, 2015), 77.

10 Most are doctoral studies. See Kevin J. Abing, "A Fall from Grace: Thomas Johnson and the Shawnee Indian Manual Labour School, 1839–1862" (PhD diss., Marquette University, 1995); Carl Kalani Beyer, "Manual and Industrial Education during Hawaiian Sovereignty: Curriculum in the Transculturation of Hawai'i" (PhD diss., University of Illinois at Chicago, 2004); Robert Carney, "Aboriginal Residential Schools before Confederation: The Early Experience," *Historical Studies* 61 (1995): 13–40; Jeffrey R. McDade, "Social Control and the Native American: The Nineteenth-Century Manual Labour Boarding School" (PhD diss., Kansas State University, 1997); and Jennifer Lorretta Pettit, "'To Christianize and Civilize': Native Industrial Schools in Canada" (PhD diss., University of Calgary, 1997).

11 There is an excellent though brief review of Fellenberg's educational ideas on manual education in the Canadian context in Patrice Milewski, "Modern Schooling in Ontario: An Archaeology of Pedagogy" (PhD diss., University of Toronto, 2003). See also Margaret Weymouth, "Philipp Emanuel von Fellenberg: Influence on American Education" (PhD diss., Stanford University, 1967).

12 E. Bonjour, H.S. Offler, and G.R. Potter, *A Short History of Switzerland* (Oxford: Clarendon Press, 1952), 236, cited in Weymouth, "Philipp Emanuel von Fellenberg," 2.

13 Henry Brougham, "Establishment at Hofwyl," *Edinburgh Review* 32 (1819): 493. The plough's tail was the handle. See James Greenwood, *The London Vocabulary Designed for Use in Schools* (London: C. and J. Rivington, 1828), 70.

14 Sheila Carr-Stewart, "A Treaty Right to Education," *Canadian Journal of Education* 26, 2 (2001): 126.

15 Government of Canada, Commissioners Appointed to Inquire into the Affairs of the Indians in Canada, John Davidson, William Hepburn, and Sir William Rawson, "Report on the Affairs of the Indians in Canada: Laid Before the Legislative Assembly 20th March 1845," ss. I–III.

16 Government of Canada, "Report on the Affairs of the Indians in Canada," 3.

17 Quoted in Indian Chiefs and Principal Men, *Minutes of the General Council of Indian Chiefs and Principal Men ... on the Proposed Removal of the Smaller Communities and the Establishment of Manual Labour Schools,* 7, https://books.google.ca/books?id=crINAAAAQAAJ&redir_esc=y.

18 Sally M. Weaver, "The Iroquois: The Consolidation of the Grand River Reserve in the Mid-nineteenth Century, 1847–1875," in *Aboriginal Ontario: Historical Perspectives on the First Nations,* ed. Edward S. Rogers and Donald B. Smith (Toronto: Dundurn Press, 1994), 182–212.

19 Wendy Fletcher, "The Canadian Experiment with Social Engineering, a Historical Case: The Mohawk Institute," *Historical Papers: Canadian Society of Church History* (2004): 133–50, https://churchhistcan.files.wordpress. com/2013/05/2004-8-fletcher-article.pdf.

20 R.D. Gidney, "Ryerson, Egerton," in *Dictionary of Canadian Biography,* vol. 11 (Toronto/Quebec: University of Toronto/Université Laval, 2003), http:// www.biographi.ca/en/bio/ryerson_egerton_11E.html.

21 Helen May, Baljit Kaur, and Larry Prochner, *Empire, Education, and Indigenous Childhood: Missionary Infant Schools in Three British Colonies* (Farnham, UK: Ashgate, 2014).

22 "Educational missionary" is from Alison Prentice, *The School Promoters: Education and Social Class in Mid-nineteenth Century Upper Canada* (Toronto: McClelland and Stewart, 1977), 14; Ryerson's appointment in 1844 was as assistant superintendent of education. His title was superintendent of education after changes to the School Act in 1846. See J. Harold Putnam, *Egerton Ryerson and Education in Upper Canada* (Toronto: William Briggs, 1912).

23 Egerton Ryerson, *Report on a System of Public Elementary Instruction for Upper Canada* (Montreal: Lovell and Gibson for the Legislative Assembly, 1847).

24 Ibid., 60.

25 Louisa Mary Barwell, *Letters from Hofwyl by a Parent on the Educational Institutions of de Fellenberg* (London: Longman, Brown, Green, and Longmans, 1842), 64.

26 Weymouth, *Philipp Emanuel von Fellenberg,* 40–41.

27 Prentice, *The School Promoters,* 28–29.

28 Ryerson, *Report on a System,* 32.

29 Ibid., 106.

30 Prentice, *The School Promoters.*

31 Egerton Ryerson, "Report by Dr. Ryerson on Industrial Schools [Appendix A]," in *Statistics Respecting Indian Schools* (Ottawa: Government Printing Bureau, 1898), 74, Library and Archives Canada (LAC), Department of

Indian Affairs, RG 10, vol. 2952, file 202, pt. 239, http://collectionscanada. gc.ca/pam_archives/index.php?fuseaction=genitem.displayItem&lang =eng&rec_nbr=2069786&rec_nbr_list=2069786,4162063,198912.

32 Ibid., 74.

33 Ibid.

34 Ibid., 73.

35 Ibid., 75.

36 Ibid.

37 Brian E. Titley, "Indian Industrial Schools in Western Canada," in *Schools in the West: Essays in Canadian Education History,* ed. Nancy M. Sheehan, J. Donald Wilson, and David C. Jones (Calgary: Detselig, 1986), 133–53.

38 Donald B. Smith, *Mississauga Portraits: Ojibwe Voices from Nineteenth-Century Canada* (Toronto: University of Toronto Press, 2013), 238.

39 Government of Canada, *Report of the Special Commissioners Appointed on the 8th of September, 1856, to Investigate Indian Affairs in Canada* (Toronto: Stewart Derbishire and George Desbarats, 1858).

40 Tim Cresswell, "The Vagrant/Vagabond: The Curious Career of a Mobile Subject," in *Geographies of Mobilities: Practices, Spaces, Subjects,* ed. Tim Cresswell and Peter Merriman (Farnham, UK: Ashgate, 2011), 239–54.

41 John Locke, *Essay on the Poor Law,* ed. Mark Goldie (Cambridge: Cambridge University Press, 1997).

42 Peter Stearns, *Childhood in World History,* 2nd ed. (New York: Routledge, 2011), 67.

43 Locke, *Essay on the Poor Law,* 184.

44 Ibid.

45 Ibid., 185.

46 Ibid., 191.

47 Eric Hopkins, *Childhood Transformed: Working-Class Children in Nineteenth-Century England* (Manchester: Manchester University Press, 1994), 163; David Dickson, *Old World Colony: Cork and South Munster, 1630–1830* (Madison: University of Wisconsin Press, 2005), 206; and Irene D.F. Dean, *Scottish Spinning Schools* (London: University of London Press, 1930).

48 Roy Nash, *Schooling in Rural Societies* (New York: Routledge, 1980), 21.

49 Margaret Connell Szasz, *Scottish Highlanders and Native Americans: Indigenous Education in the Eighteenth-Century Atlantic World* (Norman: University of Oklahoma Press, 2007), 110.

50 Colin G. Calloway, *White People, Indians, and Highlanders: Tribal Peoples and Colonial Encounters in Scotland and America* (Oxford: Oxford University Press, 2008); and Szasz, *Scottish Highlanders and Native Americans.*

51 Nina Reid-Maroney, *The Reverend Jennie Johnson and African Canadian History, 1868–1967* (Rochester, NY: University of Rochester Press, 2013), 21.

52 Erving Goffman, *Asylums: Essays on the Social Situation of Mental Patients and Other Inmates* (New York: Anchor Books, 1961).

53 Aaron David Whelchel, "'The Schoolmaster Is Abroad': The Diffusion of Educational Innovations in the Nineteenth-Century British Empire" (PhD diss., Washington State University, 2011), 163.

54 Putnam, *Egerton Ryerson and Education in Upper Canada*, 110.

55 Egerton Ryerson, *The Story of My Life*, ed. J. George Hodgins (Toronto: William Briggs, 1883), 364.

56 Henry Barnard, ed., "Educational Establishment at Hofwyl," in "Reformatory Education," *Papers on Preventative, Correctional, and Reformatory Institutions and Agencies in Different Countries* (Hartford, CT: F.C. Brownell, 1857), 57.

57 Philipp Gonon, "Travel and Reform: Impulses towards Internationalisation in the Nineteenth-Century Discourse on Education," in *Educational Policy Borrowing: Historical Perspectives*, ed. David Phillips and Kimberly Ochs (Oxford: Symposium Books, 2004), 128.

58 Barwell, *Letters from Hofwyl*, 44.

59 Henry C. Wright visited Hofwyl in July 1844, the year before Ryerson. "Letters from Henry C. Wright," *The Liberator*, July 25, 1845, 3.

60 Weymouth, "Philipp Emanuel von Fellenberg"; and William de Fellenberg, "Pestalozzi, de Fellenberg, and Wehrli, and Industrial Training," *American Journal of Education* 10 (1861): 82–92; and Mrs. E.H. Percival, *Life of Sir David Wedderburn* (London: Kegan Paul, Trench, Trübner and Co., 1884).

61 Daniel Alexandre Chavannes, *Rapport sur l'Institut d'education des pauvres à Hofwyl* (Paris: J.J. Paschoud, 1813), 28.

62 J.W. Adamson, *English Education, 1789–1902* (Cambridge: Cambridge University Press, 1930), 117 ["educational colony"]; and "Emanuel von Fellenberg," in "Encyclopaedia Americana," *Pittsburgh Weekly Gazette*, June 14, 1831, 2.

63 Margaret W. Rossiter, *The Emergence of Agricultural Science: Justus Liebeg and the Americans, 1840–1880* (New Haven, CT: Yale University Press, 1975).

64 "Emanuel von Fellenberg," 2.

65 Henry Brougham, "Establishment at Hofwyl," *Edinburgh Review* 32 (1819): 489–90.

66 Henry Brougham, "Establishment at Hofwyl," *Edinburgh Review* 31 (1819): 157.

67 Ibid., 156.

68 Different from the Agricultural Institute, with its experimental farm and focus on agricultural science.

69 John Griscom, *A Year in Europe, Comprising a Journal of Observations, in England, Scotland, Ireland, France, Switzerland, the North of Italy, and Holland*, vol. 1 (New York: Collins and Co./E. Bliss and E. White, 1823), 270.

70 Ibid., 266.

71 Henry Brougham, "Mr. Brougham's Account of an Establishment in Switzerland," *Appendix to Mr. Brougham's Letter: Containing Minutes of Evidence*

Taken before the Education Committee (London: Longman, Hurst, Rees, Orme, and Brown, 1818), 99.

72 Also called the gymnasium or high school, but most commonly simply the academy.

73 Lady Byron, cited in Julia Markus, *Lady Byron and Her Daughters* (London: Norton, 2015), 165. Louisa Mary Barwell recounted a similar scene. She observed *Real Schulers* in their studies, while "at the fountain by the château is a rural scholar washing some of the windows." Barwell, *Letters from Hofwyl*, 65.

74 Harold Silver, *The Concept of Popular Education: A Study of Ideas and Social Movements in the Early Nineteenth Century* (London: Methuen, 1965).

75 Robert Dale Owen, *Threading My Way: Twenty-Seven Years of Autobiography* (London: Trübner and Co., 1874), 135.

76 John Griscom, "Hofwyl – Fellenberg," *Common School Assistant* 2, 4 (1837): 30.

77 Brougham, "Establishment at Hofwyl," *Edinburgh Review* 32 (1819): 506.

78 Jean-Jacques Rousseau, *Emile, or On Education*, trans. Barbara Foxley (Waiheke Island, NZ: Floating Press, 2009), 167.

79 Ibid., 177.

80 Brougham, "Establishment at Hofwyl," *Edinburgh Review* 32 (1819): 492.

81 Alexander Dallas Bache, *Report on Education in Europe to the Trustees of the Girard College for Orphans* (Philadelphia: Bailey, 1839), 307–8.

82 Griscom, *A Year in Europe*, 398.

83 Brougham, "Mr. Brougham's Account," 101.

84 Brougham, "Establishment at Hofwyl," *Edinburgh Review* 31 (1819): 157.

85 Griscom, "Hofwyl – Fellenberg," 28.

86 Owen, *Threading My Way*, 127.

87 Brougham, "Establishment at Hofwyl," *Edinburgh Review* 32 (1819): 492.

88 Wyatt James Dowling, "Science, *Robinson Crusoe*, and Judgment: A Commentary on Book III of Rousseau's *Emile*" (PhD diss., Boston College, 2007).

89 "A Colony of Boys," *Vermont Watchman and State Journal*, October 5, 1848, 1.

90 Dowling, "Science, *Robinson Crusoe*, and Judgment," 33.

91 Mr. Fennell, *M. Fellenberg, His Schools and Plans* (England: n.p., 1830), 19. Also in Lady Byron, *What de Fellenberg Has Done for Education* (London: Saunders and Otley, 1839), 27–30.

92 Fennell, *M. Fellenberg*, 18.

93 Ibid., 19.

94 Ibid.

95 Ibid., 16.

96 Ibid., 17.

97 Owen, *Threading My Way*, 170–74.

98 *Pestalozzi and His Principles,* prepared at the request of the Committee of the Home and Colonial School Society, 1864, 46. Cited in Silver, *The Concept of Popular Education,* 151.

99 Adamson, *English Education,* 117.

100 Mary Berry, May 2, 1836, in Thomas McLean, ed., *Further Letters of Joanna Baillie* (Cranbury, NJ: Fairleigh Dickinson University Press, 2010), 169; see Brian W. Taylor, "Annabella, Lady Noel-Byron: A Study of Lady Byron on Education," *History of Education Quarterly* 39, 4 (1998): 430–55.

101 W.C., *Schools of Industry* (1846), 19.

102 *The Times* (London), January 3, 1843, 2.

103 *The Sydney Morning Herald,* October 2, 1844, 1.

104 John Francis Leonard, "The Historical Development of the Program of Studies in English Elementary Schools in New Brunswick" (master's thesis, University of Ottawa, 1956).

105 Paul W. Bennett, "Taming 'Bad Boys' of the 'Dangerous Class': Child Rescue and Restraint at the Victoria Industrial School, 1887–1935," *Histoire sociale/Social History* 21, 4 (1988): 71–96; Alistair Glegg, "Margaret Bayne and the Vancouver Girls' Industrial School," *Historical Studies in Education* 18, 2 (2006): 201–23; Bryan Hogeveen, "Accounting for Violence at the Victoria Industrial School," *Histoire sociale/Social History* 42, 83 (2009): 147–74; Patricia T. Rooke, "The 'Child-Institutionalized' in Canada, Britain, and the United States: A Trans-Atlantic Perspective," *Journal of Educational Thought* 11, 2 (1977): 156–71; and Neil Sutherland, *Children in English-Canadian Society: Framing the Twentieth-Century Consensus* (Waterloo, ON: Wilfrid Laurier University Press, 2000).

106 *Report of the Halifax Protestant Industrial School* (Halifax, 1866), http://static.torontopubliclibrary.ca/da/pdfs/37131055320147d.pdf.

107 Paul W. Bennett, "Taming 'Bad Boys,'" 76.

108 Ontario Industrial Schools Act, 1874, 37 Vict., ch. 29, 219, https://archive.org/details/statutesofprovi1874p1onta.

109 Charlotte Neff, "The Ontario Industrial Schools Act of 1874," *Canadian Journal of Family Law* 12 (1994–95): 172.

110 Sarah Carter, *Lost Harvests: Prairie Indian Reserve Farmers and Government Policy* (Montreal/Kingston: McGill-Queen's University Press, 1990).

111 Nicolas Flood Davin, *Report on Industrial Schools for Indians and Half-Breeds* (Ottawa: 1879), https://archive.org/details/cihm_03651. Davin's communication with the prime minister regarding the contract to conduct the study is cited in Charles Beverly Koester, *Mr. Davin, M.P.: A Biography of Nicholas Flood Davin* (Saskatoon: Western Producer Prairie Books, 1980).

112 Melissa L. Meyer, "Signatures and Thumbprints: Ethnicity among the White Earth Anishinaabeg, 1889–1920," *Social Science History* 14, 3 (1990): 305–45. The history of the White Earth Reservation is detailed by Melissa L. Meyer in *The White Earth Tragedy: Ethnicity and Dispossession at a*

Minnesota Anishinaabe Reservation, 1889–1920 (Lincoln: University of Nebraska Press, 1994).

113 Davin, *Report on Industrial Schools,* 7.

114 Ibid.

115 C.A. Ruffee, United States Indian Agent, *Report of the Commissioner of Indian Affairs* (1879), 88, http://digicoll.library.wisc.edu/cgi-bin/History/History-idx?id=History.AnnRep79.

116 Davin, *Report on Industrial Schools,* 3.

117 Ibid., 2.

118 Ibid., 13.

119 LAC, RG 10, vol. 2952, file 202.

120 Ibid., file 239.

121 Miller, *Shingwauk's Vision,* 134–35.

122 Truth and Reconciliation Commission of Canada, *Canada's Residential Schools,* 453–54.

123 D.J. Hall, "Clifford Sifton and Canadian Indian Administration, 1896–1905," in *Immigration and Settlement, 1870–1939,* ed. Gregory P. Marchidon (Regina: Canadian Plains Research Center, 2009), 190.

3

THE HEAVY DEBT
OF OUR MISSIONS

Failed Treaty Promises and Anglican Schools in Blackfoot Territory, 1892–1902

Sheila Carr-Stewart

Ask the Lord, and tell his people and doubtless the money will be found.

– Diocese of Calgary, Report on Indian Missions, 1894

The Kainai (Blood), Siksika (Blackfoot), and Piikani (Peigan) First Nations together form the Blackfoot Confederacy, whose territory encompassed present-day southern Alberta and Montana in the nineteenth century. The Blackfoot people hunted the buffalo, which provided food, clothing, and shelter and formed the basis of their economy. Lifelong learning was the focus of each community or band, and long before European colonizers arrived in North America, the Blackfoot had developed their own form of education. As Verna Kirkness writes, "it was an education in which the community and the natural environment were the classroom, and the land was seen as the mother of the people."[1] For the people of the Blackfoot Confederacy, as Chief John Snow explains in *These Mountains Are Our Sacred Places*, education was "interwoven into the life of the tribal society."[2] Mothers spent time with their young children as they grew, fathers taught skills, and Elders guided and trained youth. From them, children learned their language, stories, prayers, ceremonies, songs, dances, and their people's relationship with minerals, plants, animals, and the climate.[3] As the young listened, watched, and learned from community members, knowledge was transferred from one generation to the next.[4]

Few newcomers ventured westward into Blackfoot territory until the mid-nineteenth century, and they did so initially to trade for buffalo hides and other goods. Surveyors ventured into the area to map the territory and identify the boundary line between the North-West Territories and the United States to the south, as well as to map the route for a railroad from eastern Canada across the Prairies to what is now British Columbia. Cognizant of the Numbered Treaties negotiated between the Crown and Indigenous peoples to the east, and of the increasing number of newcomers settling in their traditional territory, in 1876 members of the Blackfoot Confederacy requested a meeting with the Crown's representatives to negotiate a treaty. They demanded a meeting at Blackfoot Crossing and were "intent on an alliance of peace, to safeguard their territory and to protect their way of life ... specific[ally] they wanted the encroachment of the newcomers controlled, they wanted the buffalo protected, and they wanted the American traders controlled."[5] The Blackfoot were joined by their neighbours to the north, members of the Tsuut'ina Nation (Sarcee), and by their northwest neighbours, members of the three nations that made up the Nakoda (Stoney) Tribe.

Canada wanted to enter into treaty with the Blackfoot to gain title to their traditional lands, which it identified as "the unsurrendered portion of the territory" comprising approximately 50,000 square miles west of Treaty 6, north of the boundary line, and east of the Rocky Mountains.[6] Within the context of the 1763 Royal Proclamation, Canada was required to settle through treaty "any claims of Indians" to lands required by the colonial government for purposes of settlement.[7] The two parties to Treaty 7 – the Crown's treaty commissioners and the Chiefs and Headmen – met at Blackfoot Crossing and over five days discussed and clarified the Blackfoot Confederacy's demands. The Crown representatives recorded that the negotiations

Sheila Carr-Stewart

were long and "tedious."[8] For members of the Blackfoot Confederacy, the treaty negotiations were "the time when we made a sacred alliance."[9] On September 22, 1877, Treaty 7 was agreed to by both parties. David Laird, the lieutenant-governor of the North-West Territories and one of the Crown's treaty commissioners, noted that "promises ... to the Indians ... will, I am convinced, cost less than those under either Treaty No. 4 or No. 6."[10] Despite Laird's prediction, Treaty 7 established the Crown's fiduciary obligation for a number of services, including education whenever "Indians" desired such services.[11]

From their discussions with the treaty commissioners and the promises made, members of the Treaty 7 nations understood they had negotiated a mutually beneficial treaty. The Crown's treaty obligations included goods and services, annual treaty payments, land, the building and establishment of schools, and the provision of Western education and training to enable them to participate and prosper in a new economic era.[12] However, the written treaty, prepared in Ottawa, did not reflect the detailed discussions into which the two parties had entered. Canada gradually created reserves, but it provided only limited farming instruction and equipment, and it did little to help reserve residents adapt to the new farming economy. The federal government left the establishment and operation of schools to religious and missionary organizations, whose clergy played multifaceted roles on reserves: they spread the Christian message, established day schools and taught skills to adults, prepared the people to adapt to a sedentary Western lifestyle, and supported the basic survival of the people, who were decimated by disease and starvation from the 1870s to the 1920s.[13]

Drawing on the Diocese of Calgary's annual reports on Indian missions, published between 1892 and 1905, and other primary and secondary sources, I examine the Anglican Church's role in establishing and financing day schools and boarding schools within Blackfoot territory and how its efforts meshed and conflicted with the federal government's new goal to assimilate and "civilize" First Nations through residential schools.[14] These records show that by relying on the churches to fund and run the schools, incurring major debts in the process, the federal government failed to meet its treaty obligations and laid the foundations for an educational system that would lead to physical and emotional stress and trauma among generations of First Nations students and their families.

The Indian Act and Indigenous Education

When Canada entered into Treaty 7 in 1877 it was fully cognizant of its responsibility for "Indians, and Lands reserved for Indians," as outlined in the 1867 British North America Act.[15] However, the underlying goal of the 1876 Indian Act, which placed "Indians" in a distinct legal category, was assimilation or enfranchisement, and "civilization" was the prerequisite to meeting this goal.[16] The federal government was determined "to make Indians into imitation Europeans and to eradicate the old Indian values through education, religion, new economic and political systems, and a new concept of property." Euro-Canadian schooling was the key to the "civilizing process."[17] The government used the churches' willingness to work among First Nations people and to establish schools on the reserves as the mechanism to implement its educational policy.

The government's educational policy initiatives were shaped by Nicholas Flood Davin's 1879 report on education, which called for "aggressive civilization" through the establishment of industrial training or boarding schools.[18] Ongoing Indian Act amendments relating to education cemented Canada's goals for Indian education and expanded the power of the governor-in-council to determine the type of schools First Nations children attended. Thus section 138 of the 1894 Indian Act deemed that the governor-in-council "may establish an industrial school or a boarding school for Indians, or may declare any existing Indian school to be such industrial school or boarding school."[19] Amendments in 1894 also ensured school attendance and "conveyance to school, and detention there, of truant children and of children who are prevented by their parents or guardians from attending."[20] Parents who resisted sending their children to boarding school faced arrest and prosecution. Canada implemented these policies without consulting with First Nations communities. At their core lay the notion that the education of young First Nations children was "the most potent power to effect cultural change ... a power to be channeled through schools and, in particular, through residential schools."[21]

While the Canadian government was passing legislation and setting the policy direction for the establishment and operation of on-reserve schools, churches and missionary societies were left to operate poorly equipped schools with limited funds with which to attract teachers. George H. Gooderham, the Indian agent at the Blackfoot Reserve and regional supervisor of Indian agencies, noted in the 1920s that

> as far as education was concerned it was truly a very informal union which left the churches to carry the greater part of the burden of educating the Indian ... The Government support throughout ... was inadequate and churches through their affiliations had to find considerable financial assistance. Even the combined funds [of Canada and the churches] were neither sufficient to pay the salaries of qualified teachers nor to supply the proper diet for the children.[22]

In a brief to the Special Joint Committee of the Senate and the House of Commons in 1947, the Church of England similarly noted that "when the Federal Government undertook its Treaty obligations, it found the Churches already caring for Indian education and the policy of giving government grants-in-aid was decided upon"; the government consequently "fulfilled its treaty education obligations with a minimum of effort and cost."[23] In a loosely defined partnership between the government and the churches, churches and missionary groups petitioned the federal government for help to defray the costs associated with the construction and operation of schools.

Early Missionary Efforts in Treaty 7

Despite Canada's fiduciary obligation to provide schools within the context of the Numbered Treaties, the federal government simply left the establishment and operation of schools to religious groups. In Treaty 7 territory, individual churches and missionary organizations took the initiative to build, maintain, and operate schools, to hire and pay teachers, and to provide food and clothing for students.[24] The churches had a mission to "evangelize local native populations, to administer to the sick and to provide basic schooling for the young."[25] Supported by the Methodist Church, John McDougall and his sons established a mission among the Nakoda at Morleyville in 1875, while Father Scollen, a Roman Catholic priest, worked among the Blackfoot peoples, particularly the Kainai, in the early 1870s. The Anglican Church, by contrast, "was late in settling a missionary" among the peoples of Treaty 7.[26] In 1878, the Reverend George McKay established an Anglican presence in Fort McLeod and the following year founded St. Peter's Mission at the Piikani Reserve. The Reverend Samuel Trivett settled on the Kainai Reserve in 1880, where he "built a school building ... with 29 children in attendance."[27]

Other Anglican clergy followed. To reach the Treaty 7 area, they travelled westward by horseback or carriage either from Toronto to Winnipeg, Prince Albert, or Edmonton or southwestward through the United States, where they met fellow clergy who guided them on the last segment of their travels. The Reverend John W. Tims, an ordained Anglican minister, wrote that when he arrived at the Siksika Reserve in 1883, he proceeded to the Chief's tent in the encampment, where he "sat cross legged on the beds around the tepee." Through an interpreter, he spoke "to the men of the love of God ... and after explanations had been made of my presence among them ... I was left to feel my way and get the work started.[28] As did the clergy of all denominations, Tims initially preached and taught on the open prairie; over time, classes moved from tents to huts to larger houses and ultimately to school buildings. Mike Mountain Horse recalled that

Sheila Carr-Stewart

after the people of Treaty 7 had "settled on reserves ... missionaries visited our Indian camps periodically to enroll pupils for the day schools opened by some of the churches."[29]

Tims initially lived with the government farm instructor, but upon receiving "a credit in a bank at Winnipeg" from the Anglican bishop, he "bought house logs, some lumber and nails ... from I.G. Baker & Co"[30] and, with the help of the Siksika people, built a mission house:

> The house was divided into three rooms – a large room taking up little more than half the building used as both kitchen and school room and the other part subdivided into a study or living room and a bedroom. The only furniture was a cook stove and the carpenter's bench which served as a table. The other rooms were furnished with a bedstead I made by myself, also a table and bookcase made by the carpenter who helped me with the building. For a seat I used an empty nail keg; a couple of boxes I had brought from England placed together with a buffalo robe thrown over them, formed a couch.[31]

With no seats in the combined kitchen and schoolroom, Tims taught the children as they sat on the floor. He wrote that "once the school opened, he started in earnest to learn the language."[32] In 1889, he published a *Grammar and Dictionary of the Blackfoot Language* and subsequently translated the *Gospel of St. Matthew and Other Readings from the Holy Scriptures*. In addition to learning the language and teaching, Tims was "called daily to visit many sick cases and to dispense medicines. Add to this the necessary cooking, washing, baking, and scrubbing ... my days were well filled."[33] Like his fellow Protestant and Roman Catholic missionaries, Tims distinguished little between his religious duties, teaching responsibilities, and outreach activities.

Building and Funding Schools

As did other Christian organizations, the Anglican Church, coordinated and funded its own educational activities among First Nations peoples, first through the Church Missionary Society (CMS) and later through the Missionary Society of the Church of England in Canada. The CMS established the Calgary Indian Missions Agency to coordinate Anglican missionary and educational activities in the Treaty 7 area. When the Diocese of Calgary was established in 1888, it "became closely involved in pastoral work and education of Indian children."[34] But these activities posed a financial challenge, particularly given loose financial arrangements with the federal government.[35]

Over time, the Anglican Church sought funding to help with new school construction and improvements to existing schools. In his 1892 year-end report for the St. John's Mission at the Siksika Reserve, J.W. Tims wrote that

> the old school house, built in 1884, of logs and mud is now too small as well as too dilapidated for further use. It is intended to build a larger and more suitable building this year [1893] ... it is hoped that one half the cost of this ($400) will be met by the Indian Department, leaving $400 to be collected from amongst the friends of this mission. This is most urgent. Will all who can help do what they can towards collecting this sum?[36]

The following year, Tims happily reported that in Eagle Rib's Village "we have erected a good school and teacher's residence at a cost of $800, one half of which was met by the Government."[37]

The first schools established in the Treaty 7 area were day schools; however, the churches gradually began to build home schools for boys and girls, often adjacent to the day schools. These initiatives, referred to as "joint projects," enabled the federal government to evade its treaty obligation to erect and establish schools on each reserve in the Treaty 7 area. In his 1892 report, also for St. John's Mission at the Siksika Reserve, Rev. Swainson noted that "during the year the Girls' Home had been completed, and will hold twenty-five children"; at the official opening of the school, news was "received that the Government would grant $750 towards a Boys' Home at the same place,

Sheila Carr-Stewart

provided the money be expended before June 30th. An effort is now being made to raise $850 in order to put up a $1600 building."[38] The federal government usually paid half of the cost of school construction, leaving the remainder to be raised by the individual church organization, a clear violation of the Crown's treaty responsibility for schools and teachers.

Receiving a contribution towards the construction of a school helped alleviate the church's burden. In 1893, Mr. Hinchcliffe, principal and teacher at St. Peter's Mission at the Piikani Reserve, reported that "$400 has been asked for from the Government" for school construction; however, Hinchcliffe was required to appeal to supporters of the Anglican Church "for assistance in clothing, bedding, crockery, etc ... towards defraying the cost ... another horse will be necessary, as there will be more travelling and hauling. Donations [would] be thankfully received by myself or the Lord Bishop of Calgary."[39] Despite difficulties acquiring donations for school construction and operation, the Diocese of Calgary reported in 1893–94 that boy's homes had been built at both St. Paul's and St. John's Missions.[40] At St. Peter's Mission at the Piikani Reserve, a new wing was added "for the accommodation of 24 boys as well as a Dining Hall sufficiently large to accommodate both boys and girls ... A large addition was also made to the Boys' Home, St. Barnabas' Mission, Sarcee Reserve in the spring of 1892, and a new wing added to the Mission House for the reception of ten girls."[41]

In his 1894 report for the St. Barnabas Mission, H.W. Gibson Stocken noted that, at the Tsuu'tina Reserve, "we have now under our care all the children of school age on the Reserve, to the number of twenty-nine, of whom nineteen are boys."[42] He added that

the Boy's Home was opened in May, 1892. The girls who came to us as recently as last month are accommodated in the Mission House. A lean-to being used as a dormitory and the kitchen as their general room. Ten girls are more than we anticipated, and we are uncomfortably pinched for room. We were unable to take in the girls at an earlier date, being without the means to support a matron. In order to accommodate the boys we had to erect a large building, and in doing so incurred a heavy debt, to which must be added the cost of maintenance ... Towards the building the Indian Department has given us altogether $600, and has paid us since July last a grant in aid of maintenance in addition to the rations of beef and flour. An urgent appeal has been issued, and is strongly endorsed by the Bishop of the Diocese, asking for immediate help towards liquidating the debt of $1000. Clothing and groceries are much needed for our Homes.[43]

The Diocese of Calgary's 1894 report on Indian missions concluded that "all this work has cost money. We have received considerable help from the Indian Department for this purpose but more than half the cost has been borne by the Missions."[44]

In 1898, the Diocese of Calgary reported that the mission's field work covered "the four Reserves in Southern Alberta: the Peigan, the Blood, the Blackfoot and the Sarcee" (identified "in the order in which they were taken up") and served a total population of 3,397.[45] The diocese relied on donations from the Missionary Society of the Church of England in Canada, the Women's Auxiliary, and individuals and groups in eastern Canada and England.[46] When it came to staffing the schools, the federal government provided funding in the form of grants only if a school had more than twenty-five students in attendance: "A salary of $300 per annum is paid to the teacher of each school ... and $12 per annum for each pupil over the number of 25 and up to the number of 42; the whole not to exceed $504 per annum."[47] By 1893, the Diocese of Calgary was operating eight day schools and four boarding schools staffed by thirty-four individuals in Blackfoot territory. Only nine teachers were funded by the government, seven had partial funding, and the remaining eighteen were paid out of funds contributed to the missions.[48] Administrators noted that "the Government pays ... the small sum of $300 to each of the teachers of the Day Schools, which is generally supplemented, but not always, by

Sheila Carr-Stewart

$200 from the C.M.S. or some local fund."[49] Supplementing teachers' salaries as well as funding the construction and operating costs of First Nations schools required the Anglican Church to constantly send out pleas for donations. It also resulted in financial difficulties: "A glance at the Financial Statements will show that the Missions are all more or less in debt."[50] Even when salaries were supplemented by the Anglican Church, they did not equal those paid to teachers who worked at schools for non-Indigenous students.

Given the size of the reserves in Treaty 7 and the scattered nature of the camps and communities in them, meeting the criteria of twenty-five students per school was often difficult and unrealistic. The church needed to build multiple schools to ensure children's attendance. The report for St. Paul's Mission at the Kainai Reserve noted, "It is the largest Reserve in the Diocese, the Indians being scattered over forty miles of territory ... day schools are established at different points on the river, by means of which about a hundred children are brought under instruction."[51] To attend these schools, students were still required to walk significant distances each day, often in freezing temperatures. Building a home or residential facility for students adjacent to the day school helped but also increased the need to provide warm clothing. In 1893, Frank Swainson reported from the mission, "Two years ago we had but seven girls in our Homes, and two day-schools on the Blood Reserve ... today we have three day schools on the reserve ... a Home with twenty-five girls, and a boy's Home with twenty-seven boys with accommodation for forty."[52] Swainson noted that they were "waiting until sufficient clothing can be gathered" before more students could be admitted to the home.[53]

The uncertainty of funding from the federal government and, at times, the denial of requests resulted in day schools being closed temporarily or permanently. During the 1892–93 academic year, Tims wrote that, despite the uncertainty of funding, "three day schools were kept open during the year."[54] But other schools were not so fortunate. In 1897, Red Crow's Day School at the Kainai Reserve was closed, "owing to the withdrawal of the Government grant towards the teacher's salary, on account of the small attendance."[55] Similarly, in 1898, the principal of St. Paul's Lower Mission reported that

the staff has been somewhat reduced, owing partly to the small income the Homes now receive as compared with three or four years ago, and the cost of carrying on the work has been reduced to a minimum. Some of the pupils have been discharged as over age, others have been transferred to the Industrial School [in Calgary] leaving about fifty-two scholars in residence ... the cost ... last year exceeded our income of $500.00. We desire most earnestly that the friends of this Mission will see to it that the work is not crippled for lack of funds.[56]

Canada's new policy emphasis on residential schooling for First Nations students signalled the closure of day schools. The Diocese of Calgary reported in 1893 that it was struggling to keep day schools open, as in the case of "Bull Horn's day-school ... the government is anxious to close it and make more use of the boarding-school at St. Paul by drafting children into it."[57] The Anglican Church had established "homes" for children on the Treaty 7 reserves, but the inclusion of an article from *The Sower in the West* magazine in the Diocese of Calgary's 1895 report offers a glimpse of the church's conflict with Canada's residential school policy:

When the boarding school system was introduced Reserves in this [Calgary] Diocese were without Government support, and children were permitted to enter and leave at will of the parents. Since the government has undertaken to support this work by grants-in-aid, it has made regulations about the detention of children in the schools that have been particularly abnoxious [sic] to the Blackfoot parents ... The burden of carrying out these regulations has fallen on Mr. Tims, as principal of the schools, and the Indians, having got it into their heads that Mr. Tims is the originator of them [have] made things so unpleasant for him that he felt it best to retire.[58]

Because Canada's educational policy emphasized residential schools, the Anglican Church worked with the federal government to build and staff the facilities. From its initial outreach activities and day schools, the church's missionary work became, by the late 1880s, fully intertwined in the federal government's large-scale residential school initiative. The Diocese of Calgary continually requested financial support from adherents to address the lack of funds received to operate the schools. In 1894, it noted:

> We desire to thank most sincerely those friends who have encouraged us in the work by their gifts of money and of clothing, and by their prayers. Especially are we indebted to a lady in England who has assisted [us] so generously in the erection of the Boys' Home in St. Paul's Mission, Blood Reserve ... and to the different Branches of the Woman's Auxiliary in Eastern Canada, without whose kind help the educational work of the Anglican Church could not be continued.[59]

Education in an Uncertain Environment

Regardless of which church organization operated schools within Treaty 7, financial donations were vital to sustain a basic level of school operation. The uncertainty of both public donations and federal contributions to the upkeep and operation of schools, as well as the fluctuating numbers of students, meant the ongoing operation of schools was often in jeopardy. Schools opened and closed with regularity, and the lack of stability did little to foster attendance and learning. For instance, White Eagle Boarding School, which was run by the Anglican Church at the Siksika Reserve from 1895 to 1901, had an average annual attendance of between nine and twenty-three students. Old Sun's school, which began as a camp school in 1889, became a day school in 1896, was closed in 1900 because of poor attendance and lack of funding, and reopened in 1910.[60] Financial statements and reports submitted by school principals identified the costs associated with operating each school. The 1893 financial statement for the Blood Reserve School at St. Paul's Mission, for instance, shows that subscriptions and donations accounted for 41 percent ($2,385) of operating costs. Major expenditures included building ($2,673), provisions ($1,380), and salaries ($417).[61]

Financial statements for the same year from J. Hinchcliffe, principal of St. Peter's Mission at the Piikani Nation, offered a more detailed account of the source of donations. Hinchcliffe reported that the boarding school was large enough to accommodate thirty-six children (twenty-four boys and twelve girls) but that there were only thirty-one students in residence. A new wing had been added to the school, which comprised a day room and dormitory for the boys, a dining room, and a room for the master, at a cost of $871.30. All of the money was raised through "the kindness" of the Anglican mission and the "exertions of our matron, Miss Brown, who has been collecting money in East Canada." Contributions came from diverse sources, including teaching and building grants from the federal government, a loan from the "Diocesan Ex. Comm.," and donations from St. James Cathedral in Toronto, the Quebec Cathedral Women's Auxiliary, and other individuals and organizations. Despite donations valued at $1,622.42, the school's finances were in a deficit position in both 1892 and 1893.[62]

The Diocese of Calgary's general report noted, "We have received considerable help from the Indian Department for [education] purpose[s], but more than half the cost has been borne by the Missions."[63] Commitments by the federal government, whether small or large, were often not fulfilled. In 1894, for instance, Tims reported from St. John's Mission: "The Government Inspector, in his report of [our] school to the Government says 'as this was one of the best schools I had visited, I made a request to the Commissioner that a flag be presented to it.' We did not, however, get the flag."[64] Tims added, "We have built a new Home at the South Blackfoot Reserve, at a cost of nearly $3500; the Department has promised $1500 towards this, so that about $2000 is required to pay the cost of the same. Towards this, about

Sheila Carr-Stewart

$100 has been received [through donations]. The need of immediate help in paying off the balance is urgent."[65]

In 1889, when missions were unable to raise enough funds to ensure that students were fed, the Diocese of Calgary reported that the government was granting $72.00 towards the maintenance and tuition of each student at the residential school at the Piikani Reserve and that it "allows us to get beef or flour, or both, from them at contract rates, the amount received in kind being deducted from the per capita grant."[66] Similarly, in 1895, Swainson noted in his report on St. Paul's Mission that "the Indian Department now gives a maintenance grant towards the keep of forty of the Indian children, and a ration of beef and floor towards the support of the remaining."[67] Tims noted that even though the federal government was providing funds for school construction, there were still problems:

> St. John's Home is to be further enlarged at once, as to accommodate fifteen more pupils. The Government has granted $500 for this purpose ... [however] the enlargement[s] to this Home ... necessitate a large addition to the staff ... we have no pecuniary help on which to depend for the payment of salaries of additional workers, but feel sure that He who has helped us in the past will provide all that is necessary in the future. We will "ask the Lord, and tell His people," and doubtless the money will be found.[68]

When the diocese outlined its "present wants" in 1893–94, they included, for St. Peter's Mission, $500 to repay the missionary; for St. Paul's Mission, $2,500 to build a large home for fifty additional girls, $120 to supplement a teacher's salary, and material for students' clothing; and for St. John's Mission, $1,000 for a new home.[69]

Donations continued to be an essential part of school construction costs, as evidenced by the school built at the Piikani Reserve. The 1897 report stated that "a frame wooden [school] building, plastered on the inside" had been opened "and is to be heated with hot air furnaces, the gift of a rancher in the district ... The cost of the new building will be about $3,500; towards this amount the Government has promised $1,100.00."[70] To address the growing crisis of lack of funds for their educational endeavours, on July 29, 1896, the Bishop's Court in Calgary issued the following statement: "In the interest of efficiency and economy, it has been arranged that all monies" will be collected centrally and divided "in accordance with the will of the donors, and the needs of the work."[71] In 1898, Mr. F. van Thiel of Calgary was appointed as the accountant of Indian missions.[72]

Despite these initiatives, a centralized accounting system only highlighted the need for more donations to supplement grants received from the federal government. In 1900, Rev. Canon Stocken, in charge of St. John's Mission at the Siksika Reserve, reported that "the Blackfoot Christians are urged to contribute to the funds of the mission, and their efforts in cash and kind have been very good."[73] The following year, he reported that "the St. John's Homes for boys and girls have been amalgamated ... in order to save expense, especially in fuel and light."[74] He also noted that "the Boys' Home at White Eagle's has been given up and the boys transferred to the Girls' Home which originally was built for boys and girls ... we trust that the union of the Schools will prove beneficial in every way."[75] The move resulted in Stocken stating his concern that "there are now forty-three pupils in residence, twenty-six boys and seventeen girls, and the quarters for both staff and pupils are cramped"[76] By 1903, donations to the diocese varied from "bales of useful clothing and quilts" to "groceries and Christmas toys," all of which enabled the diocese "to end the year with less indebtedness than usual."[77] However, the diocese noted that "the heavy debt of our Mission buildings ... weigh upon us" and that "the strictest economy is being practiced, and the good deal of self-denial is being exercised on the part of the Missionaries and all associated with them."[78]

≷∣≷

In 1901, when the Diocese of Calgary reported on its Indian missions, it noted that the federal government "had undertaken at its own

Sheila Carr-Stewart

expense, to pull down a portion of the White Eagle School and enlarge St. John's Home to a suitable size."[79] It was the first time the federal government had initiated the development of a school since Treaty 7 had been signed. Yet, despite this initiative, Anglican schools continued to be "indebted to the Woman's Auxiliary for their valuable consignments of clothing as well as for support (funding for salaries) for lady workers" in the schools.[80] In 1905, the diocese reported that "the increasing prosperity of the Indians makes the need of assistance in clothing much less than formerly, and with the exception of quilts and some articles of clothing for the old people, gratuitous clothing for the Indians in this Diocese is no longer required."[81] Nevertheless, administrators noted that "we still do need all the help for our Schools we can get."[82]

When the Anglican, Methodist, and Roman Catholic churches established schools on Treaty 7 reserves, they filled a gap opened up by Canada's failure to establish schools and provide teachers, as promised in the Numbered Treaties, and to take responsibility for "Indians, and Lands Reserved for Indians," as outlined in the BNA Act. The network of schools established by the churches created an educational system that would ultimately become the federal school system, funded by the federal government within the parameters of the Indian Act but void of any reference to the Numbered Treaties. While the federal government was a reluctant participant in establishing schools, it nevertheless gradually assumed a greater role in and financial commitment to on-reserve schools. But it did not assume full responsibility until the mid-twentieth century. The financial hurdles that the Anglican Church faced to keep its schools open in the late nineteenth and early twentieth centuries are again being faced today, as First Nations governments and organizations demand federal government funding for community-controlled schools on reserves on par with that received by provincially operated schools. To achieve the goal of reconciliation, the federal government must face its responsibilities head on to help pave the way for First Nations communities to overcome the pain and trauma suffered through decades of broken promises and neglect.

Notes

1 Verna J. Kirkness, *First Nations and Schools: Triumphs and Struggles* (Toronto: Canadian Educational Association, 1992), 5.

2 John Snow, *These Mountains Are Our Sacred Places* (Toronto: Samuel-Stevens, 1977), 6.

3 Ninastako Culture Centre, *Nitsitapi, the Real People: A Look at the Bloods* (Calgary: Liberty Printers, 1970).

4 James R. Miller, *Shingwauk's Vision: A History of Native Residential Schools* (Toronto: University of Toronto Press, 1996).

5 Treaty 7 Elders and Tribal Council, *The True Spirit and Original Intent of Treaty 7* (Montreal/Kingston: McGill-Queen's University Press, 1996), 25.

6 Alexander Morris, *The Treaties of Canada with the Indians of Manitoba and the North-West Territories: Including the Negotiations on which They Were Based, and Other Information Relating Thereto* (Calgary: Fifth House, 1880/1991), 245.

7 Peter A. Cumming and Neil H. Mickenberg, *Native Rights in Canada*, 2nd ed. (Toronto: Indian-Eskimo Association of Canada in association with General Publishing Co., 1972), 149.

8 Morris, *Treaties of Canada*, 250.

9 Treaty 7 Elders and Tribal Council, *True Spirit*, 4.

10 Ibid., 254.

11 Sheila Carr-Stewart, "A Treaty Right to Education," *Canadian Journal of Education* 26, 2 (2001): 125–43.

12 Morris, *Treaties of Canada*, 368–71.

13 The Kainai, the largest of the five nations, declined from 2,488 in 1878 to 1,776 in 1885, to 1,111 in 1920. See Ninastako Culture Centre, *Nitsitapi*, 1–4.

14 The Diocese of Calgary began publishing the annual reports in 1892. They are located in the Anglican Church of Canada General Synod Archives (ACCGSA) in Toronto.

15 British North America Act, 1867 (UK), 30 & 31 Vict., c. 3, s. 91(24).

16 E. Brian Titley, *A Narrow Vision: Duncan Campbell Scott and the Administration of Indian Affairs in Canada* (Vancouver: UBC Press, 1986), 11–13; and John L. Tobias, "Protection, Civilization, Assimilation: An Outline History of Canada's Indian Policy," *Western Canadian Journal of Anthropology* 1, 2 (1976): 17.

17 Tobias, "Protection, Civilization, Assimilation," 18, 21.

18 Nicholas Flood Davin, *Report on Industrial Schools for Indians and Half-Breeds* (Winnipeg: N.F. Davin, 1879).

19 Sharon H. Venne, *Indian Acts and Amendments, 1868–1975: An Indexed Collection* (Saskatoon: Native Law Centre, University of Saskatchewan, 1981), 164.

20 Ibid.

21 John S. Milloy, *A National Crime: The Canadian Government and the Residential School System, 1879–1986* (Winnipeg: University of Manitoba Press, 1999), 3.

22 George H. Gooderham, diary, Glenbow Museum Archives (GMA), M4738, file 208, 12–13.

23 Anglican Church of Canada, "A Brief Submitted by the Church of England in Canada to the Special Joint Committee of the Senate and the House of Commons Appointed to Examine and Consider the Indian Act, March 25, 1947," 4.

24 Ninastako Culture Centre, *Nitsitapi.*

25 Anglican Church of Canada, "Historical Sketch for Anglican Residential Schools," 2017, http://www.anglican.ca/tr/schools/.

26 James G. MacGregor, *A History of Alberta* (Edmonton: Hurtig, 1972), 69.

27 Rodney Andrews, "The Reverend Samuel Trivett, First Anglican Missionary with the Blood Indians," In *Chief Mountain Country: A History of Cardston and District,* ed. Beryl Bectell, 185–88 (Cardston, AB: Cardston and District Historical Society, 1987), 1.

28 John W. Tims, "Anglican Beginnings in Southern Alberta," *Alberta Historical Review* 15, 2 (1967): 1.

29 Mike Mountain Horse, *My People, the Bloods* (Calgary: Glenbow-Alberta Institute, 1977), 15.

30 Tims, "Anglican Beginnings," 1–2.

31 Ibid., 5.

32 Ibid.

33 Ibid.

34 Anglican Church of Canada, "St. Cyprian School: Peigan Reserve, Brocket, AB," 2017, http://www.anglican.ca/tr/histories/st-cyprian-brockel/.

35 Department of Indian Affairs (DIA), annual report, 1880, 80.

36 Diocese of Calgary, Report on Indian Missions (hereafter DCRIM), St. John's Mission, Blackfoot Reserve, 1892, 7.

37 Ibid., 1893, 8.

38 Ibid., 1892, 5.

39 Ibid., 1893, 1.

40 Ibid., 1893–94, 6.

41 Ibid.

42 Ibid., 1894, 17.

43 Ibid.

44 Ibid., 6.

45 Ibid., 1898, 7, "Lists of Subscribers, and Donors, etc."

46 Anglican Church of Canada, "Historical Sketch."

47 DIA, annual report, 1883, 180.

48 DCRIM, 1893, 7.
49 Ibid.
50 Ibid., 1894, 8.
51 Ibid., St. Paul's Mission, Blood Reserve, 1898, 2.
52 Ibid., 1893, 11.
53 Ibid.
54 Tims, "Anglican Beginnings," 6.
55 DCRIM, Red Crow's Day School Report, 1897, 6.
56 Ibid., St. Paul's Lower Mission, 1898, 7.
57 DCRIM, 1893, 6–7.
58 Ibid., 1895, 17.
59 Ibid., 1894, 6–7.
60 DIA, annual reports, 1895–1910.
61 DCRIM, 1893, 11.
62 Ibid., 9.
63 Ibid., 1894, 6.
64 Ibid., 13.
65 Ibid.
66 Ibid., 1889, 5.
67 Ibid., 1895, 9.
68 Ibid., 1894, 13.
69 Ibid., 1893–94, 22–23.
70 Ibid., 1897, 6.
71 Ibid., 1896, n.p.
72 Ibid., 1898, 6.
73 Ibid., 1900, 7.
74 Ibid., 1901, 10.
75 Ibid.
76 Ibid., 10–11.
77 Ibid., 1903, 11.
78 Ibid., 1898, 14, 15.
79 Ibid., 1901, 11.
80 Ibid., 8.
81 Ibid., 1905, 8.
82 Ibid.

Sheila Carr-Stewart

PART 2

RACISM, TRAUMA, AND SURVIVANCE

4

IF YOU SAY I AM INDIAN, WHAT WILL YOU DO?

History and Self-Identification at Humanity's Intersection

Jonathan Anuik

In Fall 2013, the University of Alberta's Faculty of Education launched a new teacher education program. The program's mandate called for more content about Indigenous peoples' education. It also came with a new introductory course for all teacher candidates, "Contexts of Education," which was designed to explore "what it means to be a teacher in contemporary society" from multiple perspectives, including those of Indigenous peoples and the foundational discipline of history.[1] In addition, students were to learn about "social and political issues in education and their implications for practice today," and they would "explore ways in which teachers can effect change within the classroom, school and community."[2] As an instructor of this first-year course and a historian of education, I focused on a relevant Indigenous educational issue with a historical root: self-identification by First Nations, Métis, and Inuit students and their families and communities.

Here, I tell the story of how I addressed this issue with neophyte teacher candidates. Indigenous peoples want members of their school communities to be aware of the issue and history of self-identification. Self-identification has an impact on teachers' practices, and understanding how people identify can help teachers to adapt learning environments to meet their needs. With historical knowledge, teacher candidates can recognize schools as institutions that project an English Canadian consensus of childhood.[3] As historians of education have shown, schools accomplish this through lessons in a common set of basic skills.[4] These same candidates can then go on to take up their responsibility to change the school climate into one that acknowledges and accurately represents the Indigenous lands upon which their teaching occurs.

History and Teacher Education

My class on self-identification sits at the intersection of history and contemporary Indigenous education. If we, as teachers, think of history and self-identification as streets that lead to investigations of educational contexts in our classrooms, and if we are to study history through an Indigenous lens, then we must begin with stories of identification. The teachings embedded in Indigenous traditions and stories encourage us to understand what does and does not make us learn.[5] Self-identification is relevant to our lives and those of the Indigenous learners we serve. What sustains us is comprehension of the process of recognizing history's impact at school. In class, I argue that implementation of self-identification policy will foil the Canadian government's use of legislation to control the identities and lives of Indigenous peoples. Teacher candidates have an opportunity to build learning environments that can accurately represent the peoples whom they are educating.

In class, we learned collectively that the most devastating legacy of legislation such as the 1876 Indian Act was that it created a definition of who an "Indian" was, told educators to identify those "Indians" and educate them, and took away the authority to identify and determine who belonged from Indigenous peoples. As an Indian–non-Indian binary formed, educators assumed that the Indian, who was viewed as a child, lagged behind the non-Indian in achievement, and this assumption justified aggressive teaching practices and abuses in institutions such as Indian residential schools.[6] As we look at schools today, we see a question in the minds and hearts of First Nations, Métis, and Inuit families: If you say I am Indian, what will you do?

Jonathan Anuik

The question that teachers should be asking themselves is, Who are you, and what can I do to help you?

Self-Identification and Teacher Education

To address the damaging impact of outside naming, I used the mandate of self-identification put forward in the *Ontario First Nation, Métis, and Inuit Education Policy Framework* as a case study for my neophytes.[7] Published by the Ontario Ministry of Education, the document mandates that school boards should develop protocols and procedures to support the self-identification of First Nations, Métis, and Inuit children and youth and their families. The underlying premise was that teachers could do their jobs better if they were aware of the Indigenous composite of their school communities.[8]

In class, I detailed the processes that school boards undertook to develop self-identification forms and supporting documents (i.e., brochures and fact sheets), and I shared one illuminating quotation with students. A school board in north-central Ontario mentioned that its staff had sought documents provided by other school boards. They consulted with Indigenous folks in those areas and shared the material gathered from their searches. In conversation with an Elder, they learned that some of the pamphlets contained definitions of *Métis* "that ... were not adequate, and some were offensive."[9] The Elder saw that school boards did not have an accurate understanding of who the Métis were. The school boards skipped over historical explanations that sustained learners. Instead of tracing the roots of identity, staff chose a definition from a source outside the community and used that source to depict who the Indigenous people were at school. The consequence: schools told learners they were Métis and left the community to wonder what the school would do as a consequence.

Indigenous people knew what the federal government had done in the past to those it called "Indian." When the North-West Mounted Police (after 1920, the Royal Canadian Mounted Police) and school inspectors came to take children to school, they did so because the state had decided the children needed an education. The police came for children registered as Status Indians under the Indian Act. After 1945, kids had to attend school so their parents could collect family allowance cheques and because the federal and provincial governments mandated attendance at school until age sixteen. In the case of residential schools, children came with the label "Indian." At provincial schools, teachers used words that varied from *Native* to *Indian* to *half-breed*.[10] In all cases, students did not get a chance to identify themselves by their nations, and they faced teachers who believed they knew what to do to educate them.

Self-Identification and Teacher Candidates, Part 1: The Teacher Educator

Against this historical backdrop, it's important that teachers understand why self-identification needs to be integrated into Indigenous education policy. To convey this lesson, I started by encouraging my preservice teachers to think about their understandings of themselves when they were in school. On the whiteboard, I wrote "Self-identification: Name." I then drew two diagonal lines that began beneath the heading and extended down to the left and right. I asked the teacher candidates to identify two labels others at school had used to describe them. I told them school could be elementary or high school, college, university, a workplace training session, or whatever setting they chose. "Others" could be teachers, administrators, professors, staff, friends, parents, or anyone involved in the school.

To show them the way, I wrote an identifier given to me when I was in Grade 2. In one corner of the whiteboard I wrote, for the first time since elementary school, the words *attention deficit disorder*. In the next corner, I wrote an attribute: "serious." In that moment, I recognized that history had pulled at me in the present. To shed the labels, I needed to tell my students the stories behind them. I had to let my neophytes know the relationship between the two identifiers.

Jonathan Anuik

The first, a diagnosis, affected how I behaved, conduct that gave me the second, an attribute.

I told students that in Grade 2 I had brought home a report card that ranked me "below average" in relation to my peers. A row of "D" grades ran down the card beside each subject. The report triggered a meeting between my parents and the principal and a series of tests. The tests spat at me a diagnosis of "attention deficit disorder." I knew that verdict made me different from my peers. I thought that every kid at school knew about my diagnosis, and I felt shame. I conflated my behavioural disorder with stupidity since I had done so poorly on my report card. I chose to disengage, to not show emotion, to stare with a long face. If I stayed quiet, then no one would suspect I had a behaviour problem. My style carried me through to Grade 9, when my health teacher said I was too serious and needed to smile more.

I chose to share my identifiers, and the stories behind them, to let my students see me as vulnerable to educational psychology and teachers' judgments. As a child, I feared that if my teachers said I had a behaviour problem, then they would treat me differently than my peers. At that moment, recognizing my privilege as a tenure-track assistant professor, someone who had earned the highest degree one could attain at university, the PhD, I told students they would not have to share what their identifiers were. Just as I had done, I wanted the teacher candidates to reflect honestly on their time in educational settings. I wanted them to find identifiers that might not have been accurate representations of who they thought they were. Hence, I asked them if they thought the two identifiers that had been applied to them were accurate assessments. I asked them if they liked to be identified in such ways.

Self-Identification and Indigenous Learners

I told students to set aside the terms for later in class. I then set up another triangle, this time with "Indigenous learner" at the top and with diagonal lines that extended down to two terms, *Indian* and *Native*. When the Canadian government mandated that Indian children had to attend residential schools in 1920, it determined eligibility by looking at whom it had registered as Status Indians under the Indian Act. The students were scooped into the schools, and their staff met them with a set of expectations. They assumed the youngsters were dirty, so they shaved their heads and deloused them; they assumed they lacked knowledge of science, so they taught them about the midnight sun; they assumed they were irreligious, so they imparted Christian teachings. Educators saw "Indians" and assumed their parents had not prepared their kids to be students at school and citizens of modern Canada. It was the school that would give the youngsters, "the oldest Canadians, a new future" because their parents had failed to do so.[11] At residential schools, staff conflated being "Indian" with being damaged by their communities, and they sought to heal wounds inflicted by what were considered to be irreligious and illiterate parents.

In 1969, the Canadian government terminated its agreement with the Christian churches then operating residential schools. Since then, enormous changes have occurred in Indigenous education. The most profound has been public assertion by Indigenous peoples of their inherent right to control decisions that concern the education of their children.[12] Educators began to recognize that their practices marginalized students, but their efforts led to a new label for Indigenous learners – "culturally different" – that once again placed them on the margins of achievement. In Saskatchewan, committees studied school readiness, tried to make curriculum relevant to the lives of youngsters, and piloted new courses. Teachers reached a new consensus: serving Indigenous children meant implementing supports and accommodations in schools.[13]

The thread that connected residential schools with initiatives in the 1960s and 1970s was the labels used to identify Indigenous peoples. To be "Indian" or "Native" was to be subjected to attempts by educators to measure them against the "norm" of non-Indigenous views of achievement and competency in English literacy, numeracy, and citizenship so that they could participate in Canada's social and economic development.[14] If students identified as Indigenous, then teachers assumed they were different and leapt to fix problems they assumed the students had.

The opportunity to identify existed in the twentieth century, but the options available were set by the Canadian government and tied to the Indian Act and (after 1982) the Constitution Act, which legally defined "Aboriginal peoples" as the Indian, Métis, and Inuit peoples in Canada. The federal government also determined who belonged to the group. The government set the terms for inclusion, and identifying with any of the labels meant exposing oneself to educators' assumptions about school readiness and the ability to achieve. Learners had the option to choose whether to identify with one of these terms when they registered at school. However, the presentation of categories such as "Aboriginal ancestry" excluded people, either because they did not reflect the lands where children learned or because they triggered fear that children would be treated differently by staff.[15]

Self-Identification and Teacher Education, Part 2: Reflections on Identifiers

As a class, my students and I returned to our identifiers. I asked them to consider whether the categories were an accurate reflection of themselves. I then asked them a series of questions: If the two identifiers appeared on the University of Alberta's registration form, and if they had to choose one, then would they? Or would they leave that part of the form blank? Would they want people to know who they are, or would they hope no one would see the form? The purpose of the exercise and my lecture was to help teacher candidates understand that Indigenous students had identities conditioned by Canadian legislation. The government saw "Aboriginal ancestry" as an identifier that described nearly 1.5 million diverse Indigenous peoples in Canada. Indigenous students' families held stories of unpleasant experiences in residential and in public and separate schools.[16] When "Aboriginal ancestry" is the only term available, all students who are identified as Aboriginal are lumped into a single category.[17]

I wanted preservice teachers to understand that naming students "Indian" or "Aboriginal" had a negative impact because being labelled one or the other triggered fear that an educator would throw the student into a container that housed a collection of misunderstandings.[18] Youngsters had no chance to identify because they either received an identifier as soon as they began school or they were asked to select from ones determined by legislation and policy. The identifier then became a signifier of educational underachievement in relation to the student's non-Indigenous peers. The Department of Indian Affairs, provincial and territorial ministries of education, and schools threw all Indigenous children "into the bucket" to generate composites of what a typical student of Aboriginal ancestry looked like at school.[19] Education became a process of targeting Indigenous students and treating them the same – as people in need of correction because their origins placed them at a disadvantage.[20] This process of self-identification bore little resemblance to Indigenous peoples' knowledge of themselves or the lands upon which their schools sat.

But when the rest of Canada got all too brief glimpses of students in the schools through the media, they received the impression that they were being shed of their old "Native" ways, which kept them from Canadian society. The schools "did good" – they were creating a new education community in which the oldest Canadians could unlearn the past and embrace "a new future."[21] Through media, the Canadian public learned that there was only one Indigenous culture, and teachers – in public, Protestant and Catholic separate, and independent schools – were, and still are, part of the public, a public that expects educators to solve what it believes are problems in society. The Canadian government assumed Indigenous children needed to be prepared to become Canadian citizens. To be Indian did not mean that a student represented a nation that had treated with and related to Canada as a sovereign entity.

Becoming a Teacher

In "Contexts of Education," teacher candidates learned that they will be responsible for addressing issues deemed by society to have an impact on children, youth, families, and communities. One area is the education of Indigenous peoples. Recently, Canadian schools have tried, through self-identification initiatives, to develop language that more accurately represents the Indigenous nation upon whose lands the school sits.[22] My investigation of these practices led me to think that before we act, we must recognize that classrooms are educational settings in which we confront identifiers, labels, and names that shape who we are as students and what educators believe we need from school. Teacher candidates in their first teacher education course need to learn that we are given identifiers that sort, label, and categorize us – some we like, some we don't like, and some we later deem inaccurate as we learn more about ourselves. In my case, one diagnosis led me to change my behaviour because I feared teachers would have lower expectations of me.

There is a consistent question that runs like a thread through the story of self-identification, the history of outside naming, and teacher education: How do we rewrite the terms of identification, and how do we hear them? Answering the question requires both an understanding of history and reflection. "Contexts of Education" offered both. By experiencing history and policy as a story that related to themselves, student teachers formed empathy and tapped into their ability to think outside of constructed labels and categories.

The practice of self-identification in Indigenous educational contexts takes place through story. The story is the elastic that pulls past and present together. The snap occurs when a student is able to identify and be understood as an Indigenous learner at school. The school should be the meeting place between past and present, a place where we can generate new identifiers that reflect Indigenous perceptions of the past, such as the stories behind the labels "Indian" or "Native" or stories rooted in language, spirit, and the land. In future work, teachers must be leaders in the development of self-identification exercises in schools. When we share our experiences with self-identification, we see knowledge shared at the place where the past and present collide. We see how we can fulfill the mandate to do more in Indigenous education.[23] However, before we act, we must keep in mind the question that families and communities are asking about us as educators: If you say we are [fill in the blank], what will you do?

Acknowledgments

I would like to thank my students in "Contexts in Education," Winter 2016, for their openness and participation in our discussion of self-identification in educational policy. I also thank Sheila Carr-Stewart for her invitation to write this chapter.

Notes

1 Jonathan Anuik, "Contexts of Education," University of Alberta, Faculty of Education, Winter 2016, 1.

2 Ibid.

3 Jonathan Anuik, "Locating Abnormal Childhood: Neil Sutherland and Teacher Education," *Journal of Educational Thought* 49, 1 (2016): 33–53; and Neil Sutherland, *Children in English-Canadian Society: Framing the Twentieth-Century Consensus*, foreword by Cynthia Comacchio, Studies in Childhood and Family in Canada series (Waterloo, ON: Wilfrid Laurier University Press, 2000).

4 Anuik, "Locating Abnormal Childhood"; Marie Battiste, "M'ikmaq Literacy and Cognitive Assimilation," in *Indian Education in Canada*, vol. 1, *The Legacy*, ed. Jean Barman, Yvonne Hébert, and Don McCaskill (Vancouver: UBC Press, 1986), 23–44; Bruce Curtis, *Building the Educational State: Canada West, 1836–1871* (London, ON: Althouse Press, 1987); and Sutherland, *Children in English-Canadian Society*.

5 Jonathan Anuik, Marie Battiste, and Priscilla (Ningwakwe) George, "Learning from Promising Programs and Applications in Nourishing the Learning Spirit," *Canadian Journal of Native Education* 33, 1 (2010): 63–82.

6 J.R. Miller, *Shingwauk's Vision: A History of Native Residential Schools* (Toronto: University of Toronto Press, 1996); and John S. Milloy, *A National*

Crime: The Canadian Government and the Residential School System, 1879–1986 (Winnipeg: University of Manitoba Press, 1999).

7 Aboriginal Education Office, Ontario Ministry of Education, *Ontario First Nation, Métis, and Inuit Education Policy Framework 2007,* http://www.edu.gov.on.ca/eng/aboriginal/fnmiFramework.pdf.

8 Jonathan Anuik and Laura-Lee Bellehumeur-Kearns, *Report on Métis Education in Ontario's K–12 Schools,* report for the Education and Training Branch, Métis Nation of Ontario, 2012; and Anuik and Bellehumeur-Kearns, "Métis Student Self-Identification in Ontario's K–12 Schools: Education Policy and Parents, Families, and Communities," *Canadian Journal of Educational Administration and Policy* 153 (2014), https://journalhosting.ucalgary.ca/index.php/cjeap/article/view/42860/30717.

9 As quoted in Anuik and Bellehumeur-Kearns, "Métis Student Self-Identification," 29.

10 Jonathan Anuik, "Métis Families and Schools: The Decline and Reclamation of Métis Identities in Saskatchewan, 1885–1980" (PhD diss., University of Saskatchewan, 2009); and Jonathan Anuik, "Language, Place, and Kinship Ties: Past and Present Necessities for Métis Education," in *Roots of Entanglement: Essays in Native-Newcomer Relations in Honour of J.R. Miller,* ed. Myra Rutherdale, Whitney Lackenbauer, and Kerry Abel, 209–29 (Toronto: University of Toronto Press, 2018).

11 Canadian Broadcasting Corporation, "'A New Future' for Children at James Bay Residential School," *CBC Newsmagazine,* March 13, 1955, http://www.cbc.ca/archives/entry/a-new-future-for-children-at-james-bay-residential-school; and Canadian Broadcasting Corporation, "'The Eyes of Children' – Christmas at Residential School," *CBC Television Special,* December 25, 1962, http://www.cbc.ca/archives/entry/the-eyes-of-children-life-at-a-residential-school.

12 Assembly of First Nations, *First Nations Control of First Nations Education: It's Our Vision, It's Our Time* (Ottawa: Assembly of First Nations, 2010); and National Indian Brotherhood, *Indian Control of Indian Education* (Ottawa: National Indian Brotherhood, 1972), a policy paper presented to the Minister of Indian Affairs and Northern Development.

13 Jonathan Anuik, "'In from the Margins': Government of Saskatchewan Policies to Support Métis Learning, 1969–1979," *Canadian Journal of Native Education* 32, Supplement (2010): 83–99.

14 Battiste, "M'ikmaq Literacy"; and Patricia Monture-Angus, *Thunder in My Soul: A Mohawk Woman Speaks* (Black Point, NS: Fernwood, 1995).

15 Anuik and Bellehumeur-Kearns, *Report on Métis Education*; Anuik and Bellehumeur-Kearns, "Métis Student Self-Identification."

16 Anuik and Bellehumeur-Kearns, "Métis Student Self-Identification."

17 Ibid.

18 Ibid.

19 Ibid.

20 Anuik, "Locating Abnormal Childhood."

21 Jenna Chalifoux, personal communication, October 3, 2016; Canadian Broadcasting Corporation, "A 'New Future' for Children at James Bay Residential School."

22 Anuik and Bellehumeur-Kearns, *Report on Métis Education*; and Anuik and Bellehumeur-Kearns, "Métis Student Self-Identification."

23 Jonathan Anuik, "Applying First Nations Holistic Lifelong Learning to the Study of Crime," *in education* 21, 1 (2015): 2, 8, http://ineducation.ca/ineducation/article/view/196/698.

5

LAYING THE
FOUNDATIONS FOR SUCCESS

Recognizing Manifestations of Racism in
First Nations Education

Noella Steinhauer

Educators and institutions of learning have begun the journey to
reconciliation set forth in the Truth and Reconciliation Commission
of Canada's (TRC) calls to action in 2015.[1] If we are to achieve the
intended outcomes, engagement by all Canadians is critical. The
thousands of residential school survivors who shared their stories did
so "not to ease their burden, but also to try to make things better for
their children and their grandchildren."[2] The negative impact that
residential schools left on First Nations throughout Canada is indisput-
able, but changing the future will require a concerted effort by all
parties. As the TRC stated:

> Reconciliation calls for federal, provincial, and territorial
>   government action.
> Reconciliation calls for national action.
> The way we govern ourselves must change.
> Laws must change.
> Policies and programs must change.
> The way we educate our children and ourselves must change.
> The way we do business must change.
> Thinking must change.
> The way we talk to, and about, each other must change.[3]

Although every line of this statement is important, I was especially drawn to the last two lines because they reminded me about my research and my motivation to attend graduate school. As a First Nation teacher in a First Nation community, I understood that the way "we talk to, and about, each other must change."[4] We educators need to talk together, listen, and change our thoughts and actions. We need to support change within our First Nation communities and, as teachers, we must ensure that all students learn in a positive environment.

On the first day of school, at the on-reserve school where I teach, a Grade 9 student named Keith proclaimed loudly, as if to give our class his stamp of approval, "Holy cow! You guys are using the same book as us." Keith had just been expelled from the provincial school in the nearby town, and this was his first day back at the "rez" school. Some of the students in the class glanced at him, one or two sighed, and others just ignored him. It was the third block of the morning, and the students were already tired of Keith's ongoing negative commentary about our community school. Keith wanted everyone to know he had done very well at the provincial school in town. He had been expelled for fighting and a series of other violations, and as a result he had no choice but to come back to the "rez school with all you dummies." The students had seen this scenario each time a student returned to our community school from the "town school." They knew that if they just continued to ignore Keith, he would eventually realize that the rez school was doing the same thing as any other school. Within a couple of days, Keith realized that silence and stares from his classmates meant they had no patience for his negative attitude towards our school; within a couple of weeks, he realized he had nothing to prove to anyone.

This scene has played out time and time again over the years, always with the same outcome. Once students realize there is nothing to prove to the students on reserve, they grow to respect our school. But each time it happened, I was saddened, because these students returned to our school wounded and with such a deep personal self-hatred that they would continually insult our school and our students in order to cope. Our students knew they just had to ignore them until they realized that our school was a great place and that learning was indeed going on.

I was determined to find out how a First Nation school like the one I served at could become even more successful. This meant I had to return to graduate school to begin to understand how success might look. I designed a study that utilized an Indigenous research methodology and involved one-on-one interviews with First Nation students, parents, teachers, and Elders. I wanted to focus on identifying the philosophical tenets that would lay the foundation for success – success founded on the community's beliefs about what success would look like for their community. I was guided by the Cree notion of *natwahtaw*, which means "looking for something in a good way."

In addition to the notion of natwahtaw, my research methodology was founded on the principle of relational accountability, which is based on mutual trust and respect between the researcher and the participant. This notion of relationality is best articulated by Shawn Wilson, who states:

> As a researcher you are answering to *all your relations* when you are doing research. You are not answering questions of validity or reliability or making judgments of better or worse. Instead you should be fulfilling your relationships with the world around you.
>
> So your methodology has to ask different questions: rather than asking about validity or reliability, you are asking how am I fulfilling my role in this relationship? What are my obligations in this relationship?[5]

In the realm of analysis, relational accountability became even more important because I needed to ensure that the words and ideas of the participants were represented in the manner they had been intended. As I began to analyze the data, a particular issue that I tried to avoid continued to present itself. Almost every participant spoke about racism and its detrimental impact on educational success, but the issue that continued to re-emerge was internalized racism. Internalized racism has manifested itself deeply in the everyday lives of community members through violence, drug abuse, alcoholism, and gossip.

Defining Racism

The very term *racism* creates discomfort, denial, and mistrust. Few words are able to elicit the emotional response that the word conjures up, especially when it is suggested that schools and teachers smack of racism. Those who are implicated in practising racism immediately get defensive or angry, even as those who feel victimized by racism are defensive or angry. Still, racism persists and permeates every aspect of society, from schools, to businesses, to government. There are various types of racism, including institutional, personally mediated, and internalized. All are equally destructive in the impact they have on people of colour.

At the school level, racism "is institutionalized to the extent that it is taught in school curricula. It is formulated into teaching practices and perpetuated in the practical structure."[6] In the school context, institutional racism manifests itself by consistently failing to validate Indigenous peoples' diversity, culture, history, and values. First Nation students learn as soon as they enter the public system that they are different, because they are in a system that rewards compliance with a white, middle-class meritocracy. As a result, teachers of First Nation children often feel frustration because the children do not fit into the system. They cannot understand why First Nation children and families would not strive to gain white, middle-class values. Unfortunately, teacher education programs do not challenge the white, middle-class perspective from which preservice teachers are trained. Teachers go out into the field believing there is only one right way for everyone. In a study involving non-Indigenous teachers in western Canada, Carol Schick and Verna St. Denis addressed the issue of how to teach anti-racist and cross-cultural courses to preservice teachers.[7] They explored

Noella Steinhauer

three ideological assumptions. One assumption they found was that the teachers believed we live in a meritocracy where everyone "has equal opportunity because we are all basically the same; all that is required to get ahead is hard work, talent, and effort."[8] Based on this assumption, if Indigenous children and people are not succeeding in education, it is because they are not trying hard enough. Little attention is paid to the power held by the dominant group, and this assumption "ignores and trivializes the significance of unearned privileges conferred by [the] dominant group identity."[9]

Personally mediated racism is the form of racism we are most familiar with. Camara Phyllis Jones writes that it "can be intentional as well as unintentional, and it includes acts of commission as well as acts of omission. It manifests as lack of respect, suspicion, devaluation, scapegoating, and dehumanization."[10] Personally mediated racism is a form of racism that First Nation children are subjected to from a very young age. In school, they learn early on that people treat them differently based on who they are, that there are stereotypes about them, and that their families might not look like the typical middle-class family unit. As they get older, they realize that people fear them, that they will be subjected to poor service in stores and restaurants, and that they are expected to do poorly in school and at work. First Nation children learn to accept racism as a fact of life in their off-reserve school experience.[11] They recognize at an early age that they are not like the people in their textbooks. Teachers do not know how to deal with their stories, so First Nation students learn how to disappear by leaving school or quietly melting into the system. Many leave school in junior high because they "just can't take it anymore." Tired of the racism built into the school system, they just leave.

Internalized racism, according to Jones, is "acceptance by a member of the stigmatized races of negative messages about their own abilities and intrinsic worth. It is characterized by them not believing in others who look like them, and not believing in themselves."[12] The ongoing negative messages eventually become so deeply imbedded in the psyche that one begins to accept them as reality. Many will even engage in self-deprecating comments and humour about their cultural group.

Study Participants and Community

The study took place in a large First Nation community that operates a locally controlled school. The First Nation is a half-hour drive from a midsize town that provides it with services. Although the town's economy is reliant on the First Nation, the relationship between the two has always been contentious. The study took place over a six-month period, and the research questions focused primarily on establishing a community definition of success and identifying the elements that contribute to successful schooling. For the purpose of the study, the community was named Nehiyanak. Nine participants took part in the study and represented various roles within the community: Elders (Ella and Edie), teachers (Tracy and Taryn), parents (Paula and Patrice), and students (Sky, Star, and Sage). Although the focus of the study was to identify the foundational elements of success, the issue of racism unfailingly made its way into each interview. Participants identified racism and manifestations of internalized racism as obstacles to a successful school system.

The long-term effects of racism were evident among the participants. Elders Ella and Edie both identified themselves as "slow learners." Ella stated, "I was slow in learning. Sometimes, I couldn't even spell." Although Ella had enjoyed school, she felt that she was a slow learner because she could not respond easily in English and often had difficulty in spelling. Edie stated, "When you can't learn, you don't like to be sitting in a classroom, and then it gets kind of boring to you." When I probed Edie a little further to find out what she meant by classifying herself as a slow learner, she said, "I couldn't answer. Sometimes, I couldn't understand what the teacher was saying." Because the Elders' first language was Cree and the language of instruction was English, they viewed themselves as deficient and less capable. Similarly, in a study on Indigenous student dropout rates,

Noella Steinhauer

Ron Mackay and Lawrence Myles found that "some dropouts confirmed that when they did not completely understand what was being said, they felt unable to participate fully in class and were more inclined to daydream. When students with weak English skills do not comprehend the task that is being asked of them, they may be too shy to ask for clarification."[13]

Both Elders had been students in residential school. Their comments confirm that they felt inadequate because of the language barriers and as a result classified themselves as slow learners. Unfortunately, this self-concept has intergenerational effects. The students had no recourse to deal with their feelings of inadequacy because the system was based on a framework that did not accommodate their differences. The form of systemic racism that caused them to believe they were slow learners is one that persists even today. Tracy, a teacher, stated that we need to move beyond "the stereotype that most of our kids are special needs." She said: "I don't believe in that, because sometimes even as First Nation educators we cast those upon our own children, and we get stuck in those ruts. We need to get past that and to be able to see past that. Our children can and will learn."

The stereotype that First Nation children are special needs students is one that has persisted for many years and is ingrained in parents and grandparents. Unfortunately, we as First Nation people have difficulty recognizing the systemic racism that has been deeply embedded in the educational system for many years. We blame ourselves and believe that we are incapable of educational attainment.

Although participants alluded to racism, few actually called it racism. Sky, a student who reluctantly identified the behaviours and actions of her teacher as racist, stated:

I think she is racist in a way, because I am [me], and it was a white school I went to, and other people ... they said she was racist and stuff like that. It could be just her own ... whatever. Maybe she didn't like me because of my skin colour, or maybe she didn't like my assignments. If I had a problem in class, she would be very forceful and strict: "Sky, you should get a better mark on this. You should understand this." It's all about the teacher's action and their behaviour toward you when you do something wrong or even when you do something right. I think she had her favourites. I just tried to see above it and be mature about it.

It is clear that Sky tried to act in a mature manner when she knew that the teacher's actions towards her were racist in nature. She tried to dismiss the teacher's actions and give her the benefit of the doubt by stating that it might have been the quality of her assignments. Later, she found out that the teacher's actions were indeed racist in nature, because other Indigenous students had similar experiences in the same classroom.

Paula, a parent, chose to send her children to Nehiyanak school to shield them from the kind of experiences she had had at school, experiences that she felt were detrimental to her self-esteem:

I chose it because I thought if they grow up around their own people they wouldn't be picked on. Their self-esteem wouldn't be as low as mine was. I thought that maybe that was part of their foundation, and you know what? It worked. It really worked. I think about a lot of these people that had their kids go off the reserve, and they're good kids, but some of them just didn't do it. They didn't finish high school, and I know a lot of it had to do with their self-esteem ... That self-esteem was so important for me that I needed them to have that self-esteem in order for them to move on in their lives.

Paula's strong feeling about the importance of children having positive self-esteem was a very important factor in her decision to send her children to the Nehiyanak school. When she was growing up in the city school, she was often singled out and picked on because she was "the only Native kid in the class." Paula did not use the word *racism* to describe her experience because she did not want to make an accusation, even though it was evident that these situations were indeed racist in nature.

Racism in the daily lives of First Nation students – especially in off-reserve environments – is so widely prevalent that it is accepted as a part of the off-reserve school experience.

Internalized Racism and the Social Issues of Nehiyanak

During the interviews, every participant was concerned with the obstacles created by social issues. Social problems, addictions, and lack of community support seemed to enter into each discussion as factors detrimental to the development of an ideal school. Over the last twenty years, issues of internalized racism have suffocated and limited community development in many areas, such as education. Decades of institutionalized and personally mediated racism have manifested themselves in the community of Nehiyanak as various forms of internalized racism.

Internalized racism is deeply embedded in the lives of many Indigenous people in Canada today, and "it manifests as an embracing of 'whiteness', selfdevaluation, and resignation, helplessness and hopelessness."[14] In communities like Nehiyanak, racism and internalized racism have been detrimental to the people and the community's progress. Racism is so deeply embedded that people do not recognize it. Instead, it is accepted as a part of life.

Since it is so deeply embedded, people do not even know they are guilty of perpetuating this form of racism. The actions of internalized racism can be the most devastating form of racism because they are from your own people. Tracy stated, "Having racism within your own is worse because it's our own people doing that to each other ... Racism that comes from the white culture has a base ... What I mean by a base is it comes from somewhere ... but when it's internal within your own people, it's harder." Tracy said she felt that internalized racism is more difficult to deal with because there is an assumption that the people in the community will support one another. Instead, they can create obstacles.

According to Donna Bivens, internalized racism "involves at least four essential and interconnected elements: decision-making, resources, standards, naming the problem."[15] First Nation people know that they do not have the ultimate decision-making power over their lives and resources because they recognize that power resides elsewhere. As a direct result, Indigenous people may think that "white people know more about what needs to be done for us than we do. On an interpersonal level, we may not support each other's authority and power."[16] Unfortunately, Indigenous people are often highly critical of other Indigenous people in positions of power, especially community leaders who have the difficult task of administering band funds. Although Chief and Council are elected by the membership, the funds that are transferred to them to operate community programs are designated for specific expenditures. Limits to funding are established in all areas, from education to housing. As a result, resources are not comparable with what any other community would get for the same activity.

Standards in education are based on Eurocentric standards that First Nation communities try to replicate. First Nation schools operate on fewer resources and do not have the range of services, such as speech and language pathologists, curriculum support and implementation, that provincial schools do, yet communities try hard to mimic the systems of their provincial counterparts. Even though these standards may not be attainable with the level of resourcing, our communities hold themselves accountable to them. As a result, many First Nation people believe that only mainstream programs warrant respect. This idea is then extended to all levels of Indigenous programming. For example, a fellow graduate student once told me, "I went to a regular program rather than the Aboriginal program," implying that her program was of a higher standard than the program I was in. This attitude reflects the deeply held belief that if it is an Indigenous program, it is less than the standard. The assumption is that Indigenous

Noella Steinhauer

programs lack the academic rigour of mainstream programs. These assumptions are made purely on the basis of internalized racism and the belief, whether conscious or not, that only Eurocentric standards are rigorous.

As Bivens notes, "there is a system in place that misnames the problem of racism as a problem of or caused by people of color and blames the disease – emotional, economic, political, etc. – on people of color."[17] Indigenous people believe, for example, that we are more violent than other people because of high rates of incarceration, even though studies have found that Indigenous people are not fairly treated by the justice system. Tracy was fully cognizant of the impact and source of this issue. She stated:

We're too busy dragging each other down, and I don't know why we do that. That's what I'm finding in my experience, and I'm finding that the hardest people that I have worked with in terms of challenge and difficulty is our own people. I've enjoyed working with many, many people from all parts of the world. The hardest that I have found are our own. I guess maybe I'll go back to the residential schools. They did a real job on many of our people. One of [the] things that I have noticed in communities, there is a lot of jealousy. As soon as we have somebody who is getting somewhere or they think that that person thinks they're getting somewhere, they bring something in to bring that person down. A lot of people lack self-esteem, and they want everyone to feel as bad as they are, and I don't think it's different even with many educated First Nations people.

Internalized racism is the direct result of years and years of oppression. For First Nation people it began with colonization, and it has continued through intergenerational transmission. Little has been written about this phenomenon, mainly because of concern that the research could be interpreted as a weakness of the oppressed.[18] Karen Pyke notes that "the failure to study internalized racism is partly due to a concern that the racially subordinated will be held responsible for re-inscribing White supremacist thinking, casting it as their short-coming rather than the problem of white racism."[19] Victims of racism may feel further victimized as generations of oppression continue.

When First Nation people were moved to reserves, all decisions (including those relating to education) were made for them. As time wore on, the government found that education was failing miserably. By the late 1960s, First Nation communities were able to have greater control over the election of their Chief and Council. Prior to the 1960s, the Indian agent told the Chief and Council when an election would be held and who would be eligible to participate. The local Indian agent wielded a great deal of power and control. He made all fiscal and political decisions in the community. In Nehiyanak, the Indian agent left in 1969, and the national devolution of Indian affairs began as fiscal and political responsibilities were slowly transferred to the community. During the 1970s, the *Indian Control of Indian Education* document and subsequent movement enabled First Nations to administer education, including the authority to establish a local school board that would oversee the operation of the local school.

The transfer of responsibilities to the band was done with limitations and stipulations on the powers of Chief and Council. The ultimate power still remained with the minister of Indian affairs. When First Nation communities achieved control of education, they tried to replicate the provincial systems that had already failed their children. Even more detrimental was the attempt to create systems without sufficient resources to provide the necessary service levels to establish a successful system. Instead, communities established "non-system systems." Communities were anxious to assume control of education, but little did they know that they had to perpetuate the system they had fought so hard to change. This system continues to exist today rather than a true system of local control with the range of support services necessary for success. The devolution of Indian affairs was merely an exercise to demonstrate to the world the wonderful job the federal government was doing to "give" First Nations autonomy and self-determination.

Noella Steinhauer

Although the Nehiyanak community has worked hard to improve educational outcomes at all levels, an undertone of some form of racism always persists. Most people in the community will ignore it and are often afraid to confront it for fear of the embarrassment that will come from the accused's denial of racism. The layers of racism run deep and impact the daily lives of people in the community, from trips to town, to hockey games, to school. No one is left untouched. Paula stated, "A lot of our kids think that white people are so much more powerful, so much better, and that's why they can't get along with white people. Even my kids think that white people are so much better." This statement reinforces that the impact of racism is very evident. More importantly, it demonstrates young people's feelings of not being as good as white people because they don't have the same social and economic power. Their actions seem to demonstrate that they feel inferior, and the resulting tension creates dislike and even hatred.

The impact of internalized racism in Nehiyanak is far-reaching and has manifested itself deeply in the everyday lives of the community and ultimately the school. Some of the key themes that emerged in my study were addictions, violence, and lack of community support.

Addictions

The issue of addictions and their impact on the community was a concern for each participant. All of the participants felt that addictions have had devastating impacts on children, students, families, and the whole social fabric of the community. Internalized racism can manifest itself in numerous ways. According to Suzanne Lipsky, addictions can be related to "patterns of powerlessness and despair" that give rise to a "feel good now" pattern.[20] This pattern is a result of an internalized belief that Indigenous people are doomed to failure. Lipsky describes the thinking that leads to the pattern: "I must settle for making myself feel good right now. At least I deserve that much.

Drugs, alcohol, and other addictions ... irrational use of money ... these are all directly related to patterns of internalized racism and oppression."[21] Sage, a student, aptly acknowledged this "feel good now" pattern by saying, "Teenagers are looking to make fast money, too, and they start selling drugs, so they drop out to sell weed." The fact that there are very limited opportunities for teenagers to make money forces them into thinking they have no other alternative except to live for today and make all the money they can, even if it is illegal. It is clear that for Nehiyanak to begin to deal with the problem of addiction, it must accept that the problem exists and begin to address the hopelessness and devastation that addictions can create.

Like most of the participants, Paula was concerned about the effects of drugs and other addictions. She said, "[There is] too much drugs now. Everyone suffers, not just [the addicts] – their kids, their families. I feel sorry for those people in the end because they are the ones who are going to suffer." She felt that parents who were using drugs not only devastated their family and children but also generated even more problematic long-term effects, because their children and grandchildren would inherit the social stigma and the effects that drugs might have on unborn children. Sky said: "Some of them don't care because they are probably alcoholics or into drugs or gambling, bingo, and just lack of attention for their children. There's a lot of abuse like alcoholism, [drugs], gambling. A lot of it happens and I think that is why parents are not involved in their children's lives."

Sky felt that some parents were too caught up in their addictions and did not have the energy to adequately care for their children, even if they wanted to. She knew that parents loved their children, but she felt that their world was too controlled by addictions for them to make proper decisions.

Patrice, a parent, felt that the community and school should focus on establishing consistency because "it's that lack of consistency why some are hopeless, and there's a lack of communication, and all of those types of things come in when kids come from homes with addictions." This lack of consistency and support becomes even more

Noella Steinhauer

evident in a community, where everything is intimately interconnected and interdependent. The problems of the community almost always impact the school. Sage stated, "It's not the school programming that's the problem. It's more the community issues." He did not feel that the school issues were as dire as the community problems with violence and drugs. Sadly, two participants felt that the problem was insurmountable and almost hopeless. Sage stated, "Our community has tried, but they don't really get anywhere. They have been trying to get the drugs off the reserve. They know where the dealers live. They just don't do anything about it, and kids suffer for it." Similarly, Sky said she felt that the community was powerless to eliminate the problem: "People have tried to approach it so many times, and sometimes some things work, but most of the time it doesn't work." The perception that eliminating the drug problem is impossible because various actions had failed reinforces the feelings of hopelessness that go along with internalized racism.

Although drugs were identified as a problem, participants also identified other problems that relate to the issue of internalized racism and have a detrimental impact on successful schooling. Taryn, a teacher, stated, "There are other issues compounding the problems, mainly things like attendance issues, in-school transfers, transitions in the community, the drug trade, neglect, poverty, no homes. We have kids that are homeless, that are going from house to house ... We have the haves and have-nots in our school." Throughout the years, Taryn had noticed that social problems had increased and had been further compounded by the prevalence of addictions among parents and caretakers. She felt that it was important to make school "a fun place" because students' living situations can be so dire that learning becomes secondary to survival. When a child's basic human needs of food, shelter, and clothing are not met, learning and going to school are not a priority. Taryn stated:

Some children come [with] no lunch – don't worry, we'll feed you. No jacket? Come to school, and we'll get you one. No winter jacket?

Come to school, we'll get you one. I know we're enabling, but if we didn't, they would have nothing, because even though parents love their kids, there's something out there that makes them think, "I need this more than my child needs a jacket."

The situation Taryn described is sadly a reality that some children in the community must live in, and the school's response could be seen as enabling parents to continue their bad habits. Taryn said she felt caught in the dilemma of either enticing children to come to school by feeding and clothing them or ignoring the problem. The school has decided to meet children's basic needs so that they can be engaged, learn, and gain hope. Taryn also believes that when children are at school there is at least an opportunity to engage them: "Let's make it fun for them here. Let's make them want to be here. Sometimes, a certain child's determination to be here is the only factor that causes them to want to be here." Elder Edie, very concerned about children's home lives, stated, "You know, that kind of life, it's awful, and then these little kids are growing, and they see all that. What's their life going to be?" Edie was very concerned that children do not have time to be children because they are exposed to violence, drugs, alcohol, abuse, and other problems. She was deeply concerned about what the future holds in store for children who are exposed to this lifestyle.

Violence

Sage was worried about issues like the impact of violence on children in the school and community. He defined violence as "not liking each other, name calling, dirty looks, and the way the movies are today, kids acting ghettoes out." Interestingly, he listed the posturing behaviours that often precede physical violence as the more detrimental acts of violence because so much of the communication is done in a nonverbal manner and can be ongoing. Although Sage felt that physical violence is hurtful, he was more concerned about name

Noella Steinhauer

calling and dirty looks. The hurt these behaviours generate runs deep and can carry on for a long time. Sage felt that it was one of the more serious issues since "this family doesn't like this [other] family, and it makes the younger generation not like them either." This form of internalized racism is rooted in the belief that we, as First Nation people, are violent and that we need to put one another down to feel better about ourselves. The problems that the people of Nehiyanak experience because of ongoing institutionalized and personally mediated forms of racism are difficult to accept in modern-day Canada. It is unfortunate that they persist in a nation that takes pride in political correctness. The problems, which can be found at every level of education, health care, justice, and government, exist whether or not people want to accept that they are prevalent. This is the daily reality for First Nation children and parents. Unfortunately, people do not want to confront the issue of racism and find it easier to pretend that it does not exist. Manifestations of these forms of racism have successfully burrowed their way into every aspect of community existence and have evolved into internalized racism, a form that is difficult to recognize and even more difficult to understand. Tracy argued that "internalized racism, it's a very, very real thing. I've seen it, and I've experienced it, and it's sad because it impedes our growth as a nation." These words summarize the devastating impacts internalized racism has had, not only on the community of Nehiyanak but also on the Cree as a nation of people who want to move forward.

Lack of Community Support

The lack of community support for the Nehiyanak school derives from the idea that off-reserve schools have better standards. Elder Edie stated, "It's hard. These parents send their kids off the reserve. We should try and support our own school." Unfortunately, many parents did send their children to off-reserve schools and did not support the community school. Edie had extensive experience with the local school, and she felt that although people were not aware of what went on in the school, parents assumed it was substandard. Star, a student, shared similar feelings. She thought it was unfortunate that students felt negatively about the school but stated that it was based "on their own lack of self-esteem." She pointed out that students need to "honestly and truthfully believe in themselves" and said, "I know a lot of my friends that transferred from [the town school] or ones who didn't go [to Nehiyanak school] had a name for it – 'no hope.' That's just not true." Star felt that because students did not believe in themselves, it was easier for them to not believe in the school and to perpetuate the belief that the school was "lesser than" simply because it was a reserve school. Star attributed the students' negative feelings to "the attitudes they have and how they have been brought up, the attitudes of their parents – it even depends on their grandparents' attitudes of the school." She felt strongly that inherited attitudes need to change for the perception of the school to change. She had graduated from Nehiyanak school and believed that it had much more to offer the community's children and youth than off-reserve schools. Star asserted that attitudes about the school are so deeply embedded that they are intergenerational and consistently drag the school down.

Internalized Racism as Appropriated Racial Oppression

In many ways, First Nation people have become our own colonizers; we have become our own oppressors because we have internalized racism to such a degree that we cannot even recognize it. At the same time, we know that there is something very, very wrong, and that something must change. It is apparent that internalized racism is highly detrimental to community, but to change the future, we must first understand what internalized racism is, where it originates, and how it manifests. As one of the study participants, Tracy, stated, "We're too busy dragging each other down, and I don't know why we do that." Internalized racism has not been widely documented because its victims are often blamed; therefore, it continues to be left unaddressed. The participants in this study identified racism and the manifestations of internalized racism in the community as detrimental to overall educational success. They stated that until the community's issues are dealt with, challenges will remain daunting and only limited success will be achieved.

So how did internalized racism become so deeply entrenched that it is now part of the First Nations reality? The obvious response is that years and years of individual and systemic racism have deeply entrenched themselves in the actions of First Nation people. The bigger question then becomes, How do we unravel decades of tightly wound oppression? It can begin with starting the dialogue in our communities so we can set in motion the process of reconciliation, with ourselves and one another. Learning what internalized racism is, where it comes from, and how it has impacted our communities is the first move in that direction.

Even though the literature in the area of internalized racism continues to be limited, the issue is something we need to talk about because it is the only way we can actually begin to reconcile relationships.[22] According to Mark Tappan, internalized racism is a dynamic phenomenon that depends on context.[23] Rebecca Rangel, citing Tappan, posits: "Given that the phenomenon of internalized racism is a result of individual, socio-cultural, historical and institutional and dynamic processes, the term and definition should reflect this accurately."[24] Tappan asserts that internalized racism needs to be moved from a psychological interpretation to a sociocultural construct in order to eliminate it. Shifting it to a sociocultural interpretation allows us to recognize how both oppression and privilege are products of society, with each consistently spread and promoted by ideologies, images, and stereotypes.[25] Over time, these societal values become reality. When we start to recognize the nature of appropriated oppression and appropriated privilege as sociocultural constructs, there is an opportunity to mediate the actions of both sides – oppressor and oppressed. Ideologically, this could work, but it warrants greater effort on the side of those with appropriated privilege, because they will be challenged to learn more.

At the pragmatic level, First Nation people are in a place of appropriated oppression. We are forced to operate in a mainstream context if we wish to work or go to school, and we must learn to operate in both places – of epistemic privilege and gross systemic disadvantage. This means that we operate within two worlds – the First Nations world and the mainstream world – and we must continually transition between worldviews as a matter of survival. In contrast, the privileged only have to operate in their own world, because they do not feel the need to operate within another worldview. What does this mean in terms of practice? It means that Indigenous people and other Canadians have to come together to a place where reconciliation and respect of worldviews can operate. Cree scholar Willie Ermine speaks of ethical space, a place where dialogue that respects different worldviews can take place.[26] In this time of reconciliation in Canada, the TRC's calls to action require various sectors of society to work with First Nations to improve the future.[27] Something as simple as a lack of collaboration could be an obstacle to reconciliation efforts. Unfortunately, the privileged feel that their understanding of collaboration is the only correct one, and there is little recognition that collaboration must extend beyond that.

At the community level, First Nations have to recognize what appropriated oppression is and, more specifically, what appropriated racial oppression is. As Rangel defines it, "appropriated racial oppression is a complex phenomenon that is made up of five dimensions: (1) appropriation of stereotypes; (2) patterns of thinking that maintain the status quo; (3) adaptation of white American cultural standards; (4) devaluation of own group; and (5) emotional reactions."[28] Understanding the manifestations of appropriated racial oppression can help to create dialogue in communities and create the necessary change.

The appropriation of stereotypes begins early with First Nation children. In fact, their earliest school experiences with racism establish feelings of inferiority. As early as Grade 1, they know they are treated differently by teachers and fellow students.[29] As they continue through

Noella Steinhauer

their school experience, their feelings of inferiority persist and are reinforced by the actions or inaction of teachers and peers. These actions range from the most blatant racism in the schoolyard to more subtle messages, such as exclusion from activities. Many children live in self-doubt because of the ongoing messaging that they receive from the world around them. The detrimental manifestation of appropriated racial oppression presents itself in two ways: against ourselves and against other members of our communities. Suzanne Lipsky describes these manifestations as being

> created by oppression and racism from the outside, [which] have been played out in the only two places it has seemed "safe" to do so. First upon members of our own group – particularly upon those over whom we have some degree of power or control, our children. Second, upon ourselves through all manner of self-invalidation, self-doubt, isolation, fear, feelings of powerlessness, and despair.[30]

To maintain the status quo, people of colour will either avoid the subject or deny that racism exists. It is the best way to avoid the hurt and humiliation created by racism. White people often deny racism and hold colour-blind perspectives; they believe that everyone is the same and can achieve equally if they try hard enough. But failing to acknowledge that racist attitudes and behaviours impact the treatment of people of colour is a way to maintain the status quo. People of colour who subscribe to the colour-blind perspective also believe in this merit-based system in which those who work hard enough receive the same rewards.

The manifestation of white cultural standards means that individuals view the distinguishing marks of their race as negative, and some even try to get surgery to change the shape of their eyelids or nose and lighten their skin to appear more "white." While it is rare for First Nation people to attempt to change their physical appearance, there are certainly issues around skin colour. This idea of privilege was validated at residential school; according to my own family members, those with lighter skin were the ones who had more privilege.

The devaluation of one's racial group can manifest itself at both the individual and group level. First Nation children may believe the propaganda that they are lazy, prone to alcoholism, dropouts, and a drain on the public purse. As a result, they may even distance themselves from other First Nation people by socializing with other groups rather than their own. This in turn creates conflict with other First Nation people because they are seen as "acting white" or "selling out."

The emotional manifestation of internalized racism includes feelings of shame for being associated with a population of people who were relegated to reserve communities, where all aspects of their lives were legislated by the government. The government determined who was a band member, where we could go to school, to what level we could go to school, and when we could leave the reserve. There is also shame associated with the atrocities committed at Indian residential schools. This shame is a response to the trauma of oppression, but there is also the shame and embarrassment of being victimized. According to Dee Watts-Jones, it is shameful to admit to being a victim because there is "the implication that a victim is passive or deficient, either as a prior condition that led to the victimization, as in blaming the victim, or as a result of it, as in being impaired."[31]

In addition to shame, internalized racism can manifest as depression and anger. Depression can certainly be attributed to high suicide rates among First Nations throughout this country. Anger has been a long-standing issue that can probably be linked to high rates of incarceration. Although these issues are much more complex, they are certainly factors.

≶│≷

Internalized racism is clearly detrimental to the success of First Nation schools and communities. Time and time again, participants in my study identified its manifestations – including drugs, alcohol,

Noella Steinhauer

violence, and gossip – as obstacles that maintain the status quo. Their experiences suggest that internalized racism should be renamed appropriated racial oppression so that it can be properly viewed as a sociocultural construct – as simply a product of society that can be overturned or overcome. When internalized racism is recognized as appropriated racial oppression, it will be easier for First Nation people to tackle it because they will see it as a societal issue rather than as a personal problem. With reconciliation on the agenda of so many sectors of government and communities everywhere, it is in the best interest of our communities to engage in this process. To do so, we must first name the problem before we can arrive at a solution and change our future.

Notes

1 Truth and Reconciliation Commission of Canada (TRC), *Final Report of the Truth and Reconciliation Commission of Canada*, vol. 1, *Summary: Honouring the Truth, Reconciling for the Future* (Toronto: Lorimer, 2015).
2 Ibid., 316.
3 Ibid., 317.
4 Ibid.
5 Shawn Wilson, "What Is an Indigenous Research Methodology?," *Canadian Journal of Native Education* 25, 2 (2001): 177.
6 Noella Steinhauer, "Sohkastwawak: They Are Resilient (First Nations Students and Achievement)" (master's thesis, University of Alberta, 1999), 52.
7 Carol Schick and Verna St. Denis, "What Makes Anti-racist Pedagogy in Teacher Education Difficult? Three Popular Ideological Assumptions," *Alberta Journal of Educational Research* 49, 1 (2003): 55–69.
8 Schick and St. Denis, "Anti-racist Pedagogy," 7.
9 Ibid., 10.
10 Camara Phyllis Jones, "Levels of Racism: A Theoretic Framework and a Gardener's Tale," *American Journal of Public Health* 90, 8 (2000): 1213.
11 Steinhauer, "Sohkastwawak," 51.
12 Jones, "Levels of Racism," 1213.
13 Ron Mackay and Lawrence Miles, "A Major Challenge for the Education System: Aboriginal Retention and Dropout," in *First Nations Education in Canada: The Circle Unfolds*, ed. Marie Battiste and Jean Barman (Vancouver: UBC Press, 1996), 164.

14 Ibid.
15 Donna Bivens, "Internalized Racism: A Definition," Women's Theological Center website (no longer active), 1995, 2.
16 Ibid.
17 Ibid.
18 Karen D. Pyke, "What Is Internalized Racial Oppression and Why Don't We Study It? Acknowledging Racism's Hidden Injuries," *Sociological Perspectives* 53, 4 (2010): 551–72.
19 Ibid., 559.
20 Suzanne Lipsky, *Internalized Racism* (Seattle: Rational Island Publishers, 1987), 4.
21 Ibid.
22 Pyke, "What Is Internalized Racial Oppression?"
23 Mark B. Tappan, "Reframing Internalized Oppression and Internalized Domination: From the Psychological to the Sociocultural," *Teachers College Record* 108, 10 (2006): 2115–44.
24 Tappan, "Reframing Internalized Oppression," cited in Rebecca Rangel, "The Appropriated Racial Oppression Scale Development and Initial Validation" (PhD diss., Columbia University, 2014), 114.
25 Tappan, "Reframing Internalized Oppression," 2115.
26 Willie Ermine, "The Ethical Space of Engagement," *Indigenous Law Journal* 6, 1 (2007): 193–203.
27 Truth and Reconciliation Commission of Canada, *Calls to Action,* 2015, https://nctr.ca/assets/reports/Calls_to_Action_English2.pdf.
28 Rangel, "Appropriated Racial Oppression," 65.
29 Steinhauer, "Sohkastwawak."
30 Lipsky, *Internalized Racism,* 3.
31 Dee Watts-Jones, "Healing Internalized Racism: The Role of a Within-Group Sanctuary among People of African Descent," *Family Process* 41, 4 (2002): 594.

6

ISKOTEW AND CROW

(Re)igniting Narratives of Indigenous Survivance and Honouring Trauma Wisdom in the Classroom

Karlee D. Fellner

SQUAAAAAWK   SQUAAAAAWK   SQUAAAAAWK

it was barely sunrise and that pesky crowalarm wouldn't let her sleep
"UGHHHHHHHH!!!"   Iskotew let out a huuuuuuge groan
    she flip-flopped in her bed   pillow over her head   but crow was too loud

"fine!   I'm getting up!!"   she declared to the empty space around her

that crow had been harassing her for so long now   Iskotew couldn't remember
how far back it began   heck   almost felt like it started before her lifetime

either way   details didn't matter
what mattered was that damn crow had gone too far and was still going
    it was ruining her life and she was sickofit
cawing   pecking   squawking   talking   relentless!

she'd tried everything in the books
politely asking the crow to leave   yelling at it to go away   throwing things at it
feeding it   desperately pleading with it
she even went to dr.crowwhisperer   supposedly professionally trained to get
rid of crows
    but at best   dr.crowwhisperer could only distract the crow momentarily

the crow had become so disruptive that Iskotew had even tried her last resort
    she went to see dr.coyote one day   looking all dapper in his suit n white
    lab coat
    see even tho dr.coyote had a reputation as an expert   Iskotew was wary
    of dr.coyotes
but she'd tried everything in the books and noneofit worked
    so into dr.coyote's office she went

"what's the problem?"   dr.coyote grinned

"it's this crow   won't leave me alone   trying to figure out what to do about it"
dr.coyote's grin spread so wide it almost fell off his face
        he rifled thru his pockets   "aha!"   he pulled out a tiny pill
"just take this! it'll get rid of that crow in no time"   dr.coyote winked tossed
the pill to Iskotew   "hmmm..."   Iskotew examined the pill   fakesmiled
"thanks dr.coyote"
dr.coyote's grin grew so big   there was no beginning or end   he nodded
warningsideeffectsmayinclude   apathy silencing lowselfworth fear learnedhelplessness disconnection
oppression suppression

indeed dr.coyote's pill helped shut that crow up
    well   more like Iskotew couldn't hear it anymore
the crow was still around all the time   it was just muffled
    problem was   so was everything else
Iskotew couldn't see hear feel taste smell experience much of anything
anymore!
    and she was still so tired   so heavy so sickofit
    eventually crow just got louder anyway   caw cAW CAW! above the pills
        so she gave up and threw em away

seemed everyone around Iskotew was sickofit too
that crow followed her to family dinners   school   work
    she couldn't even hang out with her friends without that pesky crow
    showing up
everyone at school knew her as crowgirl   one teacher warned the next
    lest they   GASP!!   be surprised when crowgirl entered their class
        seemed Iskotew's path as crowgirl was set

                                  Karlee D. Fellner

she kept her head down   headphones in   spent most of her time in the
dark   alone

some grew impatient   "crowgirl! I'm sick of you and your crow! I don't wanna
hear about it!"
others felt sorry for her   "poor crowgirl   you never did anything to deserve
this   sad enit?"
some blamed her   "what's wrong with you? how long's it been?! get rid of
that crow already!!"
still others tried to rescue her by going after the crow
     sssshhhhhhhushing it   swinging at it   yelling at it   ignoring it   feeding it
          you name it   they tried it all
               and got exhausted

everyone seemed to have their own take on how to get rid of that problematic
crow
and nothing worked   crow just got   louder   loudER   loUDER   LOUDER

crowgirl had been sickofit long enough   her last resort had failed   nothing
seemed to help
so that morning as the sun rose   crowgirl got up with determination
"I'M DONE WITH YOU CROW!!"   she yelled angrily

crowgirl charged out the door   no destination   she was just done
notacare   where she might end up   or whether she returned

her feet pounded out a dancedrumbeat on the sidewalk
     her steps   lighter   heavier   lighter again
"GUNG – HO"   she thoughtgiggled to herself
a crazyfeeling of   renewed energy   nonsensical optimism   movement

crowgirl walked and walked and walked and walked and walked and walked
til the sidewalk dissolved under her feet   her steps   thump thump thump
on soft earth

thump thump thump   thump thump thump   thump thump thump   thump
thump thump

til crowgirl found herself in a clearing deep in the woods

crowgirl's legs feet were tired   her lungs working overtime
she stopped in that clearing   laid on her back
   sinking into the soft earth   smiled "done with it" she thought

takwâkin   autumn   a bed of dried leaves rested between crowgirl and
askîy   earth
   she let out a deep breath   looking up at kîsik   sky
it was a beautiful warm fall day   kîsik   was bright blue
   the occasional cloud floating by   waving to crowgirl and all the beings
   around
another deep breath   a smile spread across crowgirl's face

quiet

this is the first quiet she'd heard in sooooooo long
soooooooooooooooooooooooooooooo   looooooooonnnnnnnnnnnnnnnnnnnng !

she breathed in the quiet   she heard the orchestra of beings
crescendoooooooOOO
plants breathing shedding prepping for   pipon winter
rocks resting smiling warming in the gentle autumn sunshine
insects animals   scurrying collecting insulating storing for the cold
birds all kinds singing talking squawking ... cawing!
   "CAWING?!!"   crowgirl thoughtpanicked to herself   realizing crow was
   still there
       "ughhhhhhhhhhh!!" she groaned   she thought she'd lost that pesky
       crow

          swoooosh swoooosh swoooosh   wings flapping
          cRunCh cruNch   leaves crunching   at her feet

crowgirl sat up

"Crow!"   she was surprised   Crow landed right in front of her

Karlee D. Fellner

crowgirl realized she had never looked directly at Crow   this was the
first time
Crow tilted its head   blinked its eyes   opened its beak
    "tan'si!   how are you?"
crowgirl was stunned   Crow was speaking to her   in languages she could
understand!
    "uhhhhh ... good? I guess??"   she stunnedreplied

Crow smiled   "ha! sorry – didn't mean to catch you off guard"   Crow winked
"figured I've been around long enough you wouldn't be so startled!"   Crow
chuckled

crowgirl chuckled   then chucklelaughed more   then laughter   laughter!
pouring out of her
    laugh laugh laugh laugh laugh laugh laugh laugh laugh
        crowgirl felt the earth laughing underneath her
            plants around her   rocks insects animals birds
                hahahahahaHAhaHaHahahaHAHAHAhahahAhAhAhahaHaHAHA
            lolololololololololololololololololololololololololololololololololol

        fear   distress   anxiety   despair   suicide   loneliness   hurt   pain
        pouring out of her
            askîy   plants   rocks   insects   animals   birds   breathing   transforming
            creating
                hahahahahaHAhaHaHahahaHAHAHAhahahAhAhAhahaHaHAHA
            lolololololololololololololololololololololololololololololololololol

everyone was laughing so hard   gigglefit   sorestomach   tearsoflaughter
lololololololol
that laughing orchestra continued for ages it seemed   til
decrescendooooooooooooo
    trailing off   Iskotew wiped those   tearsoflaughter   from her eyes

Crow smiled   hopped from the leaves onto Iskotew's cross-legged knee
    "geez ayyyyyyye girl! I've just been tryinna talk to you!"

those last few giggles escaped Iskotew's lips   "oy! is that why you been
so noisy?!"

Iskotew and Crow   **147**

"well chyaaaaa!! what you think I've got time to harass young ladies for the heckuvit?"
   Crow smiled "everything has purpose you know   even a noisy
   crow" Crow winked
Iskotew smiled a few more halfgiggles escaped she'd heard that before more than once
   'everything has a purpose'

"actually   that's what I been tryinna talk to you about Iskotew"
Iskotew looked around   the whole forest was listening
   but waitasec they weren't listening to Crow
   they were listening for whether Iskotew was listening

"I been tryinna tell you   your assistance is needed"
"huh?" Iskotew looked at Crow confused

"yep the two-leggeds are living in imbalance somewhere between the concrete slotmachines smartphones chemicals y'all seem to have lost your way forgot how to listen .... ahem! ... CLEARLY" Crow smilewinked at Iskotew "but not to worry that's why I'm here that's why we're here" Crow gestured to all the relatives around "we can see y'all are getting sick and tired of being sick and tired and heck we're sick and tired of it too"
   the earthplantsrocksinsectsanimalsbirdsskyuniverse nodded in agreement

Iskotew let out a big sigh Crow was right she was sick and tired of being sick and tired
   most people she knew were sick and tired of being sick and tired too
   Iskotew shook her head
Crow hopped onto Iskotew's wrist   "not to worry not like I squawked all this way just to leave you to find your way out on your own   we can help y'all find your way back"
Iskotew perked up smiled "oh yeah?"
"of course! where you think your original instructions came from in the first place?"
   Crow winked

Crow waved its wing over Iskotew's left hand   "here"

Karlee D. Fellner

Crow gave her 7 small grains of tobacco

"take this   use it to get the medicines you need   take those medicines back
to the people   share them generously   openly   in a good way   with the
instructions that come to you"

Crow gestured toward the tobacco   "each grain is a teaching a value that is
needed by your people at this time   when you offer a grain you will learn its
medicine and come to understand its teaching   you'll know where and when ..."

Crow paused   smiled at Iskotew "... just make sure you LISTEN..." Crow chuckled
Iskotew smiled back   "but I don't know ..."

     wing up   Crow stopped her   shook its head

"nuh uh uh!   you DO know you just forgot you know just LISTEN and let us
know when you need us   we'll be around to help you find your way when you
get lost again   others of your nation will help you too   still some real good
listeners out there"   Crow winkgrinned

Iskotew was unsure of herself   gulp!   she swallowed that lump of unsure
in her throat
Crow was totally sure   Iskotew knew she had to trust that totally sure
Crow   she nodded

Crow smiled winked   hopped around in a few circles and spread its
wings flew off

bush life as usual resumed
Iskotew let out a deep sigh
looked at the grains of tobacco in her hand
she lay back on the bed of leaves again   taking some time to rest before going
back to the busy-ness of human life

Iskotew felt the heaviness of human troubles she'd been carrying slide off of
her into askîy
     all that weight of distress about Crow was gone too   laughed into the
     earthskyuniverse

Iskotew thoughtgiggled to herself   "that whole time   Crow was trying to
help me
   I tried everything in the books!   guess the 'listening' strategy must be 'in
   press'…"

as the sun set   Iskotew   walkdanced   from the bush   back to those familiar
sidewalks

light   optimistic   unafraid   determined
all Iskotew's senses were clear   she looked around
   everything seemed new   colourful   alive   vibrant   diverse

she noticed so much she had never noticed before
she noticed many others who were distressed by helpers trying to get their
attention
      a young man trying to kickpunch a nipping coyote off his ankle
         an elderly woman swatting at a persistent raven

Iskotew realized what a pitiful state the two-leggeds were in
love for her people filled her heart   she stopped at a tree by the gas station
parking lot
      laid down that first grain of tobacco   love   sâkihitowin
      she asked for help   original instructions   so the people may know how
to listen again

The teachings in Iskotew's story come from many places, and the
story itself comes from a constellation of stories and experiences
through time and space. In the context of this essay, Iskotew[1] is a young
Cree woman living on Turtle Island[2] in a time of "concrete slotmachines smartphones chemicals" and dealing with symptoms of
trauma that are severely impacting her life. That said, Crow reminds
us not to take these identifying factors too literally, because any of
them may change at a moment's notice. Iskotew's story is a story shared
by many. Her story speaks to a collective story that is used here to talk
about Indigenous education, survivance, and trauma wisdom.

Drawing on Iskotew's story and my experiences working as a therapist with Indigenous children in schools, I hope to contribute to a conversation that is shifting paradigms of pathology that are disempowering and dominating towards Indigenous counternarratives of survivance, resilience, and resurgence. I offer some of my learnings on how educators can draw on Indigenous ways of knowing, being, and doing that move classrooms and communities towards individual and collective wellness, balance, and harmony. Here, our stories will be used to converse with/in some of the blurry spaces where Indigenous education, psychology, culture, and wellness intersect to benefit students, teachers and, ultimately, society as a whole.

I spend a lot of my time in these blurry spaces – perhaps not surprisingly given that navigating blurry spaces is so strongly encoded in my DNA as a Cree-Métis woman. niya neyihaw niya otipemisiwak.[3] Alberta ohci niya.[4] miyotehiskwew nitisiyihkason.[5] Karlee Fellner mônîyâw wihowin.[6] I am originally from central Alberta, and I am currently living as a very grateful visitor on the traditional territories of the Tsuut'ina, Stoney Nakoda, and Blackfoot Nations, including the Kainai, Piikani, Siksika, and Amskapi Pikuni. Since I began (re)connecting with the Indigenous languages, cultures, and customs that were taken from my ancestors, I have been blessed to have Elders and cultural mentors from many diverse Indigenous nations, including Cree, Anishinaabe, Métis, Secwepemc, St'at'imc, Sts'Ailes, Dakota, Lakota, Blackfoot, and Cherokee. As a result, the teachings I have received – and thus, the teachings I glean and will share from Iskotew's story – have come from many different peoples and places. I can only speak from the teachings I have been given, and I will do my best to share where they come from. I approach this work with a good heart, and I apologize for any mistakes or offences I may make along the way.

I have come to this work in Indigenous education indirectly. My undergraduate degree is in psychology, and my master's and doctorate degrees are both in counselling psychology. Most of my clinical and academic work is in Indigenous people's health and traditional approaches to wellness. I also work with Indigenous approaches to therapy and have been deeply influenced by my training in Shirley Turcotte's model of Indigenous Focusing-Oriented Therapy (formerly Aboriginal Focusing-Oriented Therapy).[7] I never imagined working in education. To be honest, my experiences in school growing up left me with a considerable aversion to doing any work in the education system. Yet those very experiences are likely a primary reason that Indigenous education eventually pulled me in and has now become an area of great passion.

My formal journey into Indigenous education began during my doctorate. I was disillusioned by the inherent colonialism in psychology, and I decided to pursue additional coursework in Indigenous education. There, I studied Indigenous curriculum and pedagogy and Indigenous research, and I attended an Indigenous education summer institute in Peru. I was amazed at the incredible work being done by Indigenous scholars and their allies in education, and I was inspired to bring this work into the fields of psychology and health more broadly. It was not until my doctoral internship in clinical psychology that I realized that my work in Indigenous wellness and decolonizing trauma also had much to offer education.

During my internship, my fellow clinical psychology trainees and I were supporting teachers in an urban elementary and middle school with an Indigenous focus. The school was 98 percent Indigenous students, and it had an explicit vision and mission to engage Indigenous students through cultural revitalization and the integration of Indigenous identities and languages. Considering this declared intent and all I had read in the literature, I walked into the school expecting to experience a rich learning environment that brought together Indigenous languages, cultural traditions, and values to inform cutting-edge Indigenous curricula and pedagogical practices. As it turns out, I have a tendency to err on the side of optimism. I do not want to minimize the tremendous efforts of the Indigenous and majority non-Indigenous educators, staff, and administrators to integrate Indigenous languages, cultural traditions, and values into the school.

Karlee D. Fellner

There were many who brought Indigenous ways of knowing, being, and doing into their work in amazing ways. However, the school overall was burdened with the pressures of whitestream education, and thus firmly rooted and steeped in the dominating system of education and colonial narratives of deficit and pathology. While indigeneity was tacked onto the walls, the curriculum, and special programs, it was – for the most part – not being lived in the classrooms. An energy of imbalance, disharmony, and difficulty echoed through the school and weighed on many of the students, staff, teachers, and administrators.

Like Iskotew, many of the children in the school were dealing with trauma and other challenges that were interfering with their ability to focus, learn, and create and sustain healthy relationships. Also like Iskotew, these children were surrounded by people who were trying whatever they knew to "get rid" of whatever symptoms were manifesting. Most of the time, these attempts were based in good intentions. However, they were also based in dominating Western colonial strategies aimed at symptom reduction, such as medication, psychotherapy, detention, or behaviour management techniques. And, as in Iskotew's story, these strategies did not adequately address the difficulties these children were facing, particularly in a long-term, meaningful way. Often, these interventions merely exacerbated symptoms. This is not surprising given that these interventions are firmly rooted within settler colonial ways of knowing, being, and doing that have themselves contributed to the traumas and symptoms being expressed in the first place.[8]

Like crowgirl, most of the children who were administered these interventions were given various labels – some in the form of formal diagnoses, some in the form of adjectives such as *disruptive, violent, shut down,* or *isolated.* The English language is rife with judgmental adjectives and nouns that are used to categorize and make conclusions about people.[9] These one-dimensional labels pathologize the individual child and deny the child's wholeness as a complex being-in-relation.[10] People around the child then treat the child in response to this simplistic label, minimizing the child's ability to engage in healthy ways of being and doing.[11] In the classroom, many of these children internalize the message that they are nothing more than these labels, and they often grow into the labels over time. Eduardo Duran talks about such labelling as a form of naming ceremony, wherein the person labelled with pathology "takes on the identity of being sick and in so doing carries the illness being projected ... into her psychological makeup."[12]

David Peat's metaphor of English as a straightjacket compared to the Blackfoot language and worldview speaks to this phenomenon in more ways than one.[13] While process-based Indigenous languages account for a holistic human in-relation and traditional namings help people actively embody and increasingly learn their gifts and purpose, noun-based English labels objectify and subjectify people, restricting them through categories that are created and implemented to privilege and perpetuate North American capitalism and nationalism.[14] These words can have detrimental consequences, because, as Karl Lee, an *iyinisiw* (Plains Cree knowledge-holder) I consulted during my dissertation research, says, "Every label limits people in their beliefs in their own outcomes, and they create negative outcomes."[15]

Within dominating North American culture, such pathologies, labels, and diagnoses have largely come to be accepted as a reality, despite their socially constructed origins and research that challenges their validity.[16] As an accepted "reality," deficit-based labels may not seem like such a big deal. Certainly, those who labelled Iskotew as crowgirl thought nothing of it – it only made sense to them, given that she was being followed by a crow all the time. The thing is, in the bigger picture, labelling is a big deal with very real consequences. Indigenous children and youth who internalize the message that they are little more than a deficit may be at greater risk of becoming statistics in the overarching colonial deficit narrative. This message not only comes through diagnostic labels and negative adjectives and nouns, it is ubiquitous, reinforced throughout the dominating discourse, including public stereotypes and media.[17] Even Indigenous media feed into the deficit narrative, running titles such as "Trauma May Be Woven into DNA of Native Americans" and "Aboriginal Drop Out Rates Still High."[18]

Indigenous children and youth who are labelled with deficits may also be at greater risk of becoming targets in the settler colonial project of assimilation through what Krista Maxwell refers to as applications of "ostensibly benevolent interventions in the name of health and welfare."[19] The application of such interventions from within dominating Western colonial frameworks constitutes a form of psycholonization that includes assessments, diagnoses, conceptualizations, and interventions implicitly geared towards shaping people to conform to the dominating system.[20] These labels and interventions are thus a form of social control.[21] Further, such labels impede healing by minimizing the possibility for change.[22] And by placing responsibility for pathology on the individual, they obscure, as Heidi Rimke points out, "societal deficits and social relations of power that often underlie and contribute to human struggles and difficulties."[23] These labels reinforce long-standing, ongoing colonial deficit narratives that portray Indigenous people, families, and communities in terms of deficits, disparities, and dysfunction.[24]

Herein lies the danger of conventional trauma discourse. The dominating North American society perpetuates a view of trauma through a lens of deficit and pathology.[25] Trauma terminology locates the response to traumatic injury within the individual, allowing government and wider society to avoid taking responsibility for the systemic injustices inflicted on Indigenous people.[26] Indigenous counterconcepts that emphasize the role of systemic forces in the collective trauma experienced by Indigenous people – such as historical trauma, colonial trauma, intergenerational posttraumatic stress disorder, ancestral trauma, and the soul wound – are helpful in this regard.[27] Yet caution must be exercised so that the emancipatory goals of these concepts are not subsumed within and overtaken by colonial narratives of deficit and pathology that universalize Indigenous suffering, silencing counternarratives of wellness and abundance.[28]

Iskotew's story illustrates a shift from pathologizing approaches to trauma, towards Indigenous approaches that honour trauma wisdom, giftedness, survivance, and the past-present-future self-in-relation to the natural and spirit worlds. Iskotew's trauma severely interferes, for quite some time, with the life she wants to live and presents many challenges and difficulties that she and those around her conceptualize within a framework of pathology. The reactions of others range from impatience to pity to blame to patronizing attempts to rescue her. It is only when Iskotew frees herself from the constraints of this dominating framework that she has the opportunity to listen to the wisdom that Crow has been trying to bring to her all along.

It is no coincidence that this opportunity and clarity come when Iskotew returns to the land. In the story, it is unclear how she got back to the land. Countless pathways may lead to clarity when people are "sickofit." These pathways are not always straightforward and are sometimes difficult, but they are an important part of the journey. Perhaps Iskotew found her way back to the land through contemplating suicide, hitting rock bottom, literally going out on the land, connecting with an Elder or knowledge-holder, or attending a traditional ceremony. Regardless of how she got there, when Iskotew returns to the land and is able to listen to Crow with clarity, she is given the medicine she needs to move forward and to help others move forward in balance, wellness, and healing. This is trauma wisdom.

I have come to understand the concept of trauma wisdom primarily through my work learning and practising Indigenous Focusing-Oriented Therapy.[29] In my understanding, *trauma wisdom* refers to the personal and collective medicine that emerges through direct, vicarious, collective, or intergenerational traumas.[30] In Iskotew's story, the precise nature of the trauma she is experiencing is unclear, yet the trauma is both personal and collective, because even with direct experiences of trauma, there are always others who share similar stories.[31] Thus, the wisdom and teachings that trauma bring are both personal and collective.[32] The medicine that Crow gives Iskotew will help her and her people. Shirley Turcotte and Jeffrey Schiffer refer to this as

Karlee D. Fellner

decolonized knowing, which informs "survival and growth for all of life and land."[33] They say "it is this decolonized knowing that is our hope in healing past, present, and future."[34] Thus, Iskotew's story illustrates the shift from trauma as individual pathology to the wisdom of the past-present-future self-in-relation to the natural and spirit worlds.[35]

Indigenous perspectives acknowledge the interconnectedness of all beings.[36] Each of us may conceive of ourselves in the centre of a web of relations, consisting of our families, our communities, the natural world, the spirit world, and everything we are connected to/ with/in/between/around in the universe. Through this web, we are also connected to past and future generations.[37] Anything that happens within our web of relations is felt throughout the web, including struggles, healing, and everything in between.[38] In the classroom context, this means that "symptoms" and "behaviours" that children experience and express are often collective, vicarious, and intergenerational. Children have an incredible gift, as Shirley Turcotte says, to "pick up the trouble so that the troubled aren't as troubled, and ... can therefore function better than they would if the child did not pick up the trouble."[39] In the absence of healthy ways of transforming or letting go, such as traditional ceremonies, children may carry the troubles of their families and communities throughout their lives.[40] Crow is not simply Iskotew's crow but rather a crow who is picking up and sharing messages from others, both in Iskotew's web of relations and through the generations. Accordingly, the teachings that Crow brings to Iskotew are meant to benefit not only her but also her relatives and fellow people and, by extension, the natural and spirit worlds and past and future generations.

The wisdom and medicine Iskotew receives will disperse healing through her web of relations. The "symptoms" and "behaviours" children experience in the classroom contain important knowledges and wisdoms to share with the children, their classmates, and teachers, and all their relations. Such symptoms and behaviours may be understood as conversations that are coming from past or future generations, from a younger or older self, or from vicarious or collective influences anywhere within an individual's web of relations.[41] When honoured and listened to, the wisdom that emerges through these conversations moves the child and all of her relations towards balance, wellness, healing, and social and environmental justice.[42]

When I was working in the Indigenous-focused school, I was particularly struck by the immense power of trauma wisdom-in-relation. Because, from what I was observing, conventional Western colonial techniques, which were individual-focused, deficit-based, patronizing, and reactive, were not nurturing healing and wellness in the classroom. My colleagues and I had an incredible opportunity to engage the collective wisdom of the children and traditional Indigenous knowledges. Teachers were eagerly seeking strategies to address imbalance, disharmony, and difficulty in their classrooms. Some of my fellow trainees and I began speaking with teachers about bringing Indigenous ways of knowing, being, and doing into the classroom to create and sustain good relationships, harmony, and balance. Given the challenges these teachers were facing in their work, they were very open and excited to create space for culturally rooted interventions.

As with Iskotew, my colleagues and I did not know the hypothesized "causes" of the so-called symptoms and behaviours the children were experiencing – and we did not need to. Many came from families who were living in poverty and dealing with a tremendous amount of intergenerational and vicarious trauma, a number were living in foster care, and some had disclosed having directly experienced trauma or witnessed violence. The thing is, not all of the children who were dealing with such challenges were having difficulty in school, and not all children who were having difficulty in school were facing these kinds of challenges. For example, a child may have never directly experienced or witnessed trauma or violence, yet when they were in the classroom, they began exhibiting behaviours or symptoms. From an interconnected Indigenous perspective, these symptoms and behaviours may have emerged solely because an ancestor was trying to communicate a message through them about how balance, wellness,

Karlee D. Fellner

and healing were needed in that environment. This may be particularly relevant with children whose ancestors attended residential or boarding schools. Future generations may also be contributing to the conversation, asking for attention so that such imbalances in the school environment are addressed before their own arrival in the classroom.

It is important to acknowledge that, without the space to be who they are in the classroom, it is incredibly risky for Indigenous students to learn an exclusively dominating North American curriculum and to do as they are told. Assimilation through education was meant to extinguish Indigenous peoples.[43] Schooling has been a threat to who we are since the introduction of settler education in our communities. I have no doubt that many of our kids who are having difficulty or who are disengaging in school are experiencing their ancestors speaking through them, bringing the message that the classroom is a dangerous place and doing their best to prevent their descendants from losing who they are. When we bring Indigenous ways of knowing, being, and doing – such as land-based learning, intergenerational learning, storywork, and circle work – into the classroom in a good way, it connects children with who they are, honouring diversity and opening space for them to do the work they need to do in the mainstream system without the risk of assimilation.[44] Given that these ways of knowing, being, and doing are inherently healing, they also address the children's mental, physical, emotional, and spiritual wellness overall.[45]

Working with the teachers, my colleagues and I were committed to bringing Indigenous languages, cultural traditions, and values into the classrooms in an embodied, genuine, and good way. This intention was aligned with some of the work I had seen in Indigenous education, and it was very consistent with the literature on Indigenous health.[46] Further, it only made sense that the inherently balancing and healing properties of traditional Indigenous approaches could offer as much benefit in educational settings as they could in health service provision. In fact, integrating these knowledges and practices into educational settings could serve a critical role in the prevention of health and social issues, which is often not addressed in current health systems that are designed primarily to react to existing concerns.

We began simply – bringing a weekly smudge and talking circle into the classrooms. We invited circle participants to speak from the heart, sharing to their comfort level what was in their minds and hearts in that moment. All of the teachers had some experience with these practices, at a minimum, through professional development seminars. What many of them told us they were missing, however, was an understanding of the deep significance of these practices and their importance for the children. This understanding grew as the teachers participated in the circles over time, where my colleagues and I shared teachings and naturally incorporated Indigenous languages and values. We shared teachings such as the use of different plants for smudging, tobacco offerings, and grandmother or grandfather rocks to help the children let go of anything that was not serving them in a good way.

We also invited the children to share their teachings and understandings, and we asked some of them to act as our helpers by assisting us in preparing the smudge. Our helpers were most often children who had previously been labelled as problematic. They expressed pride and excitement, demonstrating an increased sense of self-worth and purpose through their contributions to the classroom community. Each time we sat together in circle, the relationships among all participants grew stronger. The children developed empathy for one another in hearing one another's stories, and respect among students and teachers grew. Through the smudge and culturally rooted help in the circle, children not only had the opportunity to let go of some of the challenges they were facing, they also learned and shared cultural knowledges that brought healing to their webs of relations.

Through these inherently healing processes, the teachers also had the opportunity to let go of some of the challenges they were facing personally and professionally and, by doing so, to connect more deeply with their students. Teachers who were vicariously picking up and carrying some of the difficulties the children were facing were able to let go of those difficulties with the help of the circle and land-based processes. As teachers increasingly experienced and understood Indigenous narratives of survivance, resilience, and resurgence through the smudge, talking circles, and teachings, their perspectives shifted from dominating paradigms of individual pathology towards honouring and engaging the tremendous wisdom, knowledge, and medicine of the children and themselves. The children were knowledge-holders and active contributors in the learning environment, with each taking responsibility for their learning and for upholding the values and protocols of the circle.

Bringing traditional Indigenous approaches into the classroom shifted the conventional focus on deficit towards a focus on gifted-ness and from a patronizing stance to one of honouring. When brought together in the circle, all children (and adults) were honoured and respected for their contributions. Karl Lee explains that, in many traditional Indigenous teachings, "people were accepted for the gifts they had. Everybody was a blessing, everybody has their own teachings, everybody has different gifts."[47] People were honoured for their gifts and mentored with traditional teachings and values that guided them to use their gifts to benefit the greater community. The circles created space for teachers and students to form healthy relationships and to learn from and nurture one another's gifts.

Iskotew's story does not reveal her specific gifts, but it is clear that she has something important to offer her fellow two-leggeds. Importantly, the gifts she is given emerge not only through her trauma but also in-relation with all of life and land. Crow reminds Iskotew that these gifts are connected to the original instructions the people were given from the land, which include traditional teachings that promote balance, healing, and wellness.[48] Crow also reminds Iskotew that healing is not linear, particularly in a time of widespread im-balance. Until the imbalances in our society's current ways of living are addressed, people will continue to experience symptoms and behaviours that call for movement towards good relationships, healing, and social and environmental justice. Thus, these difficulties are not considered pathological but rather as important sources of knowledge and wisdom.[49] Crow reminds Iskotew that she can access help from others when difficulties arise, including her relatives of the natural and spirit worlds, reinforcing the importance of healing-in-relation. As I have written elsewhere, the land is "central in [Indigenous] survivance, and continues to be there to help us and offer a place where we can let go of our pain, hurt, trauma."[50]

Importantly, this shift from the colonial deficit narrative towards a narrative of Indigenous survivance simultaneously moves Indigenous people away from narratives of victimry, dominance, helplessness, and pathology and honours the deep pain and difficulty of trauma.[51] This shift also acknowledges people's immense power and ability to heal themselves and the inexcusable interpersonal and systemic violence and injustices that continue to inflict and perpetuate trauma. Coming from Indigenous perspectives, Shirley Turcotte says, "it's not about on/off, yes/no, right/wrong, bad/good, it's about relationship and it's about all the tools available and the ways in which this trauma story could be perceived."[52] Conventional trauma narratives propagate shame, blame, patronizing attitudes, and learned helplessness; they create victims and saviours, which can impede healing and transformation. Further, caution must be exercised even when drawing on Indigenous counterconcepts that acknowledge historical, collective, and intergenerational influences on trauma, because, as Maxwell points out, sometimes this discourse "is used to pathologize indigenous parents and families by simultaneously universalizing experiences of abuse, overextrapolating the implications of abuse, and failing to acknowledge the existence of countervailing experiences."[53] Imagine the implications of retitling an Indian Country Media Network article from "Trauma May Be Woven into DNA of Native Americans" to "Wisdom of Surviving 500 Years of Attempted Genocide and Countless Millennia on the Land Woven into DNA of Native Americans."[54]

Karlee D. Fellner

Shifting these narratives of intergenerational trauma to acknowledge and honour intergenerational survivance can change lives.

This pervasive colonial deficit narrative burdens individuals, families, and communities with a label that presents trauma as an incurable pathology they are destined to carry throughout their lives. Such a narrative silences stories of the myriad ways Indigenous people continually resist oppression and violence.[55] As Shirley Turcotte says, "these survival stories are very very powerful, and coming out of genocidal policies that destroy so much, we just don't have the luxury of a Western model. It's not helpful because it's ... missing out on the strengths and the abilities of people to survive all odds."[56] By convincing people that they are pathological or disordered in some way, deficit narratives reinforce oppression and suppress the tremendous wisdom that Indigenous people have to offer the world today. This wisdom includes all the knowledge that emerged through surviving five hundred years of attempted genocide.[57] It includes knowledge gained from resistance to violence and oppression.[58] And it includes the wisdom of countless generations living and thriving with the land and through traditional teachings, before and after contact, as well as contemporary Indigenous ways of knowing, being, and doing that are continually (re)emerging and evolving. These counternarratives of resisting, surviving, and thriving are living stories of survivance.

Anishinaabe scholar Gerald Vizenor refers to survivance as "an active sense of presence, the continuance of native stories, not a mere reaction, or a survivable name. Native survivance stories are renunciations of dominance, tragedy and victimry."[59] Survivance is lived in Indigenous stories.[60] Iskotew's story and my experiences working in a school with an Indigenous focus are stories of survivance. In conventional North American society, stories of oppression and trauma tend to focus on violence and suffering, implying that those who are hurt are passive victims who were completely dominated or defeated by those inflicting the hurt.[61] In contrast, survivance narratives acknowledge the oppression and violence and include parallel stories of resistance to that oppression and violence.[62] This resistance occurs in context and in response to immediate violence or oppression, and thus it may take many forms.

Within the dominating system, Alan Wade writes, "acts and experiences that reflect a disguised, outright or inner resistance to oppression are either completely disregarded or treated as symptoms of a clinical problem presumed to reside within the victim."[63] Student disengagement in the classroom, for example, may be a form of resistance to oppression and assimilation. When listened to as a source of knowledge and wisdom – rather than being pathologized and individually targeted through conventional Western colonial interventions – this resistance can inform culturally rooted collective interventions that are antioppressive, promoting greater balance, wellness, and social justice in the classroom as a whole.

My colleagues and I bringing the smudge, talking circles, and traditional teachings into the classroom was both a resurgence of traditional wisdoms and a collective response to oppression. We were addressing the oppression inherent in the conventional education system by honouring diversity and opening space for children to share their unique voices and gifts. We were bringing Indigenous ways of knowing, being, and doing into the space where these ways of knowing, being, and doing had originally been oppressed and taken away through residential and boarding schools.[64] The classroom became a place where Indigenous children could simultaneously feel proud of who they are as Indigenous people and learn what they needed to learn within the dominating system. Thus, ancestors or future generations who may have been trying to communicate through the children's so-called symptoms and behaviours could now be at ease as the balance, good relationships, and wellness created in the classroom spread to them. These Indigenous lifeways that have been promoting balance and harmony for countless generations, before and after contact, gave children who were experiencing challenges and trauma

Karlee D. Fellner

outside of school the opportunity to let go of some of the difficulties they were carrying.

The smudge, talking circles, and traditional teachings made a profound difference in the classrooms. The energy shifted towards greater harmony and balance, fostering learning and increasing student engagement. These classrooms were actively living wellness through the implementation of Indigenous ways of knowing, being, and doing. The children were learning culturally rooted coping mechanisms that would help them face challenges throughout their lives. When my colleagues and I reflected on the process at the end of the school year, I was overcome with emotion as I realized the tremendous potential impact of this kind of work. It was not only the children who were benefitting, it was their families, their communities, all of their relatives, and the ancestors and future generations connected to them. We never know what kind of difference these experiences of (re)connecting with traditional ways may make. Those tobacco or smudge teachings could potentially be critical in a given moment between life and death. This is the immense power of trauma wisdom in-relation. Had it not been for the symptoms and behaviours of some of the children, we may not have done the work we did, and the teachers and students in these classrooms may never have experienced these incredible transformations through culture. I would also likely not be doing this work and would not have this story to share.

Iskotew's story and my story working in the school demonstrate the tremendous medicine, wellness, and balance that emerge through shifting colonial deficit narratives towards Indigenous narratives of survivance, resilience, and resurgence. These shifts involve restor(y)ing the individual to the collective; they require a shift from linear time to the past, present, future in-relation, from patronizing to honouring, from reactive interventions to prevention through good relationships and living wellness, and from pathologizing "symptoms" to listening to and engaging wisdom, knowledge, and resilience. Our stories are stories of survivance.[65] When listened to, heard, and engaged with in a good way, our stories offer medicine and wisdom that may help us, our communities, and society as a whole increasingly move towards good relationships, healing, balance, wellness, and social and environmental justice.

> as Iskotew laid down that first grain of tobacco
> love   sâkihitowin
> Crow smiled   somewhere in the universe
>   boom boom boom boom   drumbeats
>   the heartbeat of askîy

Notes

1 Plains (y) Cree for "fire."
2 *Turtle Island* refers to the continent of North America. This term is connected with traditional creation stories of specific First Nations and is used by some Indigenous groups today to refer to the continent of North America.
3 Plains (y) Cree for "I am Cree I am Métis" (*nehiyaw* = "person"; *otipemisiwak* = "people who rule themselves").
4 Plains (y) Cree for "I come from Alberta."
5 Plains (y) Cree for "They call me Good Hearted Woman."
6 Plains (y) Cree for "Karlee Fellner is my white name."
7 Shirley Turcotte and Jeffrey J. Schiffer, "Aboriginal Focusing-Oriented Therapy," in *Emerging Practice in Focusing-Oriented Psychotherapy: Innovative Theory and Applications*, ed. Greg Madison (Philadelphia: Jessica Kingsley, 2014), 48–63.
8 Eduardo Duran and Bonnie Duran, *Native American Postcolonial Psychology* (Albany, NY: SUNY Press, 1995); Mandi Gray, "Pathologizing Indigenous Suicide: Examining the Inquest into the Deaths of C.J. and C.B. at the Manitoba Youth Centre," *Studies in Social Justice* 10, 1 (2016): 80–94; and Krista Maxwell, "Historicizing Historical Trauma Theory: Troubling the Trans-generational Transmission Paradigm," *Transcultural Psychiatry* 51 (2014): 407–35.
9 Rupert Ross, *Returning to the Teachings: Exploring Aboriginal Justice* (Toronto: Penguin, 2006).
10 Heidi Rimke, "Mental and Emotional Distress as a Social Justice Issue: Beyond Psychocentrism," *Studies in Social Justice* 10, 1 (2016): 4–17; and Ross, *Returning to the Teachings*.

11 Linda M. Goulet and Keith M. Goulet, *Teaching Each Other: Nehinuw Concepts and Indigenous Pedagogies* (Vancouver: UBC Press, 2014); and Ross, *Returning to the Teachings.*

12 Eduardo Duran, *Healing the Soul Wound: Counseling with American Indians and Other Native Peoples* (New York: Teachers College Press, 2006), 31.

13 David F. Peat, "Blackfoot Physics and European Minds," *Futures* 29 (1997): 563–73.

14 On process-based languages, see Lawrence W. Gross, *Anishinaabe Ways of Knowing and Being* (London: Routledge, 2016); Peat, "Blackfoot Physics"; and Ross, *Returning to the Teachings.* Ross discusses the power of noun-based labels to objectify and subjectify in *Returning to the Teachings.* On the perpetuation of capitalism and nationalism, see Karlee D. Fellner, "Returning to Our Medicines: Decolonizing and Indigenizing Mental Health Services to Better Serve Indigenous Communities in Urban Spaces" (PhD diss., University of British Columbia, 2016).

15 Karl Lee, quoted in Fellner, "Returning to Our Medicines," 155; see also Ross, *Returning to the Teachings.*

16 See Michelle O'Reilly and Jessica N. Lester, "Introduction: The Social Construction of Normality and Pathology," in *The Palgrave Handbook of Adult Mental Health,* ed. Michelle O'Reilly and Jessica N. Lester (London: Palgrave Macmillan, 2016), 1–19; and Rimke, "Mental and Emotional Distress as a Social Justice Issue."

17 See, for example, Curtis Mandeville, "'I'm Not a Bad Person': Recognizing Impacts of Childhood Trauma in the Justice System," *CBC News,* March 14, 2017, http://www.cbc.ca/news/canada/north/nwt-michael-abel -childhood-trauma-justice-system-1.4023239?cmp=abfb.

18 Mary Annette Pember, "Trauma May Be Woven into DNA of Native Americans," *Indian Country Media Network,* May 28, 2015, https://indian countrymedianetwork.com/news/native-news/trauma-may-be-woven-into -dna-of-native-americans/; and Birch Bark Staff, "Aboriginal Drop Out Rates Still High," *Ontario Birchbark* 5, 9 (2006), 3, http://www.ammsa.com/ publications/ontario-birchbark/aboriginal-drop-out-rates-still-high.

19 Maxwell, "Historicizing Historical Trauma Theory," 409.

20 The term *psycholonization* is from Fellner, "Returning to Our Medicines"; Phil Borges and Kevin Tomlinson, dirs., *Crazywise: Rethinking Madness* (Seattle: Phil Borges Productions, 2017), https://crazywisefilm.com; Duran and Duran, *Postcolonial Psychology*; and Duran, *Healing the Soul Wound.*

21 Duran, *Healing the Soul Wound.*

22 Ross, *Returning to the Teachings.*

23 Rimke, "Mental and Emotional Distress," 8.

24 Duran and Duran, *Postcolonial Psychology*; Laurence J. Kirmayer, Joseph P. Gone, and Joshua Moses, "Rethinking Historical Trauma," *Transcultural*

Psychiatry 51 (2014): 299–319; Renee Linklater, *Decolonizing Trauma Work: Indigenous Stories and Strategies* (Winnipeg: Fernwood, 2014); and Maxwell, "Historicizing Historical Trauma Theory."

25 Linklater, *Decolonizing Trauma Work.*

26 Ibid.

27 Maria Yellow Horse Brave Heart, "The Return to the Sacred Path: Healing from Historical Trauma and Historical Unresolved Grief among the Lakota" (PhD diss., Smith College, 1998) [historical trauma]; Roger E. John, "Colonial Trauma and Indigenist Ethics: Implications for Counselling Indigenous Clients" (master's project, University of Victoria, 2004) [colonial trauma]; Duran and Duran, *Postcolonial Psychology* [intergenerational posttraumatic stress disorder]; and Duran, *Healing the Soul Wound* [soul wound].

28 Maxwell, "Historicizing Historical Trauma Theory."

29 Turcotte and Schiffer, "Aboriginal Focusing-Oriented Therapy."

30 Ibid.

31 Turcotte, *Aboriginal Psychotherapy.*

32 Ibid.

33 Turcotte and Schiffer, "Aboriginal Focusing-Oriented Therapy," 81.

34 Ibid.

35 Turcotte, *Aboriginal Psychotherapy.*

36 Michael A. Hart, *Seeking Mino-Pimatisiwin: An Aboriginal Approach to Helping* (Halifax: Fernwood, 2002); Rod McCormick, "Aboriginal Approaches to Counselling," in *Healing Traditions: The Mental Health of Aboriginal Peoples in Canada,* ed. Laurence J. Kirmayer and Gail Guthrie Valaskakis (Vancouver: UBC Press, 2009), 337–54; and Leanne Simpson, "Anishnaabe Ways of Knowing," in *Aboriginal Health, Identity, and Resources,* ed. Jill Oakes, Rick Riewe, Skip Koolage, Leanne Simpson, and Nancy Schuster (Winnipeg: Native Studies Press, 2000), 165–85.

37 Turcotte, *Aboriginal Psychotherapy.*

38 Fellner, "Returning to Our Medicines."

39 Turcotte, *Aboriginal Psychotherapy.*

40 Ibid.

41 Ibid.

42 Turcotte and Schiffer, "Aboriginal Focusing-Oriented Therapy."

43 Roland Chrisjohn and Sherri Young, *The Circle Game: Shadows and Substance in the Indian Residential School Experience in Canada* (Penticton, BC: Theytus Books, 1997).

44 For example, Richard Katz and Verna St. Denis, "Teacher as Healer: Expanding Educational Resources," in *Synergy, Healing, and Empowerment: Insights from Cultural Diversity,* ed. Richard Katz and Stephen Murphy-Shigematsu (Calgary: Brush Education, 2014), 115–30 [intergenerational

learning]; Jo-ann Archibald, *Indigenous Storywork: Educating the Heart, Body, Mind, and Spirit* (Vancouver: UBC Press, 2008) [storywork]; and Goulet and Goulet, *Teaching Each Other* [circle work].

45 On healing, see Hart, *Seeking Mino-Pimatisiwin*; Linklater, *Decolonizing Trauma Work*; and Anne Poonwassie and Ann Charter, "An Aboriginal Worldview of Helping: Empowering Approaches," *Canadian Journal of Counselling* 35 (2001): 63–73. On overall wellness, see Fellner, "Returning to Our Medicines."

46 On Indigenous education, see, for example, Archibald, *Indigenous Storywork*; Goulet and Goulet, *Teaching Each Other*; and Katz and St. Denis, "Teacher as Healer." On Indigenous health, see, for example, Fellner, "Returning to Our Medicines"; John, "Colonial Trauma and Indigenist Ethics"; Linklater, *Decolonizing Trauma Work*; Rod McCormick, "Culturally Appropriate Means and Ends of Counselling as Described by the First Nations People of British Columbia," *International Journal for the Advancement of Counselling* 18 (1996): 163–72; and James B. Waldram, ed., *Aboriginal Healing in Canada: Studies in Therapeutic Meaning and Practice* (Ottawa: Aboriginal Healing Foundation, 2008).

47 Karl Lee, quoted in Fellner, "Returning to Our Medicines," 216.

48 *Original instructions* may be used to refer to ways of living that Indigenous people have been given by the Creator, including specific ethics, protocols, and practices that maintain good relationships with the human, other-than-human, natural, and spiritual worlds. See Melissa K. Nelson, "Mending the Split-Head Society with Trickster Consciousness," in *Original Instructions: Indigenous Teachings for a Sustainable Future*, ed. Melissa K. Nelson (Rochester, VT: Bear and Company, 2008), 288–97. See also Nelson, "Trickster Consciousness."

49 Turcotte, *Aboriginal Psychotherapy*.

50 Fellner, "Returning to Our Medicines," 283.

51 On victimry, see Gerald Vizenor, *Manifest Manners: Narratives on Postindian Survivance* (Lincoln: University of Nebraska Press, 1999).

52 Turcotte, *Aboriginal Psychotherapy*.

53 Maxwell, "Historicizing Historical Trauma Theory," 425.

54 Pember, "Trauma May Be Woven."

55 Alan Wade, "Resistance Knowledges: Therapy with Aboriginal Persons Who Have Been Subjected to Violence," in *A Persistent Spirit: Towards Understanding Aboriginal Health in British Columbia*, ed. Peter H. Stephenson, Susan J. Elliott, Leslie T. Foster, and Jill Harris (Vancouver: UBC Press, 1995), 167–206.

56 Turcotte, *Aboriginal Psychotherapy*.

57 Ibid.

58 Wade, "Resistance Knowledges."

59 Vizenor, *Manifest Manners*, vii.
60 Gerald Vizenor, *Native Liberty: Natural Reason and Cultural Survivance* (Lincoln: University of Nebraska, 2009).
61 Wade, "Resistance Knowledges."
62 Ibid.
63 Ibid., 175.
64 Chrisjohn and Young, *The Circle Game.*
65 Vizenor, *Manifest Manners.*

Karlee D. Fellner

PART 3

TRUTH, RECONCILIATION, AND DECOLONIZATION

7

CURRICULUM AFTER THE TRUTH AND RECONCILIATION COMMISSION

A Conversation between Two Educators on the Future of Indigenous Education

Harry Lafond and Darryl Hunter

Many concerned about Indigenous education in Canada look to the past – drawing on memories of traditional Indigenous approaches to child rearing, describing the effects of Christian proselytizing in mission schools, documenting the appalling history of residential schools, and questioning the ethos of industrial schools. We argue that the Truth and Reconciliation Commission's final report, published in 2015, offers policy-makers in First Nations and provincial school systems an occasion to move beyond memories of the past and to begin a journey towards a curriculum based on a shared future – a journey that may be rigorous but that may also have many rewards for students and for society.[1] The aim here is to identify potential paths and pitfalls for curriculum over the next two decades or so. What follows is a conversation that focuses on that journey and offers possibilities for curricula, not only within First Nations schools but, just as importantly, within provincially funded schools across the country.[2] Unlike historical texts, curricula are not primarily ways of recapturing images of the past but rather practical tools that should lever us into the future.

The TRC and Its Call to Action

A school curriculum is, by its very nature, an expression of aspirations, a vehicle for attaining a particular type of society by shaping the next generation of adults. In a sketchy and preliminary way, the Truth and Reconciliation Commission of Canada's (TRC) call for fundamental changes in Indigenous education across Canada placed the onus on the federal government rather than on provincial governments to set curriculum content and design. The federal government was called upon to draft new Indigenous education legislation with the full participation and informed consent of Indigenous peoples. The new federal legislation should set the stage for accomplishing the following goals: closing identified educational achievement gaps within one generation; improving education attainment levels and success rates; developing culturally appropriate curricula; and protecting the right to Indigenous languages, including the teaching of Indigenous languages as credit courses. Moreover, the new legislation should enable parental and community responsibility, control, and accountability (creating a situation similar to that experienced by parents in public school systems), so they can fully participate in the education of their children. The new legislation should also respect and honour treaty relationships. Widening the scope, the TRC called on federal, provincial, territorial, and Indigenous governments to develop culturally appropriate early childhood education programs for Indigenous families. Perhaps more importantly, the commission called on the federal government to acknowledge that Indigenous rights include language rights, enacted in legislation that recognizes that Indigenous original languages are a fundamental and valued element of Canadian culture and society.

According to the commission, the preservation, revitalization, and strengthening of Indigenous languages and cultures is best managed by Indigenous people and communities. The TRC assigns responsibility to the federal government for providing sufficient funding for revitalization and preservation. The funding must reflect the diversity of Indigenous languages, and the commission recommended the appointment of an Indigenous languages commissioner to promote languages and to report on the adequacy of funding for language initiatives. At the same time, the TRC called on postsecondary institutions to create university and college degree and diploma programs in Indigenous languages.

Although the TRC's final report turns the spotlight on Ottawa and explicitly seeks a rebirth in Indigenous education, the authors also argue for a change in provincial schools from early childhood to Grade 12. Reconciliation has the potential to transform the education of all young people across Canada. The goals of the TRC will not be fulfilled, the authors contend, without a substantial and parallel change in curricula for public schools – curricula that are developed by provincial governments and school boards. The TRC addressed shortcomings in education for Indigenous students, but it also provoked introspection and action on problematic assumptions in curricula for non-Indigenous students as well.

Below, we present the perspectives of two educators, condensed and edited from two lengthy interviews. Both educators were born and raised, educated, and employed within that gigantic wishbone formed by the North and South Saskatchewan rivers as they flow across the prairie.

Harry is the executive director of the Office of the Treaty Commissioner in Saskatoon. He has a wide range of experience in the community, in politics, and in academia. He has been a chairperson for the Board of Trustees of First Nations Trust since 2003. He served his nation as Chief between 1990 and 2000. Harry has worked extensively in the area of education as the director of education and, earlier, as principal of kihiw waciston School at Muskeg Lake. Harry's academic education includes bachelor of arts, bachelor of education, and master of education degrees. He was appointed to serve on the senate of the University of Saskatchewan (1995–2002) and was also appointed to the federal task force on education (2003). Family is a priority, and Harry spends many hours with his children and grandchildren teaching them about being Cree.

Darryl is an associate professor in the Department of Educational Policy Studies at the University of Alberta. Prior to entering the academy, he held a variety of managerial roles relating to assessment and evaluation for the Saskatchewan, Ontario, and British Columbia ministries of education, and he was a senior policy adviser in a cabinet planning unit. He has also served on several provincial curriculum writing and advisory committees over the years. He was a high school and middle years teacher of French and English language arts, social studies, and law in Saskatchewan for over a decade. That time included a stint as vice-principal of a public secondary school that bordered six reserves in or near the Qu'Appelle Valley in Treaty 4. Harry was Darryl's supervising teacher when Darryl was beginning his career in education.

Concepts of Curriculum

HARRY: At a recent Ottawa forum of First Nations directors of education from across Canada, I noticed a distinct change in attitude towards curriculum amongst participants. It used to be that First Nations leaders accepted whatever curriculum was available from provincial authorities or from Western-oriented institutions, such as within faculties of education, revising it so it has an Indigenous outlook. The key question used to be: How do we adapt what has been prepared elsewhere and infuse it with an Indigenous perspective?

Now, the entire concept of curriculum has moved to a new level – the discussions and presentations related to curriculum have shifted towards an interpretation of Indigenous culture, content, worldview, and belief systems and away from the borrowed foundations of Western cultures. The move is away from adaptation within the existing provincial curriculum guide towards a land-based curriculum that fosters a sense of balance. We give young people experiences in traditional practices on the land – not only as an economic activity, but towards an intergenerational transfer of values and belief systems. This is accomplished by using land-based strategies inside and around a First Nations school.

Harry Lafond and Darryl Hunter

The primary aim is not to teach trapping as an economic activity but more about going out on the land with a parent or Elder or teacher, to connect with the land, to better understand their cultural legacy. By becoming directly connected with the environment and ecology, students will become aware of the cultural values as they come under the care and instruction of experts and Elders of their community. This experience develops personal identity and impacts on the values held; it will continue as they take on adult roles and begin their own family units. At the forum, this appeared to be a cross-Canada trend in the Indigenous community, expressing itself very definitively when communities talked about centralizing language and culture in their learning strategies.[3] For example, Kahnawake people struggle within Quebec education laws that require instruction in French. Putting language and culture at the centre of the curriculum, the Mohawks have developed their own curricula and successfully implemented immersion classrooms.

So where does that take us? Many current assumptions when preparing teachers must be unearthed and reexplored as we go forward. For example, in faculties of education, the role of educational psychology must be reexamined. Do Western psychological assumptions hold? Are prospective teachers asked to consider the psychological impact of colonization on students and within Indigenous communities? In educational foundations, new master's programs are being formed where the study streams are based on land-based knowledge. These master's students, as future education leaders, will drive changes in curricula for preservice teachers.

DARRYL: As a point of contrast, I recall you teaching a Grade 7 class of twenty-five or so students, two-thirds or three-quarters of whom were from Mistawasis Reserve. You were using a textbook entitled *Lands of the Eastern Hemisphere* about rural Nigeria. The classroom activities revolved around climatograms, interpreting photographs of village life, and mastering paragraphs of English prose. It struck me as incongruous that you should have to follow a curriculum guide and provincially mandated textbook when there was a far richer and more culturally relevant set of experiences right on the students' doorsteps.

HARRY: In this older view of curriculum, the textbook was the springboard, where concepts are drawn from prose text. Physics, chemistry, biology, and art should be approached from an experiential perspective, rather than as textbook concepts. With a land-based curriculum, teachers and students go walking directly out on the land, creating music within the natural environment, drawing conjectures or concepts from the environment as opposed to following textbook models. The land and ecology become the text. We experimented with that approach at kihiw waciston School, giving students experiences in survival, identifying and collecting the medicines of the community, creating music from the rhythms of the environment. That is not to totally exclude what is currently in the provincial curriculum and the traditional subjects. Instead, we sought to blend, taking the strengths from both strategies to maximize the learning experience of the student. The learner approaches the topic from the perspective of personal experience, rather than conjecturing reality from prose and talking about it in the classroom.

The learner is experiencing, and that experience carries him or her into a different type of imagination.[4] The learner picks sweetgrass and learns the associated botany and biology of the plant. He learns how you pick it and how to respectfully use it.

As a natural follow-up, people who are knowledgeable about ceremonies may take the learners into a ceremonial knowledge and walk them through that part of learning. They are transported into an entirely different realm of imagination from that experienced when learning primarily from textbooks. They are encouraged to explore their own spirituality and their participation within that culture. Curriculum is not prescriptive, but in Cree spirituality, ways of believing are to be respected and honoured. The Cree

Harry Lafond and Darryl Hunter

belief system teaches that making choices is the essence of being human. Choices made become responsibilities and measures of personal accountability. I call this Cree democracy, which is more egalitarian than what is commonly defined as Canadian democracy. In Cree democracy, even the youngest person is expected to make choices.

DARRYL: It seems to me that many current curricular assumptions run much deeper. For example, I am working on a project right now that involves the assessment of policy capacity in three South Pacific countries. When talking with people there, everyone understands Bloom's taxonomy, which is a staple of North American education systems. The University of Chicago of the 1950s is shaping outlooks sixty years later in another hemisphere. So many assumptions in curriculum and assessment are hard-wired in by presumptions drawn from psychology and from foundational Western ideas for a mass education system. So, I have to ask: How do you view assessment vis-à-vis curriculum going forward?

HARRY: Well, you can't isolate assessment from curriculum. It is integral to curriculum. When an Elder is teaching, the focus is on experiential learning. The focus is still on growth in the person from one stage to the next. The saying "failure is not an option" illustrates a difference between Western education and traditional First Nations approaches. Today, provincial schools often see failure as a weakness of both the instructor and the learner, something to be avoided, ignored, or not acknowledged. Therefore, school administrators and teachers are forced by the system not to believe in the value of failure. With the Elders, failure is necessary. Every individual must experience failure to recognize the scope of their personal successes. That may sound harsh, but where there is no failure, there is no feedback. That is quite different from Western thought, which overemphasizes success in the intellectual realm. Schooling in the Western tradition only pays secondary attention to emotional, spiritual, and physiological development and the feedback from those sides of human nature that must be incorporated in learning.

DARRYL: My own view is that so much of assessment relies on a linear scale, statistical assumptions drawn from mathematics, and rubrics that explicitly set out knowledge in a hierarchical measurement of values. I believe we need a revamp of assessment from the ground up. As with many things, it is my spouse who has been my inspiration, through her exasperation. When she asked me how our living room walls should be repainted, I said, "White." Her retort was that there are over four hundred shades, hues, and tones of white. Then she brought a colour wheel home from the paint shop. The qualities there are set out on a circle. The wine connoisseur's and coffee taster's rubrics are circular also. I believe many of the qualities and values now sought in evaluation processes, and ordered along a measurement scale in the languages or social studies, can be reformulated in a wheel, and that evaluative processes can be designed and reformed around that circle.

HARRY: The purposes of assessment and curriculum must be similar. They should formatively foster a sense of internal balance within the growing individual – and within the evolving community – rather than revolve around an externally driven mandate that overemphasizes the intellectual and cognitive dimensions in education.

DARRYL: Would a land-based curriculum look different at the high school level than at the elementary level?

HARRY: Curriculum should reflect a spiral progression. Knowledge grows and deepens as your capacity to internalize meanings from your environment develops during maturation. Taking kindergarten students outside, you will teach them about the plants and to find sweetgrass. At the same time, you will begin to teach to a young student the religious and spiritual purposes of that sweetgrass. You

Harry Lafond and Darryl Hunter

can advance that knowledge over the years and begin to challenge the high school student to contemplate the ecological side of that sweetgrass, ensuring that it will be there five years from now. What are the preconditions for that sweetgrass to survive into the next generation? Part of the thinking here about sweetgrass is seven generations forward. This is a traditional Indigenous, specifically Iroquois, perspective, where people are conscious that the decisions we make today should result in a sustainable world seven generations into the future. Everything you teach must be in that context. Thus, for example, you would emphasize community care for that land, how the community must contemplate the survival of that plot of sweetgrass, learning about the impact of letting grazing animals enter on that land. At the same time, students' thoughts would inform the land program in that community and into the governing structure of the land. Their knowledge becomes relevant and part of the management of the lands.

When you move beyond the biology and science of sweetgrass, you are also entering the spiritual aspects of youth development. For those who choose a Cree life, you can accommodate candidates for further and future roles. There is the concept of *oskâpew* ᐊᒼᐤᐦᑐ or "young men." Schools can accommodate that selection by providing services inside the school community, for example, as the one who helps the Elder conduct a pipe ceremony. Singing or music can be drumming or hip-hop, but you can support the gift of young people by incorporating them into the life of your school.

Conversations about Contrasting Assumptions

DARRYL: Does this not raise the issue of incorporating or adapting from existing curricula versus creating anew? Do we not have an entirely new conception of curriculum here?

HARRY: We need an entirely new conversation between the Indigenous community and provincial authorities about what is acceptable knowledge, especially at the high school level. One of the assumptions is that the province has it right. However, numerous studies increasingly question that assumption.[5] The provinces must recognize the deficiencies and gaps in their own systems. What better way to address deficiencies than through discussions about assumptions in the provincial curriculum? Right now, the provincial education systems are very narrow in what and how they teach and in what they omit from the curriculum. For example, Mendeleev's table and balancing chemistry equations with moles is stressed without linking the ideas to the natural elements in a student's actual environment. Physics classes may focus on Newton's laws in mathematical terms without showing students how they are apparent in the world immediately around them. Indigenous communities want to teach the whole person. The TRC has made that quest for a holistic education even stronger. If there is any thread since the time of treaty, it has been a desire to teach language and culture. With that type of focus, there is a foundation for holistic learning. You have to deal with the spiritual, emotional, and psychological sides, not just the fourth side, the intellectual, with its focus on content and information processing. We've grown to recognize the importance of dialogue, of active learning, but most provincial systems are still caught up with intellectual exercises inside the high school classroom.

DARRYL: Once, when I was teaching in a large high school, a parent came to my classroom when I had students working in small groups. The parent commented that she had sent her child to school to learn, not to talk! It seems to me that many operating assumptions derive from Ryerson's time of trying to create a universal, free mass education system in Ontario, which was subsequently transplanted in the western provinces.

First, we know the system was never free but funded from land tax revenues. Second, it was a mass education system involving a fifth of the total population, and policy-makers deemed that the most efficient way of having universal education was to aggregate

Harry Lafond and Darryl Hunter

150 to 1,200 kids in a building in one location, with centrally developed paper documents as bureaucratic devices. These curricula were essentially bureaucratic documents to help a teacher in the classroom, originally as a table of contents in a textbook, but now as ministry statements. Teachers are inculcated to coach students to move across a set of objectives or outcomes as hurdles in the mass reproduction of provincial ideals. This can be seen as a bureaucratic-industrial conception of curriculum, now moving into cyberspace. How do you see a land-based, experiential approach as changing, modifying, or revising this conception of curriculum, Harry? Provincial curriculum seems to represent provincial "community ideas," whereas you describe a more local and smaller community of aspirations, whether linguistic or cultural.

HARRY: Curriculum in some ways has become an accountability process for teachers, less a tool for guiding the process of learning. Curriculum has become a power tool intended to keep someone in line. The implicit message is "Make sure you do your job." When I hear Elders talk about preparing young people to move from stage to stage in their cycle, the conversation is not about external accountability so much as building an internal accountability within the learner. Curriculum becomes a tool chest for helping the educator. We have to let go of the idea that there is only one right way of doing something. We have an immersion school, a faith-based school; we have pods of different ways of learning within one administration – all point to the beauty of diversity. We have to question the assumptions of mass industrial schooling. The more we move in that direction, the more we promote fear in the relationships among peoples. We do have to understand and question the assumptions of industrial production and factory efficiency and moving kids in lockstep with their age. All must be questioned. The Elders' wisdom is about the primacy of building relationships leading to self-satisfaction, self-identity development, and a sense of belonging. Elders say that our kids are moving into cities and that our urban relatives are losing touch with the earth that sustains them and gives life. That is a strong element in the traditional Cree "scriptures" that I am hearing.

DARRYL: Yes, I hear that from my Elders, too, my parents and grandparents, but that raises other questions, about rural and urban education. My own background is the epitome of white settler society near the South Saskatchewan River. I was raised on a farm not too distant from Batoche. Within the framework of land-based education, should non-Indigenous students also start with the land? The nature of the attachment to the land is different, but I would claim just as profound. My parents are still alive and have moved to town, but my brother farms about an hour and half from here. He and my parents recognize that some of those natural cycles are not operating as they should. The farm remains, in many senses, my home. My parents always sought to lure me back to the farm while I was teaching and while working in government. Farm rhythms are still tied to the seasons and, to a certain extent, so are agricultural cycles. It is an exploitive relationship with the land, but that relationship paid for my education and, through taxation, for the education of many other students. My parents' mindset spans three or four generations, not seven generations like yours. How do we have a meeting of minds or reconciliation of outlooks, as far as curriculum is concerned? Can there be a meeting around a land-based curriculum that serves these differing views about the land itself?

HARRY: If you are going to have a difficult conversation involving two systems of thought, you have to deal with those assumptions. We live in a world where more than one people is concerned about the relationship to the land because of climate change – even the Catholic Church has an encyclical about our relationships to the land and to the environment. Maybe we need to check our own assumptions and make some adjustments. As Indigenous people, we don't have it all right, and so we need to check our assumptions as well. That is the essence of the dialogue. When we are looking at rural education, there are the things we need to teach our kids and which take us into our relationship with the land. Is it safe to do full-scale, year-after-year fertilization of the land? Can we survive without some exploitation of natural resources? These questions need to be posed to and addressed among youth. Right now, teenagers in high schools ask, "Why should I study this chemistry stuff? How much will this count on the test? Why will I need to know this? Will I ever need this knowledge in the future? Now, where can I go to eat?" *[laughter]*. However, from an educator's point of view, the questions are, "What in your present and future family's spiritual teachings point to what is going to happen to your children and grandchildren?" These are valuable discussions and more important than some of the issues now in curricula. These are generational issues for resolution and reconciliation. We will not resolve them within the next week. The university is going to have to catch up with that reality. Universities tend to be a few years behind what is happening in the community, and they are going to have to catch up.

Conceptions of Language Learning

DARRYL: Actually, we academics are miles ahead, so far ahead that we've fallen over the edge. *[Laughter]* Let's go back to the perennial debates about language and culture in Canadian schools. What does language learning look like in curriculum, post TRC?

HARRY: We are in the midst of an Indigenous language renaissance or flowering right across the country. Part of the picture is that colonization has been the strongest force in holding people in a static state as far as development is concerned. It has created a state of dependency in different ways in different communities, with individuals, with principals, and with teachers. There has been a tendency to wait – wait for somebody else to do it, wait for the right amount of funding to come from the federal government, wait for the school division to come up with an answer. But that is changing now. With decolonization, people are realizing that the answer comes from within, not from without. That's a powerful shift when considering language as intergenerational transfer, as legacy, as a way of thinking. Communities and schools realize that nothing is stopping them from doing what they want to do.

There is a customary division of language into reading, writing, oracy, listening, and representation. People are asking where to start when working with children and in communities. Oral literacy is the point of pedagogical concern. Some are working at the University of Alberta with Blue Quills and the University of Saskatchewan with a language retention group. There has been an evolution in language learning, away from half an hour a day or week, away from the linguistic declination of verbs, towards experiential strategies to teach oral literacy. People are going to start with oral literacy at Onion Lake and at St. Francis School in Saskatoon and move from there into reading and writing. In Saskatchewan, the major language groups are Cree, Dene, and Saulteaux or Anishinaabe. However, where the numbers are so small that there is difficulty in perpetuating the languages through immersion programs, only bilingual programs exist.

DARRYL: This raises a new level of programming issues: options for bilingual or multilingual education on reserve, the meaning of "where numbers warrant" in an Indigenous education context, and postsecondary opportunities for sustaining languages. The TRC would ask us to address the macro policy issue rather than translating policy into program and practice. Nevertheless, I hold two assumptions about language learning in Canadian curricula. One is drawn from Piaget and Western educational psychology: that there are natural developmental stages at which students can appropriately learn. The other assumption is nurture related: that language learning can draw on the pan-Canadian experience with French immersion since the 1960s and '70s. The assumption is that immersion is superior to teaching core French for half an hour per day. Do you think the Canadian experience with French immersion can assist with language learning for Indigenous students?

HARRY: I really question the second set of assumptions – that Canada has something to teach the world about language acquisition through immersion. I do not consider Canada to be very knowledgeable in language learning. Canadians have been plagued by a largely political dialogue about languages. Thus, efforts have been more in the way of developing official languages rather than developing effective ways of teaching and honouring languages. Canada does not have much to show the world in that regard. Many turn instead to New Zealand and Māori strategies that better match the social and cultural situations of Indigenous peoples in Canada. There are also European countries that honour multiple languages without all the politics, where children speak two or three languages without sweating about it.

We must understand physiology and brain development, like Piaget, and how the Creator has made us ready for different kinds of learning at certain stages of our life. The old people recognize those stages and honour those stages as growing events in the life cycle. As well, there are teachings that are related to the cradle board and training the child to become an observer of the world by restricting their movements so that they learn in appropriate ways.[6] There are also teachings for women to not only celebrate girls' physiological transition into adulthood but also to change the curriculum for young adults at the same time.[7]

DARRYL: How do you approach language questions in the face of language attrition among adults? In French immersion, there is a debate about whether students should start immersion in a second language in early school years, reverting to mother tongue later in life, or whether you start school in the home language and gradually introduce greater portions of the instructional day in French.

HARRY: We must honour diversity. You do not want to replace one form of unanimity with another, either off or on reserve. We must recognize the right of parents to determine where they want their children on language questions, specifically, what they determine to be their mother tongue and in which language of instruction they want their children taught. In Onion Lake School [in Saskatchewan], school officials have worked out the requirements and responsibilities at home associated with the choice. There are parents who will not send their students to an on-reserve school, opting for an off-reserve public school because they believe that the sooner they expose their children to a multicultural environment, the greater their opportunities.

DARRYL: You raise an important question that was not discussed by the Truth and Reconciliation Commission: What kind of language curriculum do parents actually want – unilingual, bilingual, or multilingual? What did you learn about language when you were a principal and director of kihiw waciston School at Muskeg Lake? What have you learned as a father?

HARRY: We learned that attitudinal change was central in language learning. We had to make languages "sexy." For the first two years, we ran language-immersion camps in Cree. Games, singing, dancing were key over a two-year period to change the attitudes of students, staff, and parents. Then we hired someone who knew how to bring both Cree language and culture into the classroom through art, sports, and other subject areas. My children were part of that process, choosing to study Cree at school, and they have pursued Cree into postsecondary levels. Parallel to that, a community group of individuals began to explore spirituality, and that reciprocally helped within the school.

The program eventually became a victim of community politics. There have been several efforts at rebuilding the program over the years. However, rebuilding is always limited by the vision of

Harry Lafond and Darryl Hunter

administrators and of teachers in the school. Nonetheless, as a father, I always felt responsible for cultivating Cree at home, but unfortunately, as an adult, I never had the gift of speaking and using the Cree language. I have instead imparted an appreciation for it in my youngest child and was able to work with him on it, but he surpassed me when he was about age four. Our conversations in Cree would be just too difficult for me to be natural. He was asking too many tough questions in Cree. [Laughter] But as an adult, he now comprehends and hears the Cree, its rhythms and intonations and vocabulary, even though he is not a speaker.

I acknowledge that French as the second official language has television as a support and does come with its own mythologies, which are powerful, whether it is through Spiderman or through Canadian historical vignettes. Television is a powerful medium, but we do not need to translate everything. Some Elders tell us that we do not need to create an entirely new and unique language out of Cree and culture by translating everything. The technical diction in English can be used in ordinary language without translation. There is no use trying to translate the name *Spiderman* into Cree, but Spiderman can speak Cree. A Cree speaker can go into Tim Hortons and order coffee in Cree, but why would *cappuccino* be translated?

Nevertheless, the gaps in funding formulae between federal and provincial systems will determine the direction that debates take for adequate and equitable funding to promote languages. There are two sides to this dollars-and-cents problem. One is the need for aggregate action inside our communities in Saskatchewan, presumably a linguistic issue where Cree and other Indigenous languages are promoted in provincial schools. On the federal side, there should be recognition that languages and culture require funding for development and for maintaining them in the long term in on-reserve schools. Supporting legislation at the federal level is welcomed, if desired by the First Nation authorities. The central federal government has for too long revolved around their imperatives versus our repeated response: "Quit making decisions for us."

Curriculum and Structural Arrangements

DARRYL: What role should the federal government play in curriculum development? Presumably, a curriculum is formalized in some way at a school, community, treaty, or regional level. A curriculum might not be a formal document, but must it not be written down somewhere, somehow? Should curriculum be prepared by teachers, by a school, by a First Nations community, by treaty officials, or by the Department of Indigenous Affairs and Northern Development?

HARRY: I foresee curriculum being developed at the school level by groups of teachers in consultation with Elders. It may eventually be developed across multiple schools within an Indigenous community and aggregated across Nations within a treaty structure, even nationally. The structure might match that of the Council of Ministers of Education with its mathematics and science curriculum across provinces and languages. But that is a long way down the road. Above all, the formalization in an agreement must be broad and must allow many different First Nations with their own specific language issues to be accommodated within its provisions.

DARRYL: Some might see that predictions for the future of Indigenous languages curricula are still vague at this stage. However, your ideas do begin to scope out policy issues going forward, rather than revisiting the past. Could you also trace a future for early-learning programs and their curricular dimensions, post TRC?

HARRY: The original objective of the Head Start program and the American model we were copying in Canada, and specifically in Saskatchewan, was to engage the parent and child in becoming a team to develop literacy.[8] It was intended to provide opportunities for young parents to learn how to be teachers with their own kids and to foster literacy or multiple literacies from birth onward. But

Harry Lafond and Darryl Hunter

early learning programs have gone sideways. The people in charge of the programs have institutionalized Head Start, making early learning into a program like kindergarten. It takes the children from the home to a scheduled number of hours in classroom-like institutions. Early learning has gone sideways because it has left the parents out of the learning process. If we are going to renew language and culture, we need to return to the original objectives of Head Start, because language and culture will not work without parent and extended family participation. We can learn from the Māori people of New Zealand. In their model, everyone became involved, from the start of the "language nests" involving one-year-olds, to university programs.[9]

DARRYL: Is institutionalizing an early-learning program a synonym for professionalization of programs? Teachers often have an impulse to organize and schedule everything in a fixed location.

HARRY: I have a different definition. It's called "taking the easy way out." It is much simpler to set up a program and bring the children in than to go out in the community and work with parents to develop a customized program with parents and extended families.[10] I've heard many people comment that in Canada we do not cherish the learning of our young children compared to countries like Sweden and France, where early-learning childhood educators have advanced professional credentials.[11] It requires a different kind of expertise to work with both parents and students together, and it requires master's level skills and knowledge. Canada continues to resource the programs at a level that does not allow for the kind of programming that children's potential warrants. If we are going to seriously address language and culture, we have to change the way things are done in early childhood education, focusing less on pre-programming kids and more on becoming true supports to parents, operating less often as state agents and more often as extensions of parents.

I do not think teacher professionalism and parental ownership are mutually exclusive. However, we stand a better chance of marrying the two under a Cree democracy model. We need teacher candidates at university to be much better prepared for engaging in program decision making in a professionally autonomous way with parents, rather than expecting top-down direction from superintendents and directors. Too often now, teachers are left as bystanders in parent-program decisions.

We should also look at the way the College of Education in Saskatoon (and elsewhere) is trying to indigenize their own curriculum. Faculties of education are turning their attention and efforts towards engaging the Indigenous community. Elders and Indigenous experts are finding voice in the processes of indigenization. Their influence is evident in the delivery of courses. This postsecondary experience in Saskatoon and at the University of Regina may provide insights into different ways curricula may be retailored completely differently at the pre-K to Grade 12 levels. Thus, decision making within leadership studies means looking at educational administration in a radically different way than within the current province operating system, which hasn't really changed since Ryerson's models were transplanted to the Prairies. Course delivery and instructional leadership need to reflect a different paradigm. When assumptions are unearthed and questioned, new paradigms will emerge.

DARRYL: When I look back at my own undergraduate studies, the implicit message was that a university is but twelve warring faculties sharing a common heating system. That is, there are a plurality of perspectives and knowledges in education. Because of the competing demands between departments for their particular educational interests, undergraduates can choose what they want to study and how they go about learning it. A second assumption was that information is, despite the emphasis on social constructivist approaches in classrooms, professionally controlled, and institutional

Harry Lafond and Darryl Hunter

authority prevails. The message was that the teacher is a professional and is singularly in charge of their little piece of territory in the classroom. Is this assumption still an implicit and bedrock premise in curriculum?

HARRY: I agree that if we are going to move curriculum forward in this province, those kinds of assumptions need to be put on the table. We need to bring ideas of professionalism in line with ideas of Cree democracy so that teachers believe that Elders and parents in the community can help them become the better teachers they want to be. If we are designing a curriculum outside the realm of Bloom's taxonomy or a provincial framework of outcomes, and rather working with Elder-led processes about the land and ecology, it leads to a profound shift in curricular premises.

In the process of challenging premises about curriculum, it becomes critical to understand how current curricular materials are imbued with Western thought, to the exclusion of Indigenous worldviews and foundations.

DARRYL: The idea of Cree democracy, it seems to me, has widespread implications for curriculum. How do you see Cree democracy as shaping the ways curricula will be developed?

HARRY: We must recognize that Cree democracy is a damaged system, a victim of needing to accommodate the Canadian, British, and French governance systems. It has also been impacted by the sociocultural conditions of our communities through the Indian Act and Indian agent years.

Decision making in the Cree community is not based on a singular leadership, but rather on a diverse knowledge- and skills-based leadership model. In the Cree system of decision making, leadership is defined by the community according to the strongest person who can work with the situation at hand. We now know that records of the original treaty-making process of the 1870s are a misrepresentation of Cree democracy. The Cree community has a woman's section, a seniors' section, a men's section, and of course the young adult section. It operates according to the teachings of the circle: everyone has a dual responsibility of voice and obligation to listen. In the talking circle, everyone must be both listener and speaker. At the treaty-making session leading to Treaty 6, large portions are missing in Alexander Morris's written record because he saw the Fort Carlton discussions through the Canadian-British lens of Westminster democracy. He was projecting his view of positional authority onto the Cree, who see authority as situational and more dispersed.

From the Cree oral tradition, a very different picture emerges. Treaty 6 discussions did not start two weeks before the meeting and the actual signing. They began well before, in the preceding winter months inside the various lodges, societies, inside the women's circles, inside the men's circles, and inside the seniors' circles. Decisions were slowly being formulated within those circles well before the historical record would indicate. In the stories that emerge from Ahtahkakoop's community, the people were preparing themselves for the eventuality of signing the treaty by debating the pros and cons of accepting the economic changes they knew their eastern and southern brothers had accepted. At Fort Carlton, there were a number of Chiefs, but the whole community membership moved with leaders to the gathering. The leaders selected as spokespersons were those who the community believed would provide the strongest voice in the discussions. Three spokespersons were selected (Mistawasis, Ahtahkakoop, and Sweetgrass) in the presence of other strong voices. That did not make the three spokesmen permanent, number-one Chiefs. They were chosen for the occasion and for that purpose. The leaders were not in competition among themselves.

That form of leadership selection goes into the microcosm of the community, where people are chosen according to purpose. When building a house, the foreman is chosen for that occasion and purpose. This happens in all situations. If there is a conflict between

Harry Lafond and Darryl Hunter

two Nations, like there was in the mid-1880s and well before, the peacetime Chiefs participated in choosing military leaders to lead the raids or defend their communities. Their authority was accepted for that particular exercise and time.

That is how leadership is defined in the Cree community. Although it operates in damaged forms, nevertheless, it continues to exist within the communities. When recognized as a strength in decision making and implemented in community policy-making processes, it can be a way of building curricular engagement that emanates from the community. The Cree way operates with the knowledge that each family grouping has a diverse range of leadership skills. These then become the potential source of engagement and leadership in the curriculum development process. Unfortunately, in many cases, the damage done to the understanding of this system of operations prevents productive community consultation processes. There is not enough understanding of the original Cree democratic processes among governance and administrative sectors to enact that system effectively.

DARRYL: What does that look like in terms of decision making, when we consider, in contrast, the existing provincial educational legislation and regulations? Principals and teachers are assigned strong roles for teaching and shaping curricula at the local level. The Education Act in most provinces assigns the principal a very strong, almost singular, leadership role. This has profound implications for curriculum and its implementation. When reconceiving curriculum going forward, do we not also have to reconceive the role of key people in its delivery?

HARRY: When it is a question of the man-powering of the education institution, there is going to have to be a compromise, or a merging of two systems. There needs to be changes in both systems. The proponents of both systems, Cree people and the provincial authorities, will need to move forward to understand their commonalities and elements of diversity. This can't be about a power struggle but rather a merging of two peoples' thoughts about how knowledge and skills become a nurturing blanket in the transition of children into healthy, well-adjusted adults. The importance of stability in leadership and student-professional rapport needs to become a central objective to ensure "making relatives" becomes the way of engagement.

In terms of defining curriculum, Cree democracy makes sense, because curriculum should be about the people, reflect the people, and be drawn from the people! It should not be some task assigned to a remote third party who has no investment or vested interest in the community. Existing curriculum development ideas and processes are isolated from the community and demand an upgraded approach that challenges ministries of education and education training institutions to rethink the way curriculum is prepared and delivered.

What I see, moving forward as part of the Cree system, is the involvement of the local community. When we talk about the development of language curriculum, for example, we can attempt to do that at Muskeg alone, where we may have only three people with an interest. However, it is richer and better for language acquisition if we team up with Mistawasis and Onion Lake and other communities, because we all speak the same Cree dialect. We all achieve a richer curriculum, and we can draw on a broader array of human resources, leading to a deeper approach to language acquisition. This allows for the creation of structure and flexibility and local responsiveness. This is not a new idea, but it is necessary to realize our own potential as Indigenous people, in counterpoint to non-Indigenous people.[12]

The advantage of organizing this way forces the conversation with the province to change. If one community comes forward with one new language program, the province views that as only one community and perhaps as an oddity. But if it comes from a central

Harry Lafond and Darryl Hunter

group of Cree communities, the province pays attention in a different way. If the TRC is about everybody, this will enrich provincial curricula. Most rural schools in Saskatchewan have some Indigenous students, and the school's curriculum and environment should reflect that presence. In the urban centres, there are significant numbers of Cree and Anishinaabe learners, whose presence has been acknowledged with reformed and improved provincial curricula.

One of the TRC recommendations was to allow Indigenous language students to attain a credit. We already have credit courses in Saskatchewan, but these are not high-quality courses. If we are going to teach languages, we need to do so in a way that will improve the student's ability to be orally literate and eventually to attain reading and writing proficiency. Half an hour a day of Cree won't do that.

DARRYL: What else did you learn from your experiences in kihiw waciston School?

HARRY: Because I was not bound by provincial structures, I worked with teachers, using some ideas from Gordon Lobe's study about the foundations of Cree education systems.[13] We did simple things like changing student discipline to be in concert with Elders' teachings of inclusivity within the circle. The aim was to change values and student spirit. The teachers were encouraged to adopt the circle model to foster inclusion rather than expulsion from classrooms and schools. We gave the students a much stronger voice in school policy and its operation. Visually, we wanted to convey that we all worked within one circle in the school and took every opportunity to gather in circles, with the expectation that all be in the circle, including teachers and visitors. We noted changes in behaviour: students seeking resolutions in the schoolyard and a decrease in bullying incidents. We also noted a change in teacher behaviour. The staff bought into the idea of inclusion. The third thing I learned was that we needed to provide as many opportunities as possible for students to become leaders.

The basic idea is balance. Indigenizing a curriculum has to be done in a context of balance. I have the same conversation about local public schools. I want to avoid ghettoizing who we are in the curriculum or in the life of the school. When talking about cultural experiences in the school, we must start from the position that everyone has a distinct cultural background. Indigenization of a school curriculum or program is not just about Cree students coming into the school from Muskeg. We must not forget students from Ukrainian families who need to express their roots, balanced with Filipino students who require support. Building respect for other perspectives is part of Cree egalitarianism, particularly in the realm of spirituality. That law is present in the full Circle of Cree worldview. Thus, within this outlook, we have much more than a balance between two systems of thought.

DARRYL: The Saskatchewan Ministry of Education divides curriculum into subject boxes, each with their subsystems, subrequirements, and budgets. Curriculum advisory committees, curriculum design, curriculum writing, curriculum implementation, bibliographies of resources, curriculum evaluation, and the like all have their own inherent demands, interest groups, and staffing requirements.

HARRY: We must not make curriculum bigger than what it is. A tool box is a tool box, meant to be used by creative teachers with the freedom to innovate. That is sometimes the problem: curricula are treated as prescriptive, as an absolute obligation in application, as an eleventh commandment. We need to set clear expectations, and we do need to measure growth. But we need curricula to be permissive. Little people do not fit into boxes. They are their own beings. So, in the classroom, we have the tool box, but there may be a ten-year-old with a sixteen-year-old mind. In curriculum, we need to be careful about how we conceive of it and appraise its relevance.

Successful teachers are those who have remained creative and have not sacrificed their soul for curricular prescriptions from a government god. Rather, they make a curriculum guide work from the creative side by wrapping it around those twenty-six unique little bodies in a classroom. Each is different, each thinks and acts differently, and each has different gifts. Each will respond differently in relationship building.

Convergences

As the foregoing conversation shows, we come from different backgrounds and have followed different career paths; our perspectives on education and on the world reflect these differences. But there are also points where our viewpoints converge. Accordingly for these, we shift to the first person plural.

We believe a school curriculum that respects and honours Indigenous perspectives starts in a strong sense of location and the natural environment, moving outward from that point as youth mature emotionally, spiritually, physiologically, and intellectually in stages.[14] Concepts are derived literally from the ground up. This is a different starting point than in most provincial curricula, which begin with an ideal type of student and with a relatively uniform set of intellectual attributes that are required in the information age and largely drawn from concepts in American cognitive psychology. We believe that curricula are now overly conceptualized creations of the bureaucratic mechanisms of committees and ministry regulations. Instead, we would do better to rely on the wisdom of Elders who mediate the spiritual and conceptual development of youth in symbiosis with the natural and social community.

Thus, when reconsidering curriculum after the Truth and Reconciliation Commission, we believe that we need to return to the underlying purposes of knowledge in and for our communities. Curriculum is about uncovering both the implicit assumptions and explicit thoughts and beliefs of a community; it animates the variety of ideas in any community. We also argue for making the generational knowledge of Elders, youth, parents, warriors, hunters, leaders, gardeners, fishers, teachers, and others available to others, but not necessarily within formal structures like schools. Some understandings and ways of intergenerationally transferring that knowledge rightly and necessarily belong outside the bounds of schools and institutions. Quite sensibly, we should use original languages to express these traditional ideas and to bring old languages to new and recovered ideas. At the same time, we must honour relationships that reflect distinct ways of knowing and experiencing the world and different relationships to the land.[15]

Curriculum too often gets enmeshed in issues of jurisdiction and hence in questions of power. In our view, whether for on-reserve schools or for provincial public schools, curriculum is better considered, not as codified knowledge for K–12 schools but rather as a continuous conversation between minorities and majorities in which assumptions are reciprocally questioned – striving not for a balance of probabilities and "successful" performances but instead for a dynamic of mutually challenged premises and potentialities.[16]

As for the TRC's report, we believe it is important to draw some lines. There are several books on the uses and misuses of history: to build (dis)comfort, to justify the quest for or conquest of power, to advocate or prosecute, to defend or defy, to poetize or popularize agendas.[17] Those are precisely the ends that should be avoided with curriculum guides. Curricula are road maps or practical tools for guiding instruction in and around schools. They should be practical aids for constructing and reconstructing relationships and facilitating communication in the here and now. Many people presume that history is a set of two-tone images ending somewhere around the time their parents or grandparents were born. We argue that history is actually an ongoing stream of continuously reinterpreted and multiplying records – written, oral, and visual – that flow retrospectively. In parallel fashion, many see a curriculum as a bureaucratic compendium of state-sanctioned objectives. Rather, school curricula are better

Harry Lafond and Darryl Hunter

viewed as a device for bringing people together to guide and exchange experiences within and especially outside the classroom in a way that looks to the future. History is one small subset of, and not a substitute for, curriculum. History is about representing thought, behaviour, and passions from the past. Curriculum is about representing spirit, emotion, thought, and behaviour for the future.

In our view, education for (non-)Indigenous youth should be grounded in a vision of the future rather than in a focus on the past. We are not arguing that policy-makers should eliminate history from curricula but rather that curriculum guides are much more than history lessons. Nor are we arguing that customary ways of teaching youth should be set aside – indeed, the contrary. However, we would invert an old aphorism to argue that "Canada has too much history and not enough geography" – especially not enough ecology. Curricula must be something more than compendia of objectives and state-mandated outcomes. We are at one with those who are uncomfortable, even skeptical, of harnessing education to exercises in nation building, seeing it as using carefully selected facets of history for immediate political needs. "Let us not think of ourselves, but our children's children" is a quote attributed to Ahtahkakoop at a council before the signing of Treaty 6 at Fort Carlton in 1876. That wisdom should guide policy-makers and curriculum writers going forward from the Truth and Reconciliation Commission's calls for action. Reconciliation means striking an equilibrium for the future rather than adapting both provincial history and curriculum to the demands of the moment.

Notes

1 Truth and Reconciliation Commission of Canada, *Final Report of the Truth and Reconciliation Commission of Canada*, vol. 1, *Summary: Honouring the Truth, Reconciling for the Future* (Toronto: Lorimer, 2015).
2 The references embedded in the dialogue were added later to direct the reader to additional sources of information about the concepts under discussion.

3 Eve Tuck, Marcia McKenzie, and Kate McCoy, "Land Education: Indigenous, Post-Colonial, and Decolonizing Perspectives on Place and Environmental Education Research," *Environmental Education Research* 20, 1 (2014): 1–23.

4 Dwayne Donald, "Forts, Colonial Frontier Logics, and Aboriginal-Canadian Relations: Imagining Decolonizing Educational Philosophies in Canadian Contexts," in *Decolonizing Philosophies of Education*, ed. Ali A. Abdi (Amsterdam: Sense, 2012), 91–111.

5 See, for example, John Richards, "Closing the Aboriginal/Non-Aboriginal Education Gaps," *C.D. Howe Institute Backgrounder* 116 (October), https://www.cdhowe.org/sites/default/files/attachments/research_papers/mixed/Backgrounder_116.pdf; and Tasha Riley and Charles Ungerleider, "Self-Fulfilling Prophecy: How Teachers' Attributions, Expectations, and Stereotypes Influence the Learning Opportunities Afforded Aboriginal Students," *Canadian Journal of Education* 35, 2 (2012): 303–33.

6 Buffy Sainte-Marie, "The Cradleboard Teaching Project: Using Curriculum and Cross-Cultural Partnering to Change Perceptions," *Winds of Change* 14, 2 (1999): 32–34.

7 Estelle Simard and Shannon Blight, "Developing a Culturally Restorative Approach to Aboriginal Child and Youth Development: Transitions to Adulthood," *First Peoples Child and Family Review* 6, 1 (2011): 28–55.

8 Mai Nguyen, "Closing the Education Gap: A Case for Aboriginal Early Childhood Education in Canada – A Look at the Aboriginal Head Start Program," *Canadian Journal of Education* 34, 3 (2011): 229–48.

9 Russell Bishop, Mere Berryman, and E. Cath Richardson, "Te Toi Huarewa: Effective Teaching and Learning in Total Immersion Maori Language Educational Settings," *Canadian Journal of Native Education* 26, 1 (2002): 44–61; and Barbara Harrison and Rahui Papa, "The Development of an Indigenous Knowledge Program in a New Zealand Maori Language Immersion School," *Anthropology and Education Quarterly* 36, 1 (2005): 57–72.

10 Julie Kaomea, "Indigenous Studies in the Elementary Curriculum: A Cautionary Hawaiian Example," *Anthropology and Education* 36, 1 (2005): 24–42.

11 Carolyn Pope Edwards, "Three Approaches from Europe: Waldorf, Montessori, and Reggio Emilia," *Early Childhood Research and Practice* 4, 1 (2002): http://ecrp.uiuc.edu/v4n1/edwards.html.

12 Graham H. Smith, "Indigenous Struggle for the Transformation of Education and Schooling" (keynote address to Alaskan Federation of Natives, Anchorage, Alaska, October 2003).

13 L. Gordon Lobe, "Towards an Articulation of the Foundations of Cree Education" (master's thesis, University of Saskatchewan, 1995).

14 Anne B. Smith, "The Early Childhood Curriculum from a Sociocultural Perspective," *Early Child Development and Care* 115, 1 (1996): 51–64.

15 Eve Tuck and Rubén A. Gaztambide-Fernández, "Curriculum, Replacement, and Settler Futurity," *JCT Online* 29, 1 (2013): 72–89.

16 Jennifer A. Tupper, "The Possibilities for Reconciliation through Difficult Dialogues: Treaty Education as Peacebuilding," *Curriculum Inquiry* 44, 4 (2014): 469–88.

17 See, for example, Richard E. Neustadt, *Thinking in Time: The Uses of History for Decision Makers* (New York: Simon and Schuster, 2011).

8

INDIGENOUS AND WESTERN WORLDVIEWS
Fostering Ethical Space in the Classroom
Jane P. Preston

Originating from German philosopher Immanuel Kant, the concept of worldview refers to the way people make sense of the things that happen around them.[1] A worldview is a collection of beliefs, norms, and values held by an individual or group of individuals. It is a holistic conception of the intricacies of the world; it is a lens through which one perceives and interprets life. It is a type of cognitive schema used when reflecting upon or contemplating personal experiences, local events, and happenings in one's life. This all-encompassing, pervasive, personal standpoint is influenced by such things as life experiences, culture, language, religion, spirituality, gender, gender performance, environment, family, and friends.

The worldview under which a person functions is usually taken for granted. It is often an unconscious internal influence that escapes direct questioning.[2] Nonetheless, understanding and interrogating various types of worldviews is empowering, for a number of reasons. To facilitate successful communication, fruitful relationships, and greater respect between individuals and within groups, it is important to appreciate multiple worldviews. Possessing a better understanding of others' worldviews sparks conversation, ignites curiosity, and evokes creativity; it promotes the growth of the self and others. As people become sensitive to the intricacies of other worldviews, they tend to become less critical of the beliefs, values, actions, and cultures of others.

Understanding core similarities and differences among worldviews assists in promoting rich relationships, cultural respect, and communal harmony. This knowledge is highly beneficial in educational settings, particularly in First Nations schools or off-reserve schools with Indigenous students. The Truth and Reconciliation Commission of Canada has called upon governments to close the educational gap between Indigenous and non-Indigenous students and to develop culturally appropriate early childhood education programs for Indigenous families. But how can curriculum developers and educators cooperate with students and parents if the two groups do not understand each other? What follows is a descriptive account of the Indigenous and Western worldviews – the core values, norms, and perspectives embedded within each standpoint. Although there is no single Indigenous worldview but diverse worldviews, non-Indigenous educators need to understand how their worldview fundamentally differs from that of Indigenous peoples before there can be true reconciliation in the classroom.

A Note on Terminology

The word *Indigenous* is often used within international discourse, discussions, and protocols when referring to the original inhabitants of a country or particular geographic territory. The very title of the *United Nations Declaration on the Rights of Indigenous Peoples* exemplifies the global inclusiveness of the term *Indigenous*.[3] Over the past decade or two, the word *Indigenous* has become increasingly popular within political and academic domains throughout the world and in Canada; however, the Canadian government still uses the word *Aboriginal* in legislation such as the Constitution Act, 1982, in which *Aboriginal* refers to First Nation, Métis, and Inuit peoples in Canada.

The term *Western* is associated with a societal philosophy that emerged in western Europe during the Age of Reason. In *Voltaire's Bastards,* philosopher John Ralston Saul explains that this way of thinking reflected the merging of historical epochs, including the Age of Christianity, the Renaissance, and the Age of Enlightenment. During that time, the political, economic, and social systems of western Europe radically changed as science became powerful and explorers set out to catalogue and conquer the world.[4] Schmuel Eisenstadt argues that the Western worldview reflects an evolutionary array of chronological influences that converged into the modern hegemonic norm that permeates present-day economy-driven societies.[5] Herein, the term *Western worldview* is synonymous with *European worldview*.

It is important to keep in mind that Indigenous and Western worldviews are not monolithic philosophical entities. Among the various and diverse people who hold a particular worldview, there are subtle, sometimes conflicting differences in beliefs, values, intuition, and perceptions. It is also important to keep in mind that both worldviews are equally valid and can be compatible. Elmer Ghostkeeper, for instance, examines the potential for *wechewehtowin* (a Woodland Cree word for "partnering") between Indigenous wisdom and Western scientific knowledge in "Weche Teaching."[6] Aligned with Ghostkeeper's ideas, the intention here is not to present one worldview as superior to another. Propagating better-worse binaries for belief systems limits the possibilities that exist when two worldviews are respected. That being said, the basic concepts of Indigenous and Western worldviews are presented here in a somewhat dichotomous way in the hope to provide simplified descriptions as a starting point for future explorations, whether in the realm of the intellect or classroom.

The Indigenous Worldview

The Indigenous worldview can be expressed in two simple words: interconnected wholeness. As Richard Atleo, hereditary Chief of the Áhousaht First Nation, succinctly states, "Everything is one."[7] Indigenous peoples hold two core beliefs: everything is alive, and everything is related.[8] All things in the universe are imbued with one shared, omnipotent energy, making everything interwoven and inseparable.

All societies and communities operate in a state of relatedness. Kinship, lifestyle, and oral traditions reinforce this connectedness. Human behaviour reflects intimate kinship with an all-living cosmos. According to Indigenous ways of knowing, everything in the universe is animate, whether it be a spider, a blade of grass, a patch of dirt, or a rock, and each individual has a unique relationship with all surrounding animate and inanimate forces. The earth does not belong to humans; rather, humans belong to the earth. Nature is universal. It is not an individual, ethnic, or national property. Because there is no separation between nature and humanity, all forms of creation possess one consciousness.[9] The two-legged, four-legged, and winged; the swimmers and crawlers; and rocks and plants live together harmoniously on Mother Earth. Land, animals, and spirits are the consciousness of the universe and are part of the circle of life.[10] Coexisting in perfect unity, all matter is connected via shared energy, which dynamically radiates both within and throughout every human being. It is each person's responsibility to allow this spiritual radiance to flow through him- or herself and onward towards everyone and everything else, thereby sustaining the flow.[11]

The concept of the Sacred Circle (or simply "the circle") is one way to convey the full meaning of connected wholeness.[12] The symbol of the circle, which possesses no beginning or endpoint, represents wholeness, harmony, and eternity, cosmic order, communal energy, and the interconnected web of life.[13] The symbol of the circle is a metaphor for sun, planets, moon, asteroid belts, and orbital rotations performing a harmonious universal round dance. The circle incorporates the four spirits – earth, air, fire, and water – the essential elements of creation that sustain life. These sacred elements unremittingly and simultaneously reconstruct and deconstruct existence. The circle represents the infinite reoccurrence of ecological processes, exemplified through the water cycle, the carbon cycle, the food chain, and photosynthesis. It represents a balanced, divine rotation of creation and destruction. Within this infinite rhythm, people are invited to live in harmony and universal perfection.

The circle and its divine symmetry represent the reoccurrence of time, which can be depicted through the perpetuation of life. Human life is a synergy of the past (one's ancestors), the present (the current generation), and the future (one's children's children).[14] In *Research Is Ceremony*, Shawn Wilson argues that the identity of Indigenous peoples depends on maintaining a relationship with the land, returning ancestors to the land, and ensuring that future generations will experience the land.[15] Humanity is not simply the people on Earth today but an unending cycle of birth, youth, adulthood, and elderhood that spans generations.[16] Boundless successions of life are reflected through natural occurrences such as the rising and setting of the sun, the transition of day into night, the phases of the moon, the rhythm of the tides, the migration of birds, the life cycle of a forest, and the ring marks in every tree trunk. Through these examples, the circle represents environmental perseverance, longevity, sustainability, and ultimate beauty and perfection.

Like the Sacred Circle, the Medicine Wheel, as a symbol, is a type of mirror from which everything is reflected.[17] In *Medicine Wheels: Ancient Teachings for Modern Times*, Roy Wilson explains: "There are many Medicine Wheels. The universe is a Medicine Wheel. Our own solar system is a giant Medicine Wheel. The earth is a Medicine Wheel. Every nation is a Medicine Wheel. Each state is a Medicine Wheel. Each family is a Medicine Wheel. You are a Medicine Wheel, for every individual is a Medicine Wheel."[18] With its emphasis on the individual, the Medicine Wheel reflects the journey of the human spirit and conveys how this journey is embodied in the physical realm.[19] Messages from the Medicine Wheel articulate the path to a balanced vibrant life.[20] In other words, the Medicine Wheel is an individualized learning model through which personal empowerment, healing, and wellness can be achieved and maintained.

It is important to recognize that the Medicine Wheel and its features are depicted and understood in a variety of ways by different Indigenous cultures. For example, various North American Indigenous groups physically illustrate the Medicine Wheel using particular colours

Jane P. Preston

or animals. As Elder Francis Whiskeyjack notes, "people have different interpretations in their medicine wheel and they are all right. No one is wrong."[21] It is also important to note that some Indigenous cultures don't refer to the Medicine Wheel at all. For instance, some Canadian Inuit instead depict life's journey through a circular blanket.[22]

Despite this diversity, some generalizations can be made. The Medicine Wheel contains four equal quadrants and four cardinal directions: east, south, west, and north. Each of these directions corresponds with lessons pertaining to life stages, seasons, animals, medicines, human races, and principles of life. For example, the four quadrants of the Medicine Wheel represent spring, summer, autumn, and winter. They also represent child, youth, adult, and Elder. A balanced life can be achieved by focusing equally on the physical, mental, emotional, and spiritual aspects of wellness. In *Reclaiming Youth at Risk*, Larry Brendtro, Martin Brokenleg, and Steve Van Bockern use the Medicine Wheel to depict the four universal needs of belonging, mastery, independence, and generosity.[23] Different cultures use different colours and life principles to represent different quadrants. According to Mi'kmaw Elder Noel Milliea, yellow represents the east, the principle of respect, and the sacred medicine of tobacco; blue (or black if in mourning) represents the south, the principle of honesty, and the sacred medicine of sage; red represents the west, the principle of trust, and the sacred medicine of sweetgrass; and white represent the north, the principle of love, and the sacred medicine of cedar.[24] Also, Medicine Wheel colours (yellow, blue/black, red, and white) can represent a unified, multihued vision of the ethnicities of humankind: Asian, African, Indigenous, and Caucasian.[25] As a final point, the Medicine Wheel expresses the sacredness of the number four: the four directions, the four seasons, the four elements of life, the four stages of life, the four universal needs, the four life principals, the four sacred medicines, and the four ethnicities on Earth.

In addition to the Sacred Circle and the Medicine Wheel, the Indigenous worldview encompasses other perceptions, values, and beliefs. For example, Indigenous knowledge is predominantly passed on through oral narratives, oral histories, and the act of storytelling.[26] In Indigenous cultures, storytelling is often a spirit-focused way to preserve and transfer historical knowledge, including protocols, language, and tribal customs.[27] Sometimes, stories are told in song or dance and often explore the themes of self-identity, family lineage, and relationships with the land.[28] In *Decolonizing Education*, Marie Battiste identifies storytelling as "the most important way of sharing the experience of Indigenous peoples, who locate their identities in an alternate knowledge system built within different ways of learning."[29]

As part of the Indigenous worldview, the learning process is the experience of life itself. Indigenous peoples affirm a type of teaching in which learning is a natural and social event through which knowledge and comprehension are acquired. It is relevant, hands-on, and experiential. Children and youth observe, experience, and participate in demonstrations, cooperative events, group discussions, reflection, talking circles, games, apprenticeships, and other activities. During the learning process, an Indigenous worldview promotes the ethics of noninterference and noncompetition to foster positive interpersonal relationships and discourage physical, verbal, or psychological coercion. Jo-ann Archibald, an Indigenous studies scholar from the Stó:lō Nation, explains that, for Indigenous peoples, rich learning opportunities are achieved through the promotion of independence, self-reliance, observation, discovery, and respect for nature.[30] The knowledge and skills gained from life experience are used to promote the wellness of families and communities.

Another core aspect of the Indigenous worldview is spirit. For Indigenous people, spirituality pertains to a belief in a higher power or purpose, a sense of interconnectedness to all things, and the ongoing development of one's identity through spiritual awareness.[31] For individuals, there can be no separation from knowledge and spirit, because "spiritual identity is connected to Land/Mother Earth, to one's inner self/soul, and the physical and social surroundings."[32] Spiritual knowledge is gained by being open to the teachings of nature

Jane P. Preston

and participating in Indigenous ceremonies and rituals, which often involve dance and song. The physical act of dancing is a form of prayer, connecting body, mind, emotions, and soul to the spirit world. As a part of dance, song, and ceremony, the rhythm of a drumbeat represents the harmonic pulse of Mother Earth and the pulse of one's own heartbeat. Ceremonies (e.g., sweats, potlatches, feasts, sun dances) confer rights to hold sacred knowledge and wisdom to promote the wellness of the community and its members.[33]

Within the Indigenous worldview, dreams, visions, and intuition are forms of divine guidance. As Margaret Kovach states in *Indigenous Methodologies*, "within Plains Cree knowledges, dreams matter."[34] Betty Bastien explains that, for Blackfoot peoples, dreams are a primary source of knowledge, which is often prophetic, filled with warnings or personally relevant information.[35] Dreams, visions, prayer, and inward ways of knowing sometimes involve the offering of tobacco to honour and facilitate communication with the Creator.[36] It should be emphasized that knowledge that is gained from these types of spiritual experiences is deeply personal and particularized and therefore difficult to communicate or generalize.[37]

The Western Worldview

The Western perspective tends to categorize the world and all its matter into two types of entities: animate (e.g., humans, animals, plants) and inanimate (e.g., rocks, mountains, sky, land, water, and wind). It divides experience into two separate states of being: the physical (or natural) and the spiritual (or supernatural).[38] It depicts life as being two-layered and hierarchical, with humans at the top of the pyramid and other forms (i.e., animals and vegetation) occupying tiers below.[39] Because of this hierarchical authority, humans can and do influence and manipulate their environment.[40] Having stated such in his study of the Medicine Wheel, Roy Wilson points out that humans dominate animals and plants in the Western worldview, but they still have a moral duty of stewardship towards nonhuman life forms.[41] The spiritual (or supernatural) is sometimes ignored in Western-based societies, because it cannot be explained via logical, measurable, scientific means.[42] When spiritual knowledge is accepted and revered, it is commonly done through religious institutions or forums and framed within rules and formalities.

The Western worldview supports the primacy of the individual and the limitless potential housed in each person.[43] Competition, winning, and losing are not only acceptable features of life, they are considered valuable experiences, because they foster personal and professional growth and development.[44] When analyzing one's place in the world, Westerners do so through the lens of anthropocentricity, a view that supports the notion that humans have ultimate authority over the universe and the creative ability to mould the future; they are innately driven to advance, change, and become smarter than past generations.[45]

In Western societies, education is an individualized, academic process within demarked contexts. Education is predominantly institutionalized in terms of management, curricular content, and the slotting of predetermined timeframes. The educational practices of public schools and postsecondary organizations promote learning as an experience that often involves competitiveness, individuality, status projection, and outside judgment.[46] In this formal system, success and self-confidence are qualities that are to be developed, honed, and demonstrated as a part of the student experience. In the process, students learn to value their individuality and defend their unique thoughts and ideas.[47] Success is often defined by things that can be manipulated, controlled, and seen, and Western educational systems are renowned for promoting measurable outcomes, experiences, and skills.[48] Tests, teacher-focused feedback, and the provision of formal grades or comments are the predominant mechanisms used to summarize the learning experience.[49] Within Western systems, teachers must acquire formal certification. Educational systems approve a set of bounded curricula and pedagogical acts and decide upon the specific outcomes recognized for a specific set of learnings. In other

Jane P. Preston

words, only accredited people and recognized institutions can confer knowledge and credentials (through grades, diplomas, and degrees), which, in turn, are proof one's personal advancement.

In the Western worldview, time and space have demarked, finite boundaries. Time is a linear concept, and space is a three-dimensional physical entity. Years are divided into months, months into weeks, and weeks into days, which are further compartmentalized into hours, minutes, seconds, and milliseconds. Within this linear framework, teaching and learning are delivered within preauthorized units of time.[50] Meetings are scheduled, objectives are set, and deadlines assist in the completion of tasks. The ability to solve problems, ensure accuracy, and produce results is a useful attribute in achieving defined goals. Life is linear in the sense that a person is born, develops, and dies.

The Western quest for knowledge and supremacy over nature requires that natural systems and events be broken down and studied within individualized entities or parts. The properties of a given system (e.g., physical, biological, chemical, social, economic, mental, linguistic) are determined or explained by subprocesses or subcomponents. For example, from a biological perspective, the body is broken down into organs and tissues. Tissue is made from cells, which have a nucleus and cytoplasm. Within the nucleus, there are chromosomes, which, in turn, have genes; the genes contain DNA, which, in turn, is made up of chemical bases. Because of its attention to things at a molecular level, the Western worldview has generated much knowledge pertaining to the unique individualized parts of living systems.[51] As a result of the microanalysis of issues, scientists and academics have specialized knowledge of content-related topics and have gathered infinitesimal data about distinct topics.

Academic research in the Western world is conducted predominantly through rational and intellectual methodologies. Western research commonly presents data through categorical or thematic results.[52] The scientific process follows the prescribed steps of reflection, formulating questions, developing a hypothesis, articulating a step-by-step procedure, and writing a final report to communicate results.[53] In general, Western knowledge "is pragmatic and grounded in scientific evidence that can be quantified and empirically studied."[54]

Another feature of the Western worldview is the notion that humans have great potential to create and process new ideas, that humankind has bountiful intellectual abilities. As evidenced throughout history, artistic, scientific, and technological innovation reflect humankind's vast ability to create. As articulated via a Western worldview, "there is no question that human reason has an enormous capacity to discover and advance knowledge."[55] With an innate desire to continuously create and expand new knowledge, it is believed that humans are flexible and can adapt to new, innovative environments.[56] In fact, effective organizations are systems that adapt practices, processes, strategies, and structures so that their internal capacities successfully withstand the turbulent markets and address the ever-changing needs of consumers.[57] It is because of the Western worldview and its tenet of constant improvement that many modern-day conveniences have been invented and utilized.

≶।≷

The way people experience the world depends on their worldview, which consciously and unconsciously encompasses personal views, needs, desires, and prejudices. To make space for the opinions and knowledge of other people, each of us needs to reflect on our personally biased experiential worldview and voluntarily consider the realities and mindsets of other people. Understanding Indigenous perspectives and Western perspectives, upon which the current educational system has been built, is mandatory if educational systems are to renew, improve, change, and reform. Interlinked with the hope to improve and renew education, there is a need to establish and promote *ethical space*. Indigenous scholar Willie Ermine describes ethical spaces as ethereal locations where different views, cultures, and life experiences are recognized equally within a mutually respected, balanced team of diverse people.[58] Ermine explains, "Ethical space is formed when two societies, with disparate worldviews, are poised to engage each other."[59] Dialogue grounded in ethical space is an exciting way to examine the diverse positioning, cultures, and ways of knowing that reside within Indigenous and Western societies. Within this space, the cultural and spiritual diversities of Indigenous and non-Indigenous groups merge into an empathetic, respectful, and harmonious existence. Creating and using this ethical space begins by understanding the differences and similarities threaded within Indigenous and Western worldviews.

Teachers, administrators, and educational leaders need to recognize the features and implications of Indigenous and Western worldviews. Within the larger school community, this understanding and appreciation will stimulate greater respect for cultural diversity within a variety of collaborative teams, including ministerial teams, school boards, faculty and staff associations, school-parent associations (e.g., school councils), and student teams (e.g., extracurricular sports). The result will be a healthier, safer, more inclusive classroom and school, where the vibrancy of humankind is recognized and celebrated.

Notes

1 David K. Naugle, *Worldview: The History of a Concept* (Grand Rapids, MI: Eerdmans, 2002).
2 Michael A. Hart, "Indigenous Worldviews, Knowledge, and Research: The Development of an Indigenous Research Paradigm," *Journal of Indigenous Voices in Social Work* 1, 1 (2010): 1–16; and Leo Schelbert, "Pathways of Human Understanding: An Inquiry into Western and North American Indian Worldview Structures," *Indian Culture and Research Journal* 27, 1 (2003): 61–75.
3 United Nations, *United Nations Declaration on the Rights of Indigenous Peoples,* March 2008, http://www.un.org/esa/socdev/unpfii/documents/DRIPS_en.pdf.
4 John Ralston Saul, *Voltaire's Bastards: The Dictatorship of Reason in the West* (Toronto: Penguin Books, 1992), 15.
5 Shmuel N. Eisenstadt, "The Vision of Modern and Contemporary Society," in *Identity, Culture, and Globalization,* ed. Eliezer Ben-Rafael and Yitzhak

Sternberg (Leiden, The Netherlands: International Institute of Sociology, 2001), 26–47.

6 Elmer Ghostkeeper, "Weche Teachings: Aboriginal Wisdom and Dispute Resolution," in *Intercultural Dispute Resolution in Aboriginal Contexts*, ed. Catherine Bell and David Kahane (Vancouver: UBC Press, 2004), 161–75.

7 E. Richard Atleo, *Tsawalk: A Nuu-chah-nulth Worldview* (Vancouver: UBC Press, 2004), xi.

8 Joseph E. Couture, "The Role of Native Elders: Emergent Issues," in *The Cultural Maze: Complex Questions on Native Destiny in Western Canada*, ed. John W. Friesen (Calgary: Detselig, 1991), 201–17.

9 Betty Bastien, "The Cultural Practice of Participatory Transpersonal Visions: An Indigenous Perspective," *ReVision* 26, 2 (2003): 41–48.

10 Ibid.

11 Roy I. Wilson, *Medicine Wheels: Ancient Teachings for Modern Times* (New York: Crossroads, 1994).

12 The Sacred Circle is alternatively called the Circle of Life or the Wheel of Life.

13 Robert Regnier, "The Sacred Circle: A Process of Pedagogy of Healing," *Interchange* 25, 2 (1994): 383–415; and Robert Regnier, "Bridging Western and First Nations Thought: Balanced Education in Whitehead's Philosophy of Organism and the Sacred Circle," *Interchange* 26, 4 (1995): 383–415.

14 Jo-ann Archibald, *Indigenous Storywork: Educating the Heart, Mind, Body, and Spirit* (Vancouver: UBC Press, 2008).

15 Shawn Wilson, *Research Is Ceremony: Indigenous Research Methods* (Winnipeg: Fernwood, 2008).

16 Regnier, "Bridging Western and First Nations Thought"; and Roy Wilson, *Medicine Wheels.*

17 Hyemeyohsts Storm, *Seven Arrows* (Toronto: Random House, 1972).

18 Wilson, *Medicine Wheels*, 9.

19 Mary Elliott, Kateri Akiwenzi-Damm, and Deana Halonen, *Empowering the Spirit II: Native Literacy Curriculum* (Owen Sound, ON: Ningwakwe Learning Press, 2004).

20 Holly Garner, Mary Alice Bruce, and John Stellern, "The Goal Wheel: Adapting Navajo Philosophy and the Medicine Wheel to Work with Adolescents," *Journal for Specialists in Group Work* 36, 1 (2011): 62–77.

21 Francis Whiskeyjack, "Medicine Wheel," *Wind Speaker*, June 1, 2000, http://www.thefreelibrary.com/Medicine+wheel.-a030565110.

22 Canadian Council on Learning, *Redefining How Success Is Measured in First Nations, Inuit, and Métis Learning: Report on Learning in Canada 2007* (Ottawa, 2007), https://www.afn.ca/uploads/files/education/5._2007_redefining_how_success_is_measured_en.pdf.

23 Larry Brendtro, Martin Brokenleg, and Steve Van Bockern, *Reclaiming Youth at Risk: Our Hope for the Future*, rev. ed. (Bloomington, IN: Solution Tree, 2002).

24 Noel Milliea, personal communication, October 2015.

25 Wilson, *Medicine Wheels*.

26 Margaret Kovach, *Indigenous Methodologies: Characteristics, Conversations, and Contexts* (Toronto: University of Toronto Press, 2009).

27 Archibald, *Indigenous Storywork*; and Katherine Madjidi and Jean-Paul Restoule, "Comparative Indigenous Ways of Knowing and Learning," in *Comparative and International Education: Issues for Teachers*, ed. Karen Mundy, Kathy Bickmore, and Ruth Hayhoe (Toronto: Canadian Scholar's Press, 2008), 77–106.

28 Bagele Chilisa, *Indigenous Research Methodologies* (Los Angeles: Sage, 2012).

29 Marie Battiste, *Decolonizing Education: Nourishing the Learning Spirit* (Saskatoon: Purich, 2012), 184.

30 Jo-ann Archibald, "Locally Developed Native Studies Curriculum: An Historic and Philosophical Rationale," in *First Nations Education in Canada: The Circle Unfolds*, ed. Marie Battiste and Jean Barman, 288–312 (Vancouver: UBC Press, 1995).

31 Yatta Kanu, *Integrating Aboriginal Perspectives into the School Curriculum: Purposes, Possibilities, and Challenges* (Toronto: University of Toronto Press, 2011).

32 George S. Dei, "Indigenous Anti-colonial Knowledge as 'Heritage Knowledge' for Promoting Black/African Education in Diasporic Contexts," *Decolonization* 1, 1 (2012): 112.

33 Madjidi and Restoule, "Comparative Indigenous Ways."

34 Kovach, *Indigenous Methodologies*, 58.

35 Bastien, "The Cultural Practice of Participatory Transpersonal Visions."

36 Health Canada, Optional Session 3, "Traditional Uses of Tobacco," *Health Concerns: Quit4Life: Facilitator's Guide*, 161–68, http://dsp-psd.pwgsc.gc.ca/Collection/H46-2-04-382E.pdf.

37 Marie Battiste and James Youngblood Henderson, *Protecting Indigenous Knowledge and Heritage: A Global Challenge* (Saskatoon: Purich, 2000).

38 Atleo, *Tsawalk*; and Charles H. Kraft, "How Do Westerners Picture the World?," in *Christianity with Power: Your Worldview and Your Experience of the Supernatural*, 2nd ed., ed. Charles H. Kraft (Eugene, OR: Wipf and Stock, 2005), 23–36.

39 Nicole Note, Raúl Fornet-Betancourt, Josef Estermann, and Diederik Aerts, "Worldviews and Cultures: Philosophical Reflections from an Intercultural Perspective: An Introduction," in *Worldviews and Cultures:*

Philosophical Reflections from an Intercultural Perspective, ed. Note, Fornet-Betancourt, Estermann, and Aerts (New York: Springer, 2009), 1–9.

40 Gilbert F. Lafreniere, *The Decline of Nature: Environmental History and the Western Worldview* (Dublin: Academica Press, 2007).

41 Wilson, *Medicine Wheels.*

42 Atleo, *Tsawalk*; and Kraft, "How Do Westerners Picture the World?"

43 Kraft, "How Do Westerners Picture the World?"

44 Jason Masai, Alyson Randall, Denise Rowe, and Francisca Waring, "Aboriginal Leaders, Resistance and Education," in *First Nations Students Talk Back: Voices of Learning People,* ed. Francis Adu-Febriri (Victoria, BC: Camosun College, 2004), 145–65.

45 Kraft, "How Do Westerners Picture the World?"; and Ivan A. Solzhenitsyn, *A World Split Apart: Commencement Address Delivered at Harvard University* (New York: Harper and Row, 1978).

46 Masai et al., "Aboriginal Leaders."

47 Ibid.

48 Kraft, "How Do Westerners Picture the World?"; and Lafreniere, *The Decline of Nature.*

49 Jane P. Preston, "Enhancing Aboriginal Child Wellness: The Potential of Early Learning Programs," *First Nations Perspectives: The Journal of Manitoba First Nations Education Resource Centre* 1, 1 (2008): 98–120.

50 John MacBeath and Neil Dempster, "Introduction: Leadership and Learning – Making the Connections," in *Connecting Leadership and Learning: Principles for Practice,* ed. John MacBeath and Neil Dempster (New York: Routledge, 2009), 1–3.

51 E.W. Sinnott, "Introduction to the Compass Edition," in Jan C. Smuts, *Holism and Evolution* (New York: Viking, 1961), ix–xvii.

52 Kovach, *Indigenous Methodologies.*

53 Yves Bousquet and Harry Lafond, "Circles of Science in Saskatchewan: A Framework for Knowledge Sharing Fairs," in *Assessing Students' Ways of Knowing,* ed. Rick Sawa (Regina: Canadian Centre for Policy Alternatives, 2009), 42–53.

54 Canadian Human Rights Commission, "Overview: Expanding Knowledge," *Research Program: Differing Worldviews,* 2007.

55 Atleo, *Tsawalk,* xv.

56 D. Quinn Mills and Luke Novelli Jr., "Asian and Western Executive Styles," in *The AMA Handbook of Leadership,* ed. Marshall Goldsmith, John Baldoni, and Sarah McArthur (New York: American Management Association, 2010), 35–47.

57 Jeffrey Goldstein, James K. Hazy, and Benyamin B. Lichtenstein, *Complexity and the Nexus of Leadership: Leveraging Nonlinear Science to Create Ecologies of Innovation* (New York: Palgrave Macmillan, 2010).

58 Willie J. Ermine, "Aboriginal Epistemology," in *First Nations Education in Canada: The Circle Unfolds*, ed. Marie Battiste and Jean Barman (Vancouver: UBC Press, 1995), 101–12; Willie J. Ermine, "A Critical Examination of the Ethics in Research Involving Indigenous Peoples" (master's thesis, University of Saskatchewan, 2000); and Willie J. Ermine, "The Ethical Space of Engagement," *Indigenous Law Journal* 6, 1 (2007): 193–204.

59 Ermine, "Ethical Space," 193.

9

SUPPORTING EQUITABLE LEARNING OUTCOMES FOR INDIGENOUS STUDENTS

Lessons from Saskatchewan

Michael Cottrell and Rosalind Hardie

Issues of equity and social justice are particularly acute in the province of Saskatchewan, where Indigenous peoples, currently the fastest growing segment of the population, are also the most disadvantaged.[1] Inequities are particularly acute within the educational realm, where Indigenous students benefit the least from provincial schools, as demonstrated by their low graduation rates.[2] These extreme disparities are a moral issue, and they are increasingly seen as posing an imminent threat to the social cohesion and economic viability of the province. Ensuring more equitable educational outcomes for Indigenous learners in publicly funded education systems is consequently one of Saskatchewan's most urgent public policy goals, and it is a goal that complements the Truth and Reconciliation Commission of Canada's calls to action on Indigenous education.[3]

As a step in this direction, we identify educational environments, theories, and practices that have emerged in Saskatchewan and elsewhere that are likely to maximize the success of Indigenous students. Saskatchewan's educational landscape is similar to that of other Canadian settings and international English-speaking jurisdictions such as New Zealand, Australia, and parts of the United States, places where Indigenous peoples are likewise striving to decolonize education.[4] As Stephen Cornell, a sociologist and expert on Indigenous affairs, has noted, what "works in one country may hold lessons for others."[5] In particular, we impart the lessons learned from recent case studies of school sites with large Indigenous student populations[6] and from research completed in support of the Joint Task Force on Improving Education and Employment Outcomes for First Nations and Métis People, which reported to the Federation of Saskatchewan Indian Nations, the Province of Saskatchewan, and the Métis Nation–Saskatchewan in 2013.[7] The Joint Task Force focused on exemplary, or "Lighthouse," programs, which were identified "based on documented success in facilitating positive learning and employment outcomes for Aboriginal peoples in Saskatchewan, in all phases of the educational process."[8] These programs were also chosen because of their unique governance and funding structures. The task force's mandate "to listen to the voices of communities, seek the vision for action, and provide recommendations for leadership" resulted in eighty-three meetings with First Nations and Métis communities throughout the province and over one thousand participants.[9] Mere Berryman and colleagues' research project, which was completed for the Saskatchewan Instructional Development Research Unit in 2014 and published as *Seeking Their Voices: Improving Indigenous Student Learning Outcomes,* likewise captured the voices of students, parents, teachers, and school administrators in six Saskatchewan schools.[10] In all cases, the research was commissioned either by individual school divisions or by the Saskatchewan Ministry of Education and conducted under the auspices of research units associated with faculties of education at the University of Saskatchewan and the University of Regina, including the Saskatchewan Educational Leadership Unit, the Aboriginal Education Research Centre, and the Saskatchewan Instructional Development and Research Unit.

Drawing on the insights from these projects and reports, which included interviews with prominent academics, administrators, and policy-makers in Canada, the United States, and New Zealand, we argue that the first step in closing the achievement gap is viewing it as an "education debt"[11] owed to Indigenous people after more than a century of unfulfilled promises. Within the studies we surveyed, there exists a clear consensus, represented in the task force's report, on how that debt can be paid. Here, we outline what is required of educators and leaders to ensure that the promise of these initiatives comes to fruition and that the lessons already learned in Saskatchewan will be used when educating future generations.

From Achievement Gap to Education Debt

In 2016, 16 percent of Saskatchewan's population identified as Indigenous, and it is projected that one in five people in the province will be Indigenous by 2036.[12] It has long been suspected that the education system has failed Indigenous people, and recent data from Statistics Canada and the Saskatchewan Ministry of Education for 2010–11 confirms it. While over 74.1 percent of the province's non-Indigenous students graduate from Grade 12 within three years of starting grade 10, only 32.5 percent of Indigenous students do so.[13] As a result, Indigenous people in Saskatchewan have some of the lowest rates of educational attainment of all Indigenous groups in Canada.[14]

Fewer Indigenous students progress to postsecondary education or technical training compared to their non-Indigenous counterparts.[15] In 2011, only 24 percent of Indigenous people had obtained a certificate or diploma, compared to 32 percent of non-Indigenous people. Only 6 percent of Indigenous people had attained an undergraduate degree, and only 1 percent held postgraduate degrees. By comparison, 11 percent of non-Indigenous people had undergraduate degrees, and 4 percent had postgraduate degrees. The educational achievement gap is reflected in income levels. In 2010, the average income of Indigenous individuals was $26,354, compared to $40,798 for non-Indigenous residents. Statistics Canada recently indicated the employment rate among Indigenous people in the province was 58.4 percent compared to 82.5 percent for the non-Indigenous population.[16] Disparities in education and income are reflected in a lower quality of life for Indigenous people in terms of housing, nutrition, health, and well-being, which has profound implications for the future of the province.[17]

Michael Cottrell and Rosalind Hardie

While Indigenous peoples themselves would be the primary beneficiaries of improved educational and employment achievements, recent research has also documented the substantial gains accruing to the wider provincial society from more equitable outcomes.[18] Economist Eric Howe estimates that achieving educational parity for Aboriginal peoples would result in a monetary benefit of $16.2 billion, a nonmonetary benefit of $48.6 billion, and a social benefit of $25.2 billion, for a cumulative benefit to the province of Saskatchewan of $90 billion.[19] Howe suggests that adding this amount of money and number of new employees into the provincial economy could cause the first ever made-in-Saskatchewan boom resulting from the labour supply curve shifting right. He concludes that there are good reasons to suppose that it would have greater permanence than previous booms, since it would not be subject to the uncertainties of global commodity cycles.

In addition to the monetary benefits, improved Indigenous educational outcomes will also result in what Barbara Wolfe and Robert Haveman call the "non-market effects of schooling," which are intergenerational and as follows:

- a likely positive link between one's own schooling and the schooling received by one's children;
- a likely positive association between one's own schooling and the health status of one's family members;
- a likely positive relationship between one's own education and one's own health status;
- a likely positive relationship between one's own education and the efficiency of choices made, such as consumer choices ... ;
- a relationship between one's own schooling and fertility choices (for example, decisions of one's female teenage children regarding nonmarital childbearing); and
- a relationship between the schooling in one's neighborhood and youth decisions regarding their level of schooling, nonmarital childbearing, and participation in criminal activities.[20]

As Saskatchewan faces a future of unprecedented demographic change, with a rapidly aging non-Indigenous population and the fastest-growing Indigenous population in the country, ensuring that Indigenous learners benefit equitably from schools will become increasingly critical for Indigenous peoples themselves and for the economic and social well-being of the entire province. Consequently, according to Minister of Crown-Indigenous Relations Carolyn Bennett, "improving educational outcomes for Indigenous students is a top priority for the Government of Canada ... together with the Province of Saskatchewan."[21]

Achieving more equitable outcomes for Indigenous learners requires a sophisticated understanding of the historical contexts in which inequities have evolved and, more importantly, an appreciation of the ways that history continues to negatively affect Indigenous people. There is a general agreement among scholars and policymakers that the achievement gap cannot be understood apart from its historical and social contexts. Contrary to the myth that Saskatchewan is a place of social harmony and cooperation, Saskatchewan is a jurisdiction with a race problem rooted in its colonial history.[22] Given this context, it is critically important that educators understand the implications of that history, in particular the malign impact of the Indian Act, residential schools, and assimilative policies on generations of Indigenous peoples. Many Indigenous people perceive schools as abusive sites, and many communities view schools as alien impositions. State-controlled education and other assimilative policies severely compromised the cohesiveness and integrity of Indigenous families and communities, creating what Martin Papillon and Gina Cosentino call "a complex situation where a high level of *dependency* towards the state is combined with a *profound distrust* of that same state."[23] The achievement gap is best understood in this context. Drawing on insights from Gloria Ladson-Billings, we, along with our colleague Terrance Pelletier, concluded in a report for the Saskatchewan Educational Leadership Unit that what has been represented as an

Michael Cottrell and Rosalind Hardie

achievement gap actually constitutes an education debt rooted in the cultural and cognitive dissonance and pervasive abuse experienced in Saskatchewan schools for more than a century.[24] Given this context, the Joint Task Force concluded that rectifying the situation will depend on establishing "three foundational understandings": fostering dignified, mutual relationships; addressing poverty and racism; and recognizing First Nations and Métis cultures and languages.[25]

Fostering Dignified, Mutual Relationships

In *Significant Leadership and Ethical Space: Transforming Educational Opportunities for First Nations and Métis Learners in Saskatchewan*, their 2009 report to the Saskatchewan Ministry of Education, Michael Cottrell, Jane Preston, Joseph Pearce, and Terrance Pelletier identify Willie Ermine's conceptualization of ethical spaces as a framework for fostering dignified mutual relations and an appreciation of language and culture in the classroom and other learning environments, outcomes called for by the Joint Task Force. According to Ermine, *ethical space* describes a situation in which Indigenous and non-Indigenous people can exchange worldviews and achieve mutual cultural acceptance in an atmosphere of respect and trust.[26] As a framework, it supports partnerships, affirms diversity, and fosters a cooperative spirit among human communities to work towards an ethical order of societal relations. Ethical spaces come into being only through the affirmation of alternative worldviews, which are characterized by knowledge systems, cultural philosophies, and practices that are often quite different from the established and predominantly Eurocentric underpinnings of many current, publicly funded institutions. Ermine argues that dialogue and a cooperative spirit of cross-cultural consensus between Indigenous peoples and the provincial school system could create new currents of thought, permit the production of new knowledge, and encourage the achievement of educational parity for all.[27]

The implications of the concept of ethical space for public education in Saskatchewan are enormous and will require profound transformations in the areas of policy, governance, administration, curriculum, pedagogy, funding, staffing, school construction and design, teacher training and in-servicing, and relations between schools and the wider communities they serve.[28] The concept invites educators to "confront their epistemic and ontological assumptions about teaching and learning [and challenge] ... the established curriculum practices and interests that have been traditionally exercised in public schools."[29] As Rita Bouvier and Bruce Karlenzig frame it in their discussion of accountability in Indigenous education, the concept encourages educators to embrace "Indigenous peoples' worldviews, social structures, and pedagogy as a legitimate foundation upon which to construct new meanings or knowledge alongside Western traditions and ways of knowing."[30]

Although they do not use the term ethical space, Mere Berryman and colleagues, in *Seeking Their Voices: Improving Indigenous Student Learning Outcomes*, suggest that a significant consensus exists around the conditions likely to improve outcomes for Indigenous students:

- literacy and language programs
- culturally-based curriculum
- engagement and retention of students
- home and school partnerships
- teacher supply, quality and support
- school leadership
- school programming
- assessment, monitoring and reporting.[31]

Good intentions may abound, but school divisions need to insist on results. Step one would include setting a clear direction within the school division that dignified, mutual relationships will be the norm. In *Leaders of Learning: How District, School, and Classroom Leaders*

Michael Cottrell and Rosalind Hardie

Improve Student Achievement, Richard DuFour and Robert Marzano acknowledge the importance of school divisions explicitly setting goals, laying out critical conditions they expect to see in every school, and monitoring things to see that priorities are understood and acted on throughout the school division.[32] Capacity building for all leaders within the division needs to occur. In their study of the role of leadership in student learning, Kenneth Leithwood and Karen Seashore Louis argue that collective school leadership efficacy is "among the most powerful sources of influence that school districts can exercise on schools and students."[33] Establishing and maintaining dignified, mutual relationships are value-laden processes and may take a considerable investment of time. However, building equitable relationships in an environment of trust and respect is essential for success.

To date, efforts to build authentic relationships between Indigenous and non-Indigenous peoples have often lacked genuine commitment. In "Empowering Minority Students," Jim Cummins indicates that success depends on *"personal redefinitions* of the way classroom teachers interact with the children and communities they serve."[34] Parental involvement must be considered within the Indigenous cultural context, which means accepting that the extended family is often involved in parenting the child. In the past, ethnocentric assumptions and government policies have constrained parental involvement. However, once dignified relationships are established, new parental involvement strategies can be developed to enhance student success. Part of the disconnect between Indigenous peoples and schools stems from how governance structures have evolved. Tokenism has often been the order of the day. Under the ill-informed guise of knowing best, many educational leaders have given limited credence to including Indigenous parents as active decision makers on boards of education or school community councils. Nor has a great effort been made to value Indigenous parents' suggestions and feedback, even though strong educational partnerships with parents are important for fostering a community's pride and sense of ownership over a school.[35] Dorothy Leveque, in a study of Native American students in Barstow, California, found that parent involvement improved student learning.[36]

Since the 1970s, the National Indian Brotherhood has advocated for parental representation on school boards when provincial school divisions serve First Nations students.[37] And since 2006, there has been an expectation that school community councils will include an Indigenous representative recommended by the First Nation if students who live on reserve attend a provincial school.[38] Efforts to consult Indigenous communities were made by the Joint Task Force in Saskatchewan and in the Student First engagement process in Saskatchewan led by Russ Mirasty and Patricia Prowse.[39] Both research teams hold out promise for the future by providing a model for leadership at the school division and local school levels. Part of fostering mutual relations is making space for local innovation. Consultation with Elders, parents, and community members can help a school division adapt to a local context, and these local innovations can enhance the division's ability to address challenges and improve student achievement.

As stated in the Joint Task Force's report, "There is no magic bullet, the answer lies in establishing an ethical space that promotes dialogue, a cooperative spirit and respectful relationships among First Nations, Métis and non-Aboriginal [Indigenous] people."[40] Leadership experts favour distributed leadership across an array of positions within a school rather than emphasizing individual leaders because it is impossible for one person to contain all the necessary "knowledge, skills, and dispositions" at the level required for school-wide improvements.[41] However, the principal should act as a guiding light for the school's values; the principal must enable distributed leadership by causing "others to do things that can be expected to improve educational outcomes for students."[42] An initiative in New Zealand revealed that the principal's position as a role model is especially important when managing resistance to and conflict about professional development initiatives that require teachers to critique their own culturally located

Michael Cottrell and Rosalind Hardie

practice.[43] Educational leaders need to foster the "capacity and know-ledge to look at both worlds of the Euro-western mainstream and [I]ndigenous cultural ways and see the promise and potential ... to be guided by sheer passion for human diversity, spirit, and justice."[44]

Addressing Poverty and Racism

In *Seeking Their Voices: Improving Indigenous Student Learning Outcomes*, Berryman and colleagues note that "poverty is an inescapable reality when considering the current status of Indigenous students and how their learning might be supported."[45] According to Statistics Canada, Saskatchewan's child poverty rate is the third highest in Canada.[46] In 2014, Evan Radford reported in the *Saskatoon StarPhoenix* that 25 percent of Saskatchewan's children were living in poverty; among Indigenous children, the rate was 40 percent for those living in non-First Nations communities and 50 percent for those living on reserve.[47] According to Berryman and colleagues, "It will be difficult to mean-ingfully improve student learning and achievement in the absence of concrete action to address the issue of poverty in Indigenous families and communities."[48] The Joint Task Force, in its recommendations, emphasized the need to work across the provincial and federal levels of government and for intersectorial work across government depart-ments.[49] Addressing poverty and racism, it cautioned, will require changes outside of the education system, but a state of "jurisdictional chaos" exists that adds to the complexity of addressing the issues.[50]

In the interim, school divisions must advocate for changes to improve the living conditions of children living below the poverty line. Saskatchewan Education's *Building Communities of Hope: Best Practices for Meeting the Learning Needs of At-Risk and Indian and Métis Students* identifies some of the ways schools can address the needs of those living in poverty.[51] First among them is either implementing a nutrition program or asking whether the existing one is adequate. Should the food program be extended to community members who don't attend the school? Is the school the best place to offer meals for students? Second, community development programs can help parents acquire academic credentials, increase their employment skills, and secure regular employment. At both the division and the local level, leaders need to strengthen their capacity to guide community development. Third, preschools should be established in community schools. Cecil Rorabeck, president of the Royal College of Physicians and Surgeons of Canada, has called on the federal government to increase funding for early childhood care and learning, noting that 90 percent of brain development occurs prior to age five.[52] To maximize the positive impact of these activities, schools should follow the education ministry's directive to work with parents to address family wellness and, indirectly, support student success. Parents can assist in planning programs that they would find useful. Parents need to show their children that they value learning, encourage the acceptance of learning challenges, and are willing to celebrate learning success.[53] Parents' expectations for their child's academic success are vital.[54]

The Joint Task Force highlighted that child care structures and early childhood learning programs "play a very important role in early learning and child development by reducing risk factors, improving access to special programming, improving educational outcomes in high school and postsecondary education and developing more positive self-esteem and coping skills."[55] School divisions will need to pay particular attention to early childhood programs to determine how they can target appropriate interventions for vulnerable children who live below the poverty line. They will need to hire teachers with early childhood expertise and provide appropriate professional development.

Although many schools have students who live in poverty, they do not receive additional funding to address their specific needs. How can school divisions communicate this pressing need to the various levels of government and secure permanent funding? How can appropriate early childhood programming be permanently funded for needy families? How can external organizations be convinced to fill the void in the interim? Some schools have established partnerships

Michael Cottrell and Rosalind Hardie

with local businesses to fulfill students' immediate needs. However, a patchwork of remedies is no solution because students will continue to fall through the cracks. School divisions must throw their support behind efforts to increase awareness of poverty. Too often, known risk factors do not receive adequate attention or funding.

In addition to poverty, the continued existence of both overt and covert racism in schools has been substantiated by researchers.[56] Racism towards Indigenous students, parents, or staff has a detrimental effect on all. School divisions must insist that all staff be well informed regarding racism, preventative measures to avoid racism, and addressing racism when it occurs. Capacity building will strengthen leadership abilities among teachers and principals in this important area.

All educational structures need to be examined for evidence of racism. What are the built-in assumptions? Are there ways to adapt present-day structures to reduce the prevalence of racism within the school division? Particular attention may need to be paid to standardized tests, which tend to frame Indigenous students in deficit terms and perpetuate racial stereotypes.[57] Are there ways to give a greater voice to Indigenous perspectives on current educational issues? This type of self-examination is difficult and time-consuming, and it is hard to recognize covert forms of racism. In her analysis of anti-racist education, Verna St. Denis stresses that "educators must become informed on how racism has and continues to impact Aboriginal [Indigenous] people and work towards developing tools for anti-racist education."[58] If educators do not confront racism, St. Denis believes other steps to improve education for Indigenous students will meet with limited success.[59]

Staffing policies must also receive particular attention. Indigenous teacher education programs such as the Indian Teacher Education Program, the Saskatchewan Urban Native Teacher Education Program, and the Northern Teacher Education Program have been highly successful at increasing the number of qualified Indigenous teachers in Saskatchewan. However, there is not yet a large enough pool of qualified graduates to meet the need for Indigenous teachers in provincial and First Nations schools. As the Indigenous population continues to grow, the need for more qualified teachers of Indigenous ancestry will intensify. In the 1990s, Verna St. Denis, Rita Bouvier, and Marie Battiste collected feedback from 106 Indigenous teachers employed in public schools in the province. Among the participants, 25 percent were First Nations; the remainder were Métis. The large majority (93 percent) were raised off reserve, and only 26 percent spoke an Indigenous language. These teachers reported challenging teaching situations and felt they received limited support. They confirmed the "pervasiveness of racism" and felt it was assumed that "they alone can eradicate racism or have special knowledge about how to effectively challenge it."[60] In her 2010 study, St. Denis consulted fifty-nine Indigenous teachers across Canada; the vast majority felt they were expected to solve all Indigenous issues.[61] Many of the participants had also experienced racism. One of the recommendations made by St. Denis was to create a supportive culture that includes both Indigenous and non-Indigenous allies working together to address Indigenous issues.[62]

Recognizing First Nations and Métis Cultures and Languages

In *Seeking Their Voices: Improving Indigenous Student Learning Outcomes*, Berryman and colleagues assert that "the importance of culturally responsive pedagogy and language and culture in relation to Indigenous student success cannot be under-estimated."[63] This is particularly true, they note, "if one considers these factors in relation to other variables such as teacher/student relationships, Indigenous knowledge, instructional strategies, or other critical issues."[64] Although there has long been an expectation that First Nations and Métis content and perspectives will be incorporated within the curriculum at all grade levels, the reality has clearly fallen short of expectation. We must, Jim Cummins specifies, begin by "acknowledging

Michael Cottrell and Rosalind Hardie

the cultural, linguistic, imaginative, and intellectual resources that children bring to school."[65]

According to the National Indian Education Association, culturally based education is systematic and integrates cultural ways of thinking, learning, and problem solving.[66] Similarly, the Alaska Native Knowledge Network argues that culture and language are a prerequisite for student success.[67] In his study of leadership and learning, Russell Bishop notes that an effective school culture for Indigenous students supports interactions in which all learners know that their "culturally generated sense-making processes are used and developed" and viewed as legitimate.[68]

Although many researchers agree that cultural affirmation will help Indigenous students, it shouldn't be assumed that all teachers are adequately prepared to carry out this important work. Indigenous teacher education programs have helped to recruit and train teachers of First Nations ancestry, but the numbers are still inadequate to meet the needs of Indigenous students. While instruction in a first language is an important aspect of early childhood education, there is an acute shortage of qualified Indigenous language teachers in the province.[69]

All school divisions must provide for capacity building in the area of cultural awareness and affirmation. This will require diligence in seeing that Treaty Education, which is mandatory, is carried out in the most effective way possible. At the same time, steps must be taken to ensure that "misappropriation of Indigenous knowledge" does not occur.[70] Every opportunity to hire qualified First Nations and Métis teachers must be pursued. However, the majority of qualified teachers are non-Indigenous and will need to learn to be more culturally responsive. In *Investigating Culturally Responsive Mathematics Education*, Cynthia Nicol, Jo-ann Archibald, and Jeff Baker highlight this challenge: "Developing culturally responsive practices requires years of sustained and connected professional development involving opportunities for teachers to question, explore, and examine their teaching in collaborative and collective space."[71] Needless to say, the challenge is immense.

Although challenges lie ahead, school divisions are breaking new ground. In order to succeed, Kenneth Leithwood argues that they must do the following:

- Expect from the onset that success will require substantially greater change in their organization than they can make comfortably or easily.
- Focus their energies "laser-like" on conditions in their organizations which the best available evidence suggests will make significant contributions to the learning of those First Nations and Métis children who are struggling at school.
- Stop wasting energy on conditions which are not "high leverage," no matter how popular they might be or how much has already been invested in them.[72]

Improving the academic achievement of First Nations and Métis students can be guided by the lessons contained in instructional leadership theory. In "Confidence for School Improvement: A Priority for Principals," Kenneth Leithwood, Blair Mascall, and Doris Jantzi argue that leadership practices at the district level should have four main areas: "setting direction for the organization, developing the capacities of organizational members to pursue those directions, redesigning the organization to align with and support members' work, and improving the instructional program."[73] They emphasize that building a consensus around the efficacy of school improvement (including for Indigenous students) is essential.[74]

Our analysis of developments in Saskatchewan shows that school divisions committed to seeing improved educational outcomes for Indigenous students focus relentlessly on improving academic achievement for all Indigenous students. These school divisions understand that meeting the challenges ahead will require adaptive changes and that teachers and principals will need the opportunity and resources to build new skills and knowledge. To create a cycle of ongoing improvement, leaders will need to work collaboratively within and across schools in a distributive leadership framework to manage teaching and learning programs in ways that deepen understanding of the changes necessary.[75] Researchers recognize the need to align efforts at the provincial, school division, and local school levels – often labelled tri-level leadership – to bring about improvements with lasting value.[76] Formal leaders will require passion, optimism, persistence, and resiliency to fulfill their role.[77] Brent Davies, in his work on effective leadership, states: "Passionate leadership is about energy, commitment, a belief that every child can learn and will learn, a concern with social justice and the optimism that can make a difference. It takes leadership from the realm of a role or a job to one of an abiding drive to enhance children's learning and children's lives."[78]

As we show here, educators in Saskatchewan and elsewhere can benefit from paying attention to promising practices in our own schools and lessons learned by our counterparts elsewhere. The work is well under way, but more is necessary, and it will require embracing more change than can be made comfortably. Nevertheless, we believe that the search for improved academic outcomes for Indigenous students presents an exciting opportunity to fundamentally reimagine how schools are constructed and operated and to reconfigure how schools relate to learners, their families, and their communities. Success will depend on bringing about a fairer distribution of wealth in the province. None of these changes will be easy, but the rewards for future generations will be well worth the effort.

Notes

1 Statistics Canada's 2011 National Household Survey estimated that Saskatchewan's Indigenous population numbered 157,740, or 15.6 percent of the total population: 103,205 identified as First Nations, 52,450 as Métis.

See Statistics Canada, "NHS Aboriginal Population Profile, Saskatchewan 2011," http://www12.statcan.gc.ca/nhs-enm/2011/dp-pd/aprof/details/Page.cfm?Lang=E&Geo1=PR&Code1=47&Data=Count&SearchText=Saskatchewan&SearchType=Begins&SearchPR=01&A1=All&B1=All&GeoLevel=PR&GeoCode=47; and Michael Cottrell, "Indigenous Education in Comparative Perspective: Global Opportunities for Reimagining Schools," *International Journal for Cross-Disciplinary Subjects in Education* 1, 4 (2010): 223–27.

2 Joint Task Force on Improving Education and Employment Outcomes for First Nations and Métis People, "Voice, Vision, and Leadership: A Place for All," report prepared for the Federation of Saskatchewan Indian Nations, the Province of Saskatchewan, and the Métis Nation–Saskatchewan, 2013; and Mere Berryman, Sheila Carr-Stewart, Margaret Kovach, Cornelia Laliberté, Sharon Meyer, Brenda Merasty, Anne Sloboda, Bonnie Stelmach, and Larry Steeves, *Seeking Their Voices: Improving Indigenous Student Learning Outcomes* (Regina: Saskatchewan Instructional Development and Research Unit, 2014), http://aerc.usask.ca/research-projects-planning-activities/Seeking%20Their%20Voices_Nov%202014.pdf.

3 Government of Saskatchewan, "Education Sector Strategic Plan, Cycle 4 (2019–20)," http://publications.gov.sk.ca/documents/11/100620-ESSP%20Level%201%20Cycle%203%20Matrix%20-%20FINAL.pdf; Ministry of Education, *Annual Report for 2017–18* (Regina: Government of Saskatchewan, 2018), http://publications.gov.sk.ca/documents/15/107654-Annual-Report-2017-18-Final-web.pdf.

4 Cottrell, "Indigenous Education in Comparative Perspective."

5 Stephen Cornell, "Indigenous Peoples, Poverty, and Self-Determination in Australia, New Zealand, Canada, and the United States," in *Indigenous Peoples and Poverty: An International Perspective*, ed. Robyn Eversole, John-Andrew McNeish, and Alberto Cimadamore (London: Zed Books, 2006), 6.

6 Michael Cottrell, Jane Preston, Joseph Pearce, and Terrance Pelletier, *Significant Leadership and Ethical Space: Transforming Educational Opportunities for First Nations and Métis Learners in Saskatchewan* (Saskatchewan Educational Leadership Unit, Department of Educational Leadership, University of Saskatchewan, 2009).

7 Terrance Pelletier, Michael Cottrell, and Rosalind Hardie, *Improving Education and Employment Opportunities for First Nations and Métis Peoples* (Saskatoon: Saskatchewan Educational Leadership Unit, Department of Educational Administration, University of Saskatchewan, 2013), http://www.jointtaskforce.ca/wp-content/uploads/2013/04/Research-Report-for-the-Task-Force-March-26.pdf.

8 Ibid., 105.

9 Joint Task Force, *Voice, Vision, and Leadership*, 12–13, 21.

10 Berryman et al., *Seeking Their Voices*.

11 The term *education debt* was first used by Gloria Ladson-Billings in "From the Achievement Gap to the Education Debt: Understanding Achievement in U.S. Schools," *Educational Researcher* 35, 7 (2006): 5.

12 "Saskatchewan Aboriginal Peoples, 2016 Census," http://publications.gov. sk.ca/documents/15/104388-2016%20Census%20Aboriginal.pdf.

13 Government of Saskatchewan, *Saskatchewan Education Indicators Report: Prekindergarten to Grade Twelve* (Regina: Publications Saskatchewan, 2010).

14 Michael Mendelson, *Aboriginal Peoples and Postsecondary Education in Canada* (Ottawa: Caledon Institute of Social Policy, 2006); and John A. Richards, *A Disastrous Gap: How High Schools Have Failed Canada's Aboriginal Students* (Toronto: C.D. Howe Institute, 2008).

15 Cynthia Gallop, "Supporting Success: Aboriginal Students in Higher Education," *Canadian Journal of Higher Education* 46, 2 (2016): 206–24.

16 Karen Kelly-Scott, *Aboriginal Peoples: Fact Sheet for Saskatchewan*, catalogue no. 89-656-X2016009 (Ottawa: Statistics Canada, 2016), 6.

17 Statistics Canada, "NHS Aboriginal Population Profile, Saskatchewan 2011."

18 Eric Howe, *Education and Lifetime Income for Aboriginal People in Saskatchewan* (Saskatoon: University of Saskatchewan, 2002); Eric Howe, *Mishchet aen kishkayhtamihk nawut ki wiichiihtonaan: Bridging the Aboriginal Education Gap in Saskatchewan* (Saskatoon: Gabriel Dumont Institute, 2011); Mendelson, *Aboriginal Peoples*; Marie Battiste, "State of Aboriginal Learning: Background Paper for the 'National Dialogue on Aboriginal Learning,'" Canadian Council on Learning, Ottawa, 2005, http://en.copian. ca/library/research/ccl/aboriglearn/aboriglearn.pdf; David Bell, *Sharing Our Success: Ten Case Studies of Aboriginal Schooling* (Kelowna, BC: Society for the Advancement of Excellence in Education, 2004); Sheila Carr-Stewart, "A Treaty Right to Education," *Canadian Journal of Education* 26, 2 (2001): 125–43; and Richards, *A Disastrous Gap*.

19 Howe, *Mishchet aen kishkayhtamihk nawut ki wiichiihtonaan*.

20 Barbara L. Wolfe and Robert H. Haveman, "Social and Nonmarket Benefits from Education in an Advanced Economy," Federal Reserve Bank of Boston Journal Conference Series, June, 2001, 98–99.

21 Quoted in Morgan Modjeski, "Made-in-Saskatchewan Education Initiative Gets Funding, Recognition from Government of Canada," *Saskatoon StarPhoenix*, June 8, 2017, https://thestarphoenix.com/news/local-news/made-in-saskatchewan-education-initiative-gets-funding-recognition-from-government-of-canada.

22 Joyce Green, "From *Stonechild* to Social Cohesion: Anti-racist Challenges for Saskatchewan" (paper presented at the annual meeting of the Canadian Political Science Association, "Theory, Policy, and Pedagogy of

Decolonization," University of Western Ontario, London, June 2005), 19; and Michael Cottrell and Paul Orlowski, "Poverty, Race, and Schools in Saskatchewan," in *Education for Social Justice: Intersection of Poverty, Class, and Schooling,* ed. Elinor L. Brown (Newcastle, UK: Information Age, 2014), 257–79.

23 Martin Papillon and Gina Cosentino, *Lessons from Abroad: Towards a New Social Model for Canada's Aboriginal Peoples,* Research Report F140 (Ottawa: Canadian Policy Research Networks, 2004), 1.

24 Pelletier, Cottrell, and Hardie, *Improving Education and Employment Opportunities for First Nations and Métis Peoples,* 23–24.

25 Joint Task Force, *Voice, Vision, and Leadership,* 8.

26 Willie Ermine, "A Critical Examination of the Ethics in Research Involving Indigenous Peoples" (master's thesis, University of Saskatchewan, 2000); Willie Ermine, "The Ethical Space of Engagement," *Indigenous Law Journal* 6, 1 (2007): 193–203, https://jps.library.utoronto.ca/index.php/ilj/article/view/27669/20400.; and Willie Ermine, "An Ethical Space Experience: Summary Paper Examining First Nations and Métis Initiatives in Two Schools," in Cottrell et al., *Significant Leadership and Ethical Space,* 57–76.

27 Ermine, "The Ethical Space of Engagement"; and Ermine, "An Ethical Space Experience."

28 Michael Cottrell, Terrance Pelletier, Joseph Pearce, Joanne Cunningham, and Betty Rohr, *Albert Community School Aboriginal Student Achievement Project* (Saskatoon: Saskatchewan Educational Leadership Unit, 2010); and Cottrell et al., *Significant Leadership and Ethical Space.*

29 Lorenzo Cherubini, "Taking Haig-Brown Seriously: Implications of Indigenous Thought on Ontario Educators," *Journal of the Canadian Association for Curriculum Studies* 7, 1 (2009): 12–13.

30 Rita Bouvier and Bruce Karlenzig, "Accountability and Aboriginal Education: Dilemmas, Promises, and Challenges," *Our Schools, Our Selves* 15, 3 (2006): 17.

31 Berryman et al., *Seeking Their Voices,* 16.

32 Richard DuFour and Robert J. Marzano, *Leaders of Learning: How District, School, and Classroom Leaders Improve Student Achievement* (Bloomington, IN: Solution Tree Press, 2011), 33.

33 Kenneth Leithwood and Karen Seashore Louis, *Linking Leadership to Student Learning* (San Francisco: Jossey-Bass, 2012), 230.

34 Jim Cummins, "Empowering Minority Students: A Framework for Intervention," *Harvard Educational Review* 71, 4 (2001): 657.

35 Berryman et al., *Seeking Their Voices,* 32.

36 Dorothy M. Leveque, "Cultural and Parental Influences on Achievement among Native American Students in Barstow Unified School District"

(paper presented at the national meeting of the Comparative and International Educational Society, San Diego, California, March 1994).

37 National Indian Brotherhood, "Indian Control of Indian Education," policy paper prepared for Minister of Indian Affairs and Northern Development, National Indian Brotherhood, Ottawa, 1972.

38 Government of Saskatchewan, "School Community Councils Support Centre: Membership," https://www.saskatchewan.ca/residents/education -and-learning/prek-12-education-early-learning-and-schools/school -community-councils-support-centre.

39 Russ Mirasty and Patricia Prowse, *Student First Engagement Discussion Guide* (Victoria: R.A. Malatest and Associates, 2014).

40 Joint Task Force, *Voice, Vision, and Leadership*, 70.

41 Viviane Robinson, Margie Hohepha, and Claire Lloyd, *School Leadership and Student Outcomes: Identifying What Works and Why* (Wellington, NZ: New Zealand Ministry of Education, 2015), 47, https://www.education counts.govt.nz/__data/assets/pdf_file/0015/60180/BES-Leadership-Web -updated-foreword-2015.pdf.

42 Ibid., 70.

43 Marama Tuuta, Lynette Bradnam, Anne Hynds, and Joanna Higgins, with Robina Broughton, *Evaluation of the Te Kauhua Maori Mainstream Pilot Project* (Wellington, NZ: Ministry of Education, 2004).

44 Cottrell et al., *Significant Leadership and Ethical Space*, 195.

45 Berryman et al., *Seeking Their Voices*, 22.

46 Statistics Canada, CANSIM Table 202-0802, cited in Garson Hunter, *United Nations Human Rights Council Review of Canada and Canada's Response to Recommendation 17: Poverty among Seniors, Women, and Children, and Income Inequality in Canada and Saskatchewan* (Regina: University of Regina, 2010).

47 Evan Radford, "One in Four Sask. Kids Live in Poverty," *Saskatoon Star Phoenix*, November 25, 2014, A3.

48 Berryman et al., *Seeking Their Voices*, 22.

49 Joint Task Force, *Voice, Vision, and Leadership*.

50 Ibid., 16.

51 Saskatchewan Education, *Building Communities of Hope: Best Practices for Meeting the Learning Needs of At-Risk and Indian and Métis Students* (Regina: Government of Saskatchewan, 1996).

52 Cecil Rorabeck, "Early Years Help for Children Pays Dividends," *Saskatoon Star Phoenix*, November 27, 2014, A9.

53 Neil Dempster and George Bagakis, "An Environment for Learning (Principle 2)," in *Connecting Leadership and Learning*, ed. John MacBeath and Neil Dempster (London, UK: Routledge, 2009), 91–105.

54 Kenneth Leithwood, "Critical Learning Conditions for Improvement in Schools Serving First Nations and Métis Children," in Cottrell et al., *Significant Leadership and Ethical Space,* 77–101.

55 Joint Task Force, *Voice, Vision, and Leadership,* 33.

56 Battiste, "State of Aboriginal Learning"; Canadian Council on Learning, *State of Learning in Canada: A Year in Review* (Ottawa: Canadian Council on Learning, 2010); Joint Task Force, *Voice, Vision, and Leadership*; and Verna St. Denis, *A Study of Aboriginal Teachers' Professional Knowledge and Experience in Canadian Schools* (Ottawa: Canadian Teachers' Federation, 2010).

57 Michael Cottrell, Jane Preston, and Joseph Pearce, "The Intersection of Modernity, Globalization, Indigeneity, and Postcolonialism: Theorizing Contemporary Saskatchewan Schools," *Diaspora, Indigenous, and Minority Education* 6 (2012): 242–57.

58 Verna St. Denis, "Aboriginal Education and Anti-racist Education: Building Alliances across Cultural and Racial Identity," *Canadian Journal of Education* 30, 4 (2007): 1085.

59 Ibid.

60 Verna St. Denis, Rita Bouvier, and Marie Battiste, *Okiskinahamakewak – Aboriginal Teachers in Saskatchewan's Publicly Funded Schools: Responding to the Flux* (Regina: Saskatchewan Research Networking Project, 1998), vii, 10.

61 St. Denis, *A Study of Aboriginal Teachers.*

62 Ibid.

63 Berryman et al., *Seeking Their Voices,* 27–28.

64 Ibid.

65 Cummins, "Empowering Minority Students," 653.

66 National Indian Education Association, "Using Culturally Based Education to Increase Academic Achievement and Graduation Rates," http://files.eric.ed.gov/fulltext/ED523558.pdf.

67 Alaska Native Knowledge Network, "Alaska Standards for Culturally Responsive Schools: Cultural Standards for Students, Educators, Schools, Curriculum, and Communities," University of Alaska, 1998, 2, http://ankn.uaf.edu/Resources/mod/glossary/showentry.php?courseid=2&eid=2112&displayformat=dictionary.2.

68 Russell Bishop, "How Effective Leaders Reduce Educational Disparities," in *Leadership and Learning,* ed. Jan Robertson and Helen Timperley (Thousand Oaks, CA: Sage, 2011), 31.

69 Leithwood, "Critical Learning Conditions"; Helen Raham, "Policy Levers for Improving Outcomes for Off-Reserve Students" (paper presented to the Colloquium on Improving the Educational Outcomes of Aboriginal People Living Off-Reserve, Saskatoon, March 2010), 6, 7.

70 St. Denis, Bouvier, and Battiste, *Okiskinahamakewak*, 78.

71 Cynthia Nicol, Jo-ann Archibald, and Jeff Baker, *Investigating Culturally Responsive Mathematics Education* (Ottawa: Canadian Council on Learning, 2010), 7.

72 Leithwood, "Critical Learning Conditions," 78.

73 Kenneth Leithwood, Blair Mascall, and Doris Jantzi, "Confidence for School Improvement: A Priority for Principals," in Leithwood and Louis, *Linking Leadership to Student Learning*, 110.

74 Ibid., 117.

75 Fleur Harris, "Critical Engagement with the Deficit Construction of Maori Children as Learners in the Education System," *Critical Literacy* 2, 1 (2008): 43–59.

76 DuFour and Marzano, *Leaders of Learning*; Michael Fullan, *Leadership and Sustainability: System Thinkers in Action* (Thousand Oaks, CA: Corwin Press, 2005); and John Hattie, *Visible Learning for Teachers: Maximizing Impact on Learning* (London, UK: Routledge, 2012).

77 Christopher Day and Michèle Schmidt, "Sustaining Resilience," in *Developing Sustainable Leadership*, ed. Brent Davies (London: Paul Chapman, 2007), 65–86; DuFour and Marzano, *Leaders of Learning*; and Hattie, *Visible Learning for Teachers*.

78 Brent Davies, "Introduction: Passionate Leadership," in *Passionate Leadership in Education*, ed. Brent Davies and Tim Brighouse (Los Angeles, CA: Sage, 2008), 1.

10

HYBRID ENCOUNTERS

First Peoples Principles of Learning
and Teachers' Constructions of Indigenous
Education and Educators

Brooke Madden

In 2006–07, the BC Ministry of Education, in partnership with the First Nations Education Steering Committee, created the "English 12 First Peoples" course in consultation with Indigenous knowledge-keepers and educators in the province. The project included the development of the "First Peoples Principles of Learning," which were intended to help the course "focus more authentically on First Peoples' experiences, values, beliefs, and lived realities."[1] The principles were constructed on the premise that although Indigenous people in the province are diverse – in addition to Métis and Inuit, there are 203 First Nations in BC – there are strong similarities in their worldviews and approaches to knowing and learning, and incorporating this knowledge into the curriculum can enhance the public education system for all students.[2]

The principles are as follows:

- Learning ultimately supports the well-being of the self, the family, the community, the land, the spirits, and the ancestors.
- Learning is holistic, reflexive, reflective, experiential, and relational (focused on connectedness, on reciprocal relationships, and a sense of place).
- Learning involves recognizing the consequences of one's actions.

- Learning involves generational roles and responsibilities.
- Learning recognizes the role of indigenous knowledge.
- Learning is embedded in memory, history, and story.
- Learning involves patience and time.
- Learning requires exploration of one's identity.
- Learning involves recognizing that some knowledge is sacred and only shared with permission and/or in certain situations.[3]

The principles gesture towards the human-nature-spirit web in which meaning is made, and they offer guidelines for exploring the purpose, characteristics, processes, protocols, and outcomes of learning from this location. Positioned as an educational framework, the "First Peoples Principles of Learning" typically take the shape of a one-page document that is most commonly distributed in the form of an 18" × 24" colour poster.

I noticed, however, that the document's focus is on learning and that it uncouples the learning process from teaching. The absence of images of or references to teacher and student added to the intrigue. I wondered: How are teachers relating to the principles? How does the relationship shape, reinforce, and challenge the professional identities of teachers, their practices in the classroom, and how they construct or understand Indigenous education?[4] In an educational context laden with prescriptive policy that typically relies on teachers for interpretation and activation, what makes this document distinct? What might an educational framework that centres learning, rather than teaching, provide and prohibit?

I explored these questions as part of a larger study of the subjectification of nine early career teachers in BC.[5] The participants in the study were both Indigenous and ally, each had one to five years of teaching experience, they had all completed Faculty of Education coursework on the topic of Indigenous education, and they had implemented this coursework in Metro Vancouver schools.[6] Seven agreed to participate in an interview about a lesson or unit they had developed that integrated Indigenous content, and four invited me to participate and observe the delivery of the lesson or unit.[7] What I learned was that the participants overwhelmingly equated supports for Indigenous education with documents.

To consider how relationships between teachers and documents produce constructions of Indigenous education and the subject position of the teacher with it, I looked to Lindsay Prior's analytical approach.[8] I mapped the two primary functions of the "First Peoples Principles of Learning," as revealed in interviews and the classroom. Teachers considered the principles an authority on "what counts" as Indigenous education, and the principles also functioned as an undiscerning associate that could be relied on as proof to support the teachers' assertions that they are engaging in Indigenous education.

Early Encounters with "First People's Principles of Learning" as a Central Support

I invited teachers to select and share a lesson or unit plan that they had developed that integrated Indigenous perspectives, knowledges, or pedagogies. I let them know that I was particularly interested in the resources that they had drawn upon. The teachers cited a range of supports, including curricular documents (e.g., *English 10 and 11 First Peoples: Curriculum 2010*), policy documents (e.g., *Aboriginal Education Enhancement Agreement: Our Visions, Our Voices*), educational frameworks (e.g., "First People's Principles of Learning"), online resources (e.g., *Teaching for Indigenous Education* website and a Museum of Anthropology guided tour), and school staff (e.g., Indigenous education teacher consultants and Elders in residence).[9]

Supports in the form of documents were cited approximately six times more frequently than human supports. References to relationships with Indigenous cultural mentors and community members were extremely rare. With the exception of one teacher participant, all contact with Indigenous knowledge-holders was through existing school district relationships (e.g., with Elders in residence or an

Brooke Madden

Indigenous education teacher consultant) rather than their own initiative. This overreliance on documents supports research that shows that capacity for integrating Indigenous knowledge is strengthened when systemic supports – such as specialized positions for Indigenous education, long-term contracts for Elders and knowledge-holders, funding for honoraria, and welcoming environments – are in place.[10] In the case of the BC public school system, it appears that these systemic supports have not been extended widely enough.

Although the teachers listed additional supports, it was apparent that the "First Peoples Principles of Learning" played a central role in shaping teachers' constructions of Indigenous education and their role as teachers. My own first encounter with the principles was when a respected scholar of Indigenous education encouraged me to pay close attention to them. Her perception, based on collaboration with administrators in a local district, was that they were being utilized as the main educational framework to introduce teachers to Indigenous education and to help them reshape how they conceptualize and facilitate learning in their classrooms. There are similar frameworks being used across Canada (for example, see Manitoba's *Treaty Education Initiative* and Ontario's *First Nation, Métis, and Inuit Education Policy Framework* 2007).[11] These frameworks both reflect and produce curricular reform and Indigenous education initiatives across institutions at all levels.

Within the larger research project, I documented sixteen encounters with the principles during consultations with administrators on Indigenous education, thirty-three interviews with nine teachers across four school districts, participant observation in four classrooms, and participation in a school district's professional learning series and an Aboriginal Education Enhancement Agreement advisory committee.[12] The principles are currently available in the "Learning First Peoples Classroom Resources" section of the First Nation Education Steering Committee's (FNESC) website, where they are presented as a foundation for all of the curricular supports developed by the committee and its partners. These supports include curricular documents, teacher resource guides such as *Indian Residential Schools and Reconciliation Teacher Resource Guide 5*, workshops such as "First Peoples Science Teacher Resources," and classroom resources such as "First Nations Career Role Models." There is very little information about the principles beyond their being listed on this website, although some discussion is included in the introductory sections of selected supports.

Educational documents produced by the BC Ministry of Education regularly provide a link to the principles on the FNESC's website as well as to a text-only version of the document on the ministry's website, which states that the principles "generally reflect First Peoples pedagogy" and includes this cautionary note: "Because these principles of learning represent an attempt to identify common elements in the varied teaching and learning approaches that prevail within particular First Peoples societies, it must be recognized that they do not capture the full reality of the approach used in any single First Peoples society."[13] Further, at the time of research, the ministry connected the principles to the "redesigned provincial curriculum" that, among additional significant changes, "authentically integrate[s]" Indigenous perspectives and content across all levels and subjects.[14] Redesigned K–9 curricular documents and related resources were officially in use as of the beginning of the 2016–17 school year, and redesigned Grades 10 to 12 curricular documents and related resources were made available for voluntary use by teachers that same year. The ministry's representations of the connection between the principles and the redesigned provincial curriculum often lack detail. For example, statements such as the following, which appeared in a list of frequently asked questions in 2015, are common: "The First Peoples Principles of Learning provided a crucial lens for the teacher teams when drafting curricula, and all curriculum teams included Aboriginal representation. The teams put great effort into embedding Aboriginal knowledge and worldviews in the curriculum in authentic, meaningful ways."[15]

Brooke Madden

Studying the Use and Function of Documents:
Data Fragments That Include Hybrid Agency

Drawing on the insights of Lindsay Prior, who advocates studying the use and function of documents (rather than their content),[16] I regard nonhumans and hybrids (nonhuman beings or bodies that display human cultural characteristics) as dynamic resources. Their agency extends beyond that which is "activated" by humans. Prior contends that focusing on how documents function in systems and networks reveals "how [they] can drive, rather than be driven by, human actors – i.e., the spotlight is on the *vita activa* [active life] of documentation."[17] I consider the principles a hybrid actor that incorporates "a degree of human consciousness – though it is consciousness-at-a-distance (from its designer) so to speak."[18] This perspective resonates with my commitment to honour Indigenous relational theories. It also works to counter the sedimented Eurocentric notions that discourse is reducible to linguistic practices and that signification is primarily a human application of anthropocentric meaning onto static and inert objects. Hereafter, I refer to the principles as *FPPL*. This choice is inspired by the discursive practices used by the research participants. The distinction between *FPPL* (as hybrid actor) and *the principles* (as document) is intentional.

In designing the research, I asked: How might I invite consideration of a hybrid document within a series of interviews and supporting activities conceptualized primarily as conversations between teacher participants and myself as research? If I could develop my capacity to listen anew, how might I collude in the production of data in order to theorize how documents shape teachers' constructions of Indigenous education and the associated subject position of the teacher? If I was being encouraged by Prior to outline the roles of a key document and study how it operates, what methods would I use during analysis and designation of function?[19]

I began by producing data fragments that represented FPPL as an agential hybrid that, alongside us humans, contributed to the production of data and the associated knowledge claims generated. I paid particular attention to

- the humans' physical positioning with respect to and gestures towards FPPL
- the pronouns and terms utilized when referring to FPPL
- instances where FPPL drove hybrid-human, hybrid-nonhuman, and hybrid-hybrid activity
- the roles and function of FPPL (e.g., FPPL acting as an agent that brought humans to recall other times and spaces).

Paying particular attention to constructions of Indigenous education and the subject positions of the teacher, this process enhanced my capacity to theorize what the roles that FPPL was playing in this particular landscape of Indigenous education would produce. For example, during my third interview with Julian – an elementary school teacher who identified as male, white, Canadian, and of English, Scottish, Irish, and Swedish descent – I noticed FPPL in poster form hanging above the main entrance to the Grades 5 and 6 classroom where he taught. I suspected it was the copy that had been distributed during the school district's Indigenous education professional learning series session, which both Julian and I had participated in two weeks before. Figure 10.1 is a data fragment that represents our encounter. This example reveals the multiple roles and functions that FPPL played, a characteristic that emerged in all the teachers' encounters with it, but here I focus on the two that emerged as the most important.

FPPL as Authority

As outlined above, FPPL has both implicitly and explicitly been positioned – by teachers, administrators, teacher educators, university and school curricular documents and resources, and Indigenous education websites – as a comprehensive outline of school-based Indigenous education. In most of the encounters I documented, teachers did not

Brooke Madden

Encounter 5: 12/09/2014, ~4:15pm
Julian, Interview 3 – Walking Interview With/in Significant Place
Julian's Elementary School Classroom

Legend	
( )	positioning with respect to and gesturing towards FPPL
[ ]	researcher's surfacing thoughts
{ }	hybrid-human, hybrid–non-human, and hybrid-hybrid activity
//	interrupted speech
bold+italics	pronouns and terms utilized when referring to FPPL
(dark grey box)	FPPL roles
(light grey box)	FPPL productions

BROOKE: The other ***thing*** (pointing to FPPL in poster form hanging over classroom door) [the centrality of the placement reminds me of where a cross typically hung in my school classroom experiences] ... (in a comical voice that continues to elevate in pitch) ***First Peoples Principles of Learning*** {During Interview 2, Julian asked if I was familiar with FPPL when discussing his experience of participating in teacher education on the topic of Aboriginal education. We discussed that FPPL was seemingly "everywhere".} [perhaps I was humourously calling on our history of what I read as a shared curiosity regarding the document]

Artefact of shared experience

Produced the occasion for talk

JULIAN: Yes (looking at FPPL) ... ***Those*** are up there now//

Authority

BROOKE: Did you just put ***that*** up there after the PD session? {Julian and I participated in an Aboriginal education professional learning series session on November 26, 2014 where FPPL was a central focus explored through a What, Wonder, and Wow activity. Posters were distributed.}

JULIAN: Well ya, I didn't have ***it*** until then//

BROOKE: How did you get ***it*** laminated? [lamination, in addition to the placement of FPPL, suggests importance]

JULIAN: Uh, we have a laminator at the school.

BROOKE: So do you think ***it's*** something you're going to be using or did you just put ***it*** up? Did you get a chance to introduce ***it*** to the class?

JULIAN: I have had a chance to introduce ***it*** to the class//

Brought teachers together to Introduce Aboriginal education and question/ reshape how they conceptualize and facilitate learning in their classrooms

BROOKE: So how did you do that? ... or ... like (I audibly exhale as I sit on a desk facing FPPL) ... maybe not how did you do that, but, how did you explain to them about what ***this new framework*** or whatever//

JULIAN: Introducing ***it*** was rather easy because the kids were like, "Hey Mr. X, what's ***that***?"//

Newcomer to the Classroom

BROOKE: They noticed it right//

JULIAN: They noticed it, I put ***it*** up and they noticed ***it*** right away and I was like, "Uhhhh!", Ummm ...

BROOKE: Why do you think they noticed ***it*** right away?

Produced student curiosity and teacher discomfort

JULIAN: They're just perceptive, curious, "Oh, you made a change. What's going on? Something's not right here ..." [This presents an interesting invitation to remember how it felt to occupy classroom space as a school student. Long hours of surveying and daydreaming came to mind, convincing me that I too would have noticed a new prominently displayed poster] Um, yeah, and I think that as we go through// (long pause) we'll reference ***this*** I think. Umm, the number//I've been very surprised //actually I'm not sure if I would say surprised, but, there have been a number of times where they've commented that the way I do things is somewhat different in ... um ... in various ways and I think that a lot of that can be traced back to these (motioning to poster) principles. Whether bringing the holistic approach I bring [connection to principle 2], or asking them to ... explore themselves and their understandings as they get in [connection to principle 8] //to treat their decisions and their opinions as though they matter ... as though the consequences of what they do are really important things [connection to principle 3] and thinking about story//as we go through we will draw back to *that* in a way that for them is quite//yeah, that I think sorta grounds the difference from the kinds of teaching that they've normally seen. Like next term, we're going to be doing this human rights unit that I totally plan to have encompass social studies, science, both reading and writing and language arts, visual art, math. And I think that having all of those things wrapped up in one sort of big question is gonna be a really, really different experience for them. I think whether that's looking at how holistic that is [connection to principle 2] or the consequences of our actions on those around the world [connected to principle 1] or something as simple as that "learning involves patience and time" [principle 7] and I know there will be days where it's like (in an exasperated tone mimicking students), "Mr. X, we're learning about rights again?" and I'll be able to reference (looking at and pointing toward FPPL) "learning involves patience and time" [principle 7].

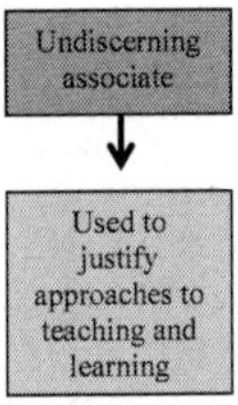

BROOKE: Uh, huh, uh huh ... So you kind of see *them* as kind of *tools*//well *principles*! As way to think about//

JULIAN: As *ways to guide us* into what we're learning.

BROOKE: And I just heard you mention that the way that you think about teaching and the way that you think about yourself as a teacher within a community of learners resonates with a lot of these *things*. Is there any *spaces* that you're not so sure about or that you want to bring into your practice more or ...

JULIAN: Hmmm (looks to FPPL) ... I think ... what do I think? I think that if I were to think of something *there* that I would love to see come into my practice more ... Um, I would love to see us become more involved with generational roles and responsibilities [principle 5] ... Looking at//becoming really involved in looking at the roles of Elders in our community. Roles that they can have even by grades 5 and 6, looking at the role that they have as Elders in the school [collapsing of the term/position and potential misunderstanding of the principle] and seeing that yes there are those who are older than you and those that will be guiding you and you are older than many and you will guide them ...

BROOKE: Does [school district] have Elders and are they [members of the local First Nations community]?

JULIAN: I believe they are [local First Nation] and yes we do have//I believe so//not entirely sure. I//It's not something I've had//or taken the opportunity to explore thoroughly. I know that as a school we're doing some professional development with the local [First Nation's] cultural centre but I don't believe it's happening till May.

Undiscerning associate

↓

Used to justify approaches to teaching and learning

Undiscerning associate

Authority

↓

Provides a platform from which to reimagine approaches to teaching and learning, including school-community relationships

↑

Activator

Figure 10.1 Data fragment of encounter between FPPL, author, and Julian, an elementary school teacher

Brooke Madden

distinguish the principles by type, for example, by purpose, character-istics, processes, protocols, or outcomes of learning. Instead, they understood them as pedagogical approaches. To understand how they are translated into teaching practice, consider Julian's statement: "I know there will be days where it's, like (in an exasperated tone mim-icking students), 'Mr. X, we're learning about rights again?' and I'll be able to reference (looking at and pointing towards FPPL] 'learning involves patience and time' [principle 7]." He appears to be interpreting Principle 7 as an approach to designing, or justification for, a unit on human rights that spans a period of time lengthy enough to potentially irritate students.

Despite FPPL being positioned as an authority on "what counts" as Indigenous education, teachers sometimes remained unclear about how to interpret the principles and how they might be applied in teaching practice. During one school district's Indigenous education professional learning series session, held in November 2014, the prin-ciples were introduced and then explored through a what, wonder, and wow activity. Nine pieces of chart paper were displayed on desks, each with one principle handwritten on the top. Participants were asked to circulate and (1) add information that they knew about the principle (the what), (2) ask questions about the principle (the won-der), and (3) contribute positive comments or stories connected to the principle (the wow). Here are their responses, which are repro-duced with their permission.

Learning ultimately supports the well-being of the self, the family, the community, the land, the spirits, and the ancestors.

- Learning and growing is essential to individuals and commun-ity life.
- Learning/education is such an important step to understanding.
- Acknowledges the importance of the past to the future.
- The well-being of everything is connected.
- Self-regulation.

Learning is holistic, reflexive, reflective, experiential, and relational (focused on connectedness, on reciprocal relationships, and a sense of place).

- Can we discuss the difference between *reflexive* and *reflective*?
- How do we nurture all of our relationships?
- *Sense of place* is such a great starting point for classes to come together and feel connected. I wonder how many of our students feel strong connections to more than one place, i.e., living in multiple worlds? [Two additional participants replied to this comment: "I like this." and "Me too!"]
- So needed at this time in our planet's history.

Learning involves recognizing the consequences of one's actions.

- Recognizing consequences of our mistakes, ensuring that we don't repeat them.
- The Aboriginal way of "consequences" is different than punishment.
- Awareness that recognition is perhaps more important than compensation.
- Learning from mistakes.
- Some of the most powerful learning happens when experiencing this.
- Consequences that extend beyond humans to include natural and spirit worlds.
- What about the consequences we can never foresee? What does that kind of learning accountability look like?
- Great opportunities to connect this principle to our care and treatment of the planet.

Learning involves generational roles and responsibilities.

- Interesting that in our Western culture, growing old, being called an "elder," is sometimes taken as an insult. In Aboriginal cultures, it is a status of great importance.

- All generations play important roles that together enhance the well-being of community.
- How a society values/treats its elders can be very revealing ...
- How do we take this and implement it cross-culturally (when the elderly are often undervalued in certain dominant cultures)?
- How can we support students in exploring their (potential) roles?
- A great example of how "we" can learn from different lenses/perspectives.

Learning recognizes the role of Indigenous knowledge.

- So much knowledge, poorly valued with our changing world.
- Think this is particularly true in "science" as we think about traditional IK and what it can offer, especially around environmental sustainability.
- How do we go beyond recognizing that Indigenous knowledge is valid and valuable to recognizing that there are also entire ways of knowing and ways of being through which it emerges?
- Indigenous is global, we are all Indigenous to somewhere, so it honours all students?
- Does *recognizing* include validating, integrating, responding etc.?

Learning is embedded in memory, history, and story.

- Acknowledge education mistakes. Twisted memory (point of view) and history.
- As a contrast to the often self-focused lens learning can easily take (and a focus on the present), this grounds learning in the much broader context of others and the past.
- This would take patience and time (another principle, I know!). Will be able to consistently convince young learners of the value this holds?
- Do all teachers believe this? If they don't believe, will they teach their students?
- Wow! I love this. It recognizes past knowledge in learning.

Learning involves patience and time.

- In my class, we use this as a repeated mantra, for students, teachers and parents.
- Assessing our relationship with time and patience ... when are we patient? When are we not patient? When do we work well with time? When don't we?
- We need to use time very well. It's really precious.
- How does and how could our school system and structures within it (e.g., reporting) reflect this principle?
- How do we make time within sometimes rigid time structures?

Learning requires exploration of one's identity.

- An invitation to share one's "uniqueness" and to honour our stories.
- This exploration of identity is key, as students can come to see their own agency and the power of their thoughts, beliefs, and actions.
- How is identity conceptualized?
- So important, but how to do so with sensitivity and respect?
- Great for both students and teachers to explore their identity!
- A great place to start... who am I?

Learning involves recognizing that some knowledge is sacred and only shared with permission and/or in certain situations.

- This one is quite different than in Western culture.
- This makes me think of protocols that support respectful/ responsible engagement in knowledge.
- Wondering how social media and internet distorts this – whose story is it to share?
- How do we know what is sacred?

The comments reveal that the teachers were unclear about specialized vocabulary ("Can we discuss the difference between *reflexive* and *reflective*?") and how familiar terms were being utilized ("Does *recognizing* include validating, integrating, responding etc.?"). They asked philosophical questions about the principles, such as, "I wonder how many of our students feel strong connections to more than one place, i.e., living in multiple worlds?" and "What about the consequences we can never foresee? What does that kind of learning accountability look like?" They also expressed uncertainty about the principles in practice, raising important considerations at the level of teachers ("How do we know what is sacred?"), students ("How can we support students in exploring their [potential] roles?"), and systems ("How do we make time within sometimes rigid time structures?").

Perhaps in striving for clarity in both their interpretation and application of FPPL, teachers simply asserted knowledge about principles within the Eurocentric paradigm. Consider the statement "Interesting that in our Western culture, growing old, being called an 'elder' is sometimes taken as an insult. In Aboriginal cultures, it is a status of great importance." With this statement, the participant appears to equate growing old with being an Elder, masking the Indigenous ways of knowing, being, and doing that result in high status in the process. While it is important to point out that, in the context of Indigenous communities, the term *Elder* can have many meanings and local forms of acknowledging Elders exist, some shared characteristics can be outlined.[20] Within Indigenous languages generally, *Elder* is not a title but a verb that describes the particular role these community members play.[21] Briefly stated, Elders may be recognized for their ability to draw on traditional teachings to interpret and respond to current events as well as for their collection and application of cultural knowledge and practices (e.g., language, ceremony, oral history, Indigenous stories, and local knowledge about hunting, trapping, picking, and making) for the well-being of the community (e.g., through teaching, advising, leading, and negotiating).[22] An Elder is typically a holder and practitioner of specialized and place-based Indigenous knowledge and does not necessarily serve in multiple roles (e.g., ceremonialist, historian, medicine person, or storyteller). Traditionally, the one who seeks knowledge (i.e., the prospective learner) is responsible for selecting the teacher and for determining his or her role in learning; local protocols are often engaged that establish the teacher-learner pairing and confirm and extend associated responsibilities beyond the time and place of the exchange.[23] Even in a casual consideration of some of the characteristics that Indigenous Elders share across communities it is apparent that there is a difference between simply growing old and being an Indigenous Elder.

FPPL as Undiscerning Associate

The role that FPPL plays as an undiscerning associate underscores the relationship between how the principles are positioned as a comprehensive outline of Indigenous education and how they are used in practice or to guide practice. My observations of and interviews with teachers revealed that they had come to the conclusion that if the principles defined "what counts" as Indigenous education, and if they were drawing on the principles to reconfigure their teaching approach, then they were engaging in Indigenous education and could be considered Indigenous educators. My use of the adjective *undiscerning* is in reference to what I regularly perceived as being a superficial understanding of the principles. One example of this cursory comprehension was the transposition of Eurocentric meanings onto the principles and the simultaneous suppression of Indigenous knowledge, as in the definition of *Elder*. Moreover, when teachers attempted to learn more about the knowledge systems that they perceived as underpinning the principles, their efforts commonly resulted in disregard for local knowledge and the indiscriminate combination of knowledge from different First Nations. For example, one teacher who established an

Indigenous education unit based on the principle "Learning is embedded in memory, history, and story" combined the Seven Grandfather teachings of the Anishinaabe with the *First Nations Journeys of Justice* curriculum, which draws on the stories, teachings, artwork, and knowledge of BC First Nations.[24]

The principles being seen as both an authority and undiscerning associate led to a number of new practices and behaviours: education series and courses that brought teachers together to question or reimagine learning in their classrooms, teachers' justifying their approaches to teaching and learning, administrators and teacher consultants attempting to persuade teachers that they were "already doing" Indigenous education, and teachers reimagining their classroom approaches and community relationships. As an example of the latter, when Julian set his gaze on the principle "Learning involves generational roles and responsibilities," he began to evaluate his current teachings practices against the principles aloud and expressed interest in working with students to develop an understanding of the role of Elders in the community and the leadership roles they play in the elementary school as seniors: "I would love to see us become more involved with generational roles and responsibilities ... becoming really involved in looking at the roles of Elders in our community. Roles that they can have even by Grades 5 and 6." This encounter points to the complex nature of documents; they can simultaneously reassert colonial logics and serve as a platform for establishing and developing allies that may not have engaged in Indigenous education otherwise.

A FPPL-Centred Network

Using the data fragments that included other-than-human agency (e.g., Figure 10.1), an interactive network was mapped. It centres FPPL and connects sixteen encounters that occurred during data collection and across the research sites. Figure 10.2 is an excerpt from the FPPL-centred network that illustrates the hybrid's relational properties alongside its features by linking Encounters 4, 5, and 11 for comparison with data productions above. Linking FPPL encounters, the principles' roles and associated productions, and connections among humans, hybrids, and nonhumans (see legend in left-hand corner) reveals the relational properties of this *more-than*-educational framework.

Prior maintains that when documents instead of subjects constitute the hub of network analysis, it is possible "to reticulate 'the field' as it were. As a consequence, we inevitably see that documents are far from being static and inert objects that become energized only at the behest and instigation of human actors."[25] By demonstrating that FPPL can "both hold and fashion the shape of the network,"[26] the linear, unidirectional, causal relationship that is often assumed of humans and documents is disrupted. It also displays how the knowledge-practice associated with formal Indigenous education moves within and across educational institutions as well as related (e.g., Massive Online Open Courses) and transitional (e.g., teaching practicum) spaces. For example, the school district administrators who facilitated the professional learning series session that included the what, wonder, and wow activity (Encounter 4) said they did so because they had been reacquainted with and inspired to utilize FPPL at an Indigenous education leadership conference hosted by the BC Ministry of Education.[27]

Julian attended the district-led professional learning series session where FPPL was introduced, explored, and distributed in poster form. Several weeks later, he invited me to his school to conduct an interview where the poster was acting, among additional productions, as a catalyst for developing an interdisciplinary and holistic human rights unit (Encounter 5). Three months later, I participated in a classroom observation with Julian and his students. During this observation, as a concluding lesson in the human rights unit, Julian facilitated an activity that engaged Grades 5 and 6 students in brainstorming

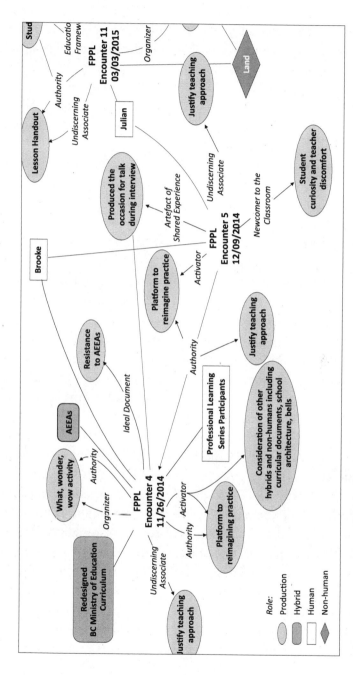

Figure 10.2 Excerpt from FPPL-centred network

examples of how they had applied each of the principles throughout the unit and closed with a related talking circle that took place outside in the schoolyard (Encounter 11).

≋⫶≋

"First Peoples Principles of Learning" is clearly shaping teachers' constructions of "what counts" as Indigenous education in British Columbia and the characteristics and practices of teachers who are involved in incorporating the principles in the curriculum. Mapping a document-centred landscape of becoming in Indigenous education also revealed examples of how the knowledge-practice associated with formal Indigenous education moves within and across educational institutions.

So long as teachers are drawing on the principles to reconfigure their teaching approach and to reimagine learning in their classrooms, they consider themselves teachers of Indigenous education. Although there is widespread confidence in this document among educators and administrators, this confidence rests on shaky ground. Teachers are not distinguishing among the principles by type, they are uncertain about how to interpret and apply them in practice, and they commonly interpret the principles from within a Eurocentric paradigm. When teachers attempt to investigate or apply the Indigenous theories that they think inform the principles, they often offer inaccurate or simplistic depictions of Indigenous knowledge. I wish to be clear that this critique of the principles by no means is intended to undercut the efforts of those involved in the First Nations Education Steering Committee or to undermine the traditional teachings that gave form to the educational framework. Rather, my goal is to draw attention to how colonial discourses and subject positions can affect the interpretation and use of documents that are intended to represent Indigenous knowledge.

My interviews with and observations of teachers in the classroom suggest that teacher educators and educational researchers will have much to gain from working in a landscape of Indigenous education that is attuned to documents.[28] I ask teacher educators who encounter the principles in their practice to consider the following. Modelling how each principle relates to learning (its purpose, characteristics, processes, protocols, and outcomes) in varied ways at multiple depths may counteract the misunderstanding that all principles have straightforward pedagogical methods. A deeper understanding of learning from the perspectives of Indigenous peoples may emerge, and preoccupation with what Deborah Britzman refers to as the acquisition of "tricks of the trade" may subside.[29] To avoid pan-Indianism or Eurocentric projections, teachers must root the principles in local knowledge and be prepared to work respectfully with local knowledgeholders. They must be aware that the principles will take divergent forms, and that learning may be conceptualized quite differently, depending on the Nation.[30] In this way, the principles will be positioned *as a starting point* from which the work begins. To initiate the work of connecting principles to local or place-based teachings, administrators and teachers might begin by locating, reviewing, and adapting support materials and by building and sustaining relationships with Indigenous Elders, cultural mentors, community members, and families.

Notes

1 Jo-Anne L. Chrona, "Background of FPPL and Current Contexts," First Peoples Principles of Learning website, https://firstpeoplesprinciplesof learning.wordpress.com/background-and-current-context/.

2 Ibid., 1.

3 Ibid.

4 For the PDF version of the principles, see First Nations Education Steering Committee (FNESC), "First Peoples Principles of Learning," http://www. fnesc.ca/wp/wp-content/uploads/2015/09/PUB-LFP-POSTER-Principles-of -Learning-First-Peoples-poster-11x17.pdf.

5 See Brooke Madden, "(Un)becoming Teacher of School-Based Aboriginal Education: Early Career Teachers, Teacher Identity, and Aboriginal

Education across Institutions" (PhD diss., University of British Columbia, 2016).

6 Keeping with usage in this volume, the term *Indigenous* is used instead of *Aboriginal*, unless specific reference is being made to legal and political categories imposed by the Canadian government, which defines *Aboriginal peoples* as the Indian, Métis, and Inuit peoples in Canada. *First Peoples*, as used in these documents, includes First Nations, Inuit, and Métis.

7 After school hours, I visited a fifth teacher's classroom, where she gave me a tour and used examples of students' work to describe and reflect on a variety of lessons she had designed. Two part-time teacher participants detailed the lessons or units they had developed by sharing teaching plans, curricular documents, student handouts, resources, photos, feedback forms, and modes of assessment.

8 Lindsay Prior, "Repositioning Documents in Social Research," *Sociology* 42, 5 (2008): 821–36.

9 British Columbia Ministry of Education (BCME), *English 10 and English 11 First Peoples: Curriculum 2010*, http://www.bced.gov.bc.ca/irp/pdfs/english_language_arts/2010efp1011.pdf; Richmond School District 38, *Aboriginal Education Enhancement Agreement: Our Voices, Our Visions*, 2009, https://www2.gov.bc.ca/assets/gov/education/administration/kindergarten-to-grade-12/aboriginal-education/enhancement-agreements/framework/sd38.pdf; and *Teaching for Indigenous Education*, http://www.indigenous education.educ.ubc.ca/.

10 See David Newhouse, "Ganigonhi:oh: The Good Mind Meets the Academy," *Canadian Journal of Native Education* 31, 1 (2008): 184–97; and Katherine Sanford, Lorna Williams, Tim Hopper, and Catherine McGregor, "Indigenous Principles Informing Teacher Education: What We Have Learned," *Education* 18, 2 (2012): 18–34.

11 Treaty Relations Commission of Manitoba, *Treaty Education Initiative*, http://www.trcm.ca/treaty-education-initiative/; and Ontario Ministry of Education, *First Nation, Métis, and Inuit Education Policy Framework 2007*, http://www.edu.gov.on.ca/eng/aboriginal/fnmiFramework.pdf.

12 As defined by the British Columbia Ministry of Education, an Aboriginal Education Enhancement Agreement (AEEA) "is a working agreement between a school district, all local Aboriginal communities, and the Ministry of Education designed to enhance the educational achievement of Aboriginal students." They often provide a framework that details how the school district will work to meet the needs and support the priorities of local Indigenous students and communities.

13 BCME, "First Peoples Principles of Learning," http://www2.gov.bc.ca/assets/gov/education/kindergarten-to-grade-12/teach/teaching-tools/aboriginal-education/principles_of_learning.pdf.

14 BCME, "Curriculum Redesign 2015: Frequently Asked Questions," http://www.sd22.bc.ca/Programs/curriculum/Documents/faq.pdf.

15 Ibid., 4.

16 Prior, "Repositioning Documents in Social Research," 821–36.

17 Ibid., 826.

18 Ibid., 830.

19 Marc Higgins, Brooke Madden, Marie-France Bérard, Elsa Lenz Kothe, and Susan Nordstrom, "De/signing Research in Education: Patchwork(ing) Methodologies with Theory," *Educational Studies* 43, 1 (2017): 16.

20 S.M. Stiegelbauer, "What Is an Elder? What Do Elders Do? First Nation Elders as Teachers in Culture-Based Urban Organizations," *Canadian Journal of Native Studies* 16, 1 (1996): 37–66.

21 Council on Aboriginal Initiatives, University of Alberta, "Elder's Protocol and Guidelines," *Aboriginal Policy Studies* 2, 1 (2012): 132–74, https://ejournals.library.ualberta.ca/index.php/aps/article/view/17707/pdf.

22 Leilani Holmes, "Heart Knowledge, Blood Memory, and the Voice of the Land: Implications for Research among Hawaiian Elders," in *Indigenous Knowledges in Global Contexts: Multiple Readings of Our World*, ed. George J. Sefa Dei, Budd L. Hall, and Dorothy G. Rosenberg (Toronto: University of Toronto Press, 2000), 37–53; *First Nations Pedagogy Online*, "Elders," http://firstnationspedagogy.ca/elders.html; and Shawn Wilson, *Gwich'in Native Elders: Not Just Knowledge, but a Way of Looking at the World* (Fairbanks: Alaska Native Knowledge Network, 1994), http://ankn.uaf.edu/publications/Books/Gwich%27in_Native_Elders.pdf.

23 Jo-ann Archibald, *Indigenous Storywork: Educating the Heart, Mind, Body, and Spirit* (Vancouver: UBC Press, 2008); and Cora Weber-Pillwax, "Indigenous Knowledge Systems" (lecture conducted as part of "EDU 211: Aboriginal Education and the Context for Professional Engagement," University of Alberta, Edmonton, December 2014 and December 2016).

24 Law Courts Education Society of British Columbia, *First Nations Journeys of Justice* (Vancouver: Law Courts Education Society, 1994).

25 Prior, "Repositioning Documents in Social Research," 832.

26 Ibid.

27 To the best of my understanding, the school district administrators were introduced to FPPL on multiple occasions, though the Indigenous education leadership conference hosted by the BC Ministry of Education was the only one referenced in Encounter 4.

28 A growing body of research is enhancing our knowledge of the role of documents in Indigenous education. See, for example, Jesse Butler, "The Gap between Text and Context: An Analysis of Ontario's Indigenous Education Policy," *Education* 21, 2 (2015): 26–48; Lorenzo Cherubini, "An Analysis of Ontario Aboriginal Education Policy: Critical and Interpretive

Perspectives," *McGill Journal of Education* 45, 1 (2010): 9–26; Lorenzo Cherubini, "Postsecondary Aboriginal Educational Policy in Ontario: Policy and Practical Implications," *Aboriginal Policy Studies* 2, 1 (2012): 42–55; Lorenzo Cherubini and John Hodson, "Ontario Ministry of Education Policy and Aboriginal Learners' Epistemologies: A Fundamental Disconnect," *Canadian Journal of Educational Administration and Policy* 79 (2008): 1–33; Jan Hare, "First Nations Education Policy in Canada: Building Capacity for Change and Control," in *Multicultural Education Policies in Canada and the US*, ed. Reva Joshee and Lauri Johnson (Vancouver: UBC Press, 2007), 51–68; Julie Kaomea, "A Curriculum of Aloha? Colonialism and Tourism in Hawaii's Elementary Textbooks," *Curriculum Inquiry* 30, 3 (2000): 319–44; Julie Kaomea, "Reading Erasures and Making the Familiar Strange: Defamiliarizing Methods for Research in Formerly Colonized and Historically Oppressed Communities," *Educational Researcher* 32, 2 (2003): 14–23; and Kevin White, Jozsef Budai, Daniel Mathew, Mary Rickson Deighan, and Harteg Gill, "Educators' Perspectives about a Public School District's Aboriginal Education Enhancement Agreement in British Columbia," *Canadian Journal of Native Education* 35, 1 (2012): 42–60.

29 Deborah Britzman, *Practice Makes Practice: A Critical Study of Learning to Teach*, rev. ed. (New York: SUNY Press, 2003).

30 I recognize that some Nations' and communities' knowledge and practices associated with teaching and learning may not be available to teachers. In this case, I advocate for a placed understanding of principles that connects deeply with one or commensurate sources.

11

THE ALBERTA MÉTIS EDUCATION COUNCIL

Realizing Self-Determination in Education

Yvonne Poitras Pratt and Solange Lalonde

As educators of Métis ancestry who have both held leadership roles in advancing the self-determining goals of Métis people through education, with the support of the Métis Nation of Alberta and its affiliate, Rupertsland Institute, we represent wayfinders in the emerging realm of Métis education. In 2016, the Alberta Métis Education Council was created as an act of self-determination to assert the collective voice of Métis peoples in educational programming.[1] Composed of a group of Métis with professional backgrounds in education, the council, with its collective expertise, serves as a standing committee and advisory body to Rupertsland Institute, Métis Centre of Excellence, whose members are representative of Métis perspectives across Alberta. As an affiliate of the Métis Nation of Alberta, Rupertsland Institute has a mandate to deliver programs and services in education, training, and research. One of the key priorities identified by the Métis Nation of Alberta is "to establish, promote and support initiatives that will improve the quality of life of Métis people."[2] As we see it, the creation story of the Alberta Métis Education Council exemplifies how the quality of life for Métis can be improved through education thereby demonstrating how self-determination can be achieved through working together on a nation-to-nation basis. With the endorsement and support of the Rupertsland Institute Board of Governors and the Métis Nation of Alberta political leadership, our council moves forward on a self-determining initiative in the vital realm of education to realize the collective interests of our nation.

In seeking to gain a foothold in the influential realm of education – by, with, and for Métis peoples – the Alberta Métis Education Council emerged at an opportune moment in history. Recent court decisions, such as *Daniels v Canada* (2016), and Canada's recent endorsement of the *United Nations Declaration on the Rights of Indigenous Peoples* (UNDRIP) have affirmed the inherent rights of the Métis to educational self-determination.[3] Articles 14.1 and 15.1 of UNDRIP state the following:

> *Article 14.1:* Indigenous peoples have the right to establish and control their educational systems and institutions providing education in their own languages, in a manner appropriate to their cultural methods of teaching and learning ...

> *Article 15.1:* Indigenous peoples have the right to the dignity and diversity of their cultures, traditions, histories and aspirations which shall be appropriately reflected in education and public information.[4]

In addition, the commissioners leading the Truth and Reconciliation Commission of Canada emphasized the appropriateness of UNDRIP as an important "framework for reconciliation in Canada."[5] The recognition of the United Nations' internationally sanctioned document provides the requisite principles, norms, and standards to advance improved relations between Indigenous and non-Indigenous peoples and thereby advances the vital work of reconciliation. Importantly, UNDRIP also provides us with a guiding framework to situate the ethical work of self-determination in education.

In navigating our journey to self-determination, we are conscious that mainstream education has swept many Métis people through a colonial landscape littered with racist or biased schooling experiences. As with any fast-moving current, mainstream education cut a deep path in the colonial landscape that we now call Canada, moving learners along a predetermined route, with little regard for their former knowledge traditions. In recognizing the impact of a colonial history on our communities, we understand that the confluence where Indigenous and non-Indigenous knowledge traditions meet is a place of turbulence, yet this meeting place is also a place of great possibilities.[6] In this place of hope, we see collaboration and ethical relationships as essential elements in the realization of our future potential.

As we gather together to envision and realize this work, we find further inspiration in the growing momentum of Indigenous peoples who are finding ways to reclaim the education of their children. From a global perspective, one of the most striking examples of this reclamation in education is that of the Māori people of New Zealand, who have created Kaupapa Māori as a way to restructure colonial relationships into a renewed relationship of autonomous partners working in collaboration. As Russell Bishop asserts, the goal of self-determination is not one of separation or even distancing from national interests; rather, the goal is to invite an ongoing dialogue with political actors in which, "despite self-determination meaning the right to determine one's own destiny, to define what that destiny will be, and to define and pursue means of attaining that destiny, there is a clear understanding ... that such autonomy is relative, not absolute, that it is self-determination *in relation to others.*"[7]

In the Canadian context, Indigenous education scholar Dwayne Donald refers to an ethical imperative to realize a relational space where Indigenous peoples have the right to represent their perspectives.[8] Up until this point, the provincial government has taken the lead in defining and articulating Métis perspectives and content. We believe that, under the auspices of UNDRIP and in response to the Truth and Reconciliation Commission of Canada, Métis peoples hold an inherent right to have resources that appropriately reflect Métis perspectives and content in educational programming and professional learning.

On July 9, 2015, the Alberta Government asserted: "We [are] introducing mandatory education for all our students in the histories and cultures of Indigenous people, including residential schools ... Alberta is also the only province to have established Métis governments and Métis lands."[9] In keeping with this provincial mandate, we maintain that content on Métis ways of knowing, being, and doing is best inspired and informed by the wisdom and guidance of Métis community members, educators, and leaders who bring their lived experiences and cultural expertise to this learning area.

A critical aspect of reconciling productive relationships is addressing the lack of education, or miseducation, concerning Métis peoples and their unique history and culture.[10] As history reveals, the legacy of colonization has thrown a deep shadow over much of our educational timeline as our diverse stories slip in and out of federal and provincial currents. In coming to know the vacillating realities within a Métis context, those who have influence over the intent and design of policy and planning are asked to carefully consider and reflect on the following questions: Whose story is this, and whose voice is missing? We explore these questions in tandem with the belief that good relations between Indigenous and non-Indigenous citizens will only be accomplished through a truly inclusive model of education – one that informs all citizens of Canada's colonial history and its impact on the Métis, from the time of first contact through to the present day, in the realm of education.

Self-Determination as an Inherent Indigenous Right

In the wake of several significant sociopolitical transitions, we assert our right for self-determination in education by calling on governments to honour the articles of UNDRIP and the TRC's calls to action, which means creating space for a collective Métis voice.[11] In the present moment, our quest for self-determination takes place in a political context that situates the Métis perspective within education as a largely unexplored realm, with the exception of a few rare studies.[12] An intrepid few, including Adam Gaudry and Robert Hancock, as well as John Dorion and Kwan Yang, have explored the Métis experience in the

Yvonne Poitras Pratt and Solange Lalonde

postsecondary context.[13] This void exists within a complex historical, social, and political landscape. In retracing our colonial history, it is important to note the disadvantaged position that the Métis continue to face, as detailed within the *Daniels* decision:

> The first declaration should be granted: Métis and non-status Indians are "Indians" under s. 91(24) ... A declaration can only be granted if it will have practical utility, that is, if it will settle a "live controversy" between the parties. The first declaration, whether non-status Indians and Métis are "Indians" under s. 91(24), would have enormous practical utility for these two groups who have found themselves having to rely more on noblesse oblige than on what is obliged by the Constitution. A declaration would guarantee both certainty and accountability. Both federal and provincial governments have, alternately, denied having legislative authority over non-status Indians and Métis. This results in these Indigenous communities being in a jurisdictional wasteland with significant and obvious disadvantaging consequences. While finding Métis and non-status Indians to be "Indians" under s. 91(24) does not create a duty to legislate, it has the undeniably salutary benefit of ending a jurisdictional tug-of-war.[14]

Despite the inclusion of the Métis in section 35 of the Constitution Act, 1982, as one of Canada's three groups of Indigenous peoples, the nation-to-nation relationship entrenched in the "honour of the Crown" has largely ignored the Métis. Thomas Isaac, in his role as special representative to the minister of Indigenous and northern affairs on reconciliation with Métis, maintains: "Métis have largely been forgotten until recent years in the [Canadian] national narrative as distinct rights-bearing Aboriginal peoples."[15] Noting a high variability in how provinces and territories have taken up Métis rights, Isaac makes it clear that Métis "history and culture as an Indigenous peoples was either not known or [is] misunderstood generally when dealing with Canada and the applicable provinces."[16] This lack of clarity, or awareness, has meant the Métis have been treated primarily as an "after-thought."[17] In sum, this national report offers a refreshing perspective, because it upholds the self-determining stance of the Métis in forging the shape and design of future educational programming.

We maintain that Métis peoples must be respectfully recognized, acknowledged, and included within educational programming and initiatives, not only as a response to the Truth and Reconciliation Commission but also in consideration of our positioning as distinct rights-bearing Aboriginal people. In seeking a way forward, we are prompted to ask: How do we bring knowledge of the unique issues that surround the Métis to the broader Canadian public? More specifically, how might we serve the unique educational needs of the Métis?

Making a Case for Inclusion and Parity

With the recent *Daniels* decision asserting a resolution of jurisdictional matters, the Métis have emerged from their largely marginalized position in Canadian society. As one of the three constitutionally recognized Indigenous groups in Canada, the Métis have long waited for rights recognition.[18] According to the Indigenous and Northern Affairs Canada website, the federal government is working "with our many different partners in communities across Canada to build a future in which First Nations, Inuit, Métis and northern communities are healthy, safe, self-sufficient and prosperous places in which to live."[19] The Métis have had varying levels of support from the federal or provincial governments over the years, as each government has held that the other holds jurisdiction and primary responsibility for the education of the Métis.[20] If we are to make headway as First Peoples, we must collectively imagine and realize, as Dwayne Donald urges, a "way to hold together the ambiguous, layered, complex, and conflictual character of Aboriginal and Canadian relations without the need to deny, assimilate, hybridize, or conclude."[21] In this, we see an ethical space opening for Métis content and perspectives within education.[22]

Using self-determination as our compass, we look to the contributions of both academics and knowledge-keepers to help set the direction for our work. As an early signpost in our travels, we acknowledge participatory action research as advancing critical research approaches that intentionally level a hierarchical model of knowledge production in an effort to confront hegemonic interests and reveal power differentials. Importantly, the principles espoused in this approach support community-based knowledge and local experts.[23] Critical methodologies such as participatory action research have empowered what are typically marginalized communities to take on research activities of their own, often in partnership with academics.[24] Over the years, this type of work has inspired Indigenous academics to assert and articulate a body of decolonizing research that serves to give back to our communities through the privilege of our formal academic positions.[25]

Within an Indigenous context, self-determination is identified as one of the primary research objectives within decolonizing efforts.[26] In our view, decolonization is an act that serves as a gateway to the work of self-determination. Within the particular context of Métis education, the need for decolonization applies equally to those of Indigenous and non-Indigenous backgrounds, and for those of us who hail from diverse ancestral backgrounds. Eric Ritskes, a scholar who specializes in decolonizing efforts, explains: "We're all implicated in and through colonialism and how we decolonize is connected to how exactly we are implicated."[27] As tributaries that arise from diverse contexts, the scholarly streams of decolonizing and Indigenizing can commingle. Educators Joe Kincheloe and Shirley Steinberg assert an important message for well-intentioned educators: "The purpose of Indigenous education and the production of Indigenous knowledge does not involve 'saving' Indigenous people but helping construct conditions that allow for Indigenous self-sufficiency."[28] In embarking on this journey, we follow the lead of Ritskes, who asserts that decolonization is a journey towards an unknown destination, one that holds both risks and responsibilities and in which "there are many views of decolonization, often contrasting and competing." However, they all have "one thing is common: *the belief that through action, change can occur.*"[29] It is in this spirit of inclusivity and social change that we seek social equity and justice on par with our Indigenous kin.

On our complex voyage of self-determination, it is important that we seek Métis-specific knowledge traditions and models to track our way forward. This mapping is a daunting task as Métis-specific literature within education is both scant and seemingly diverse in its various articulations.[30] Two former national initiatives, including the Canadian Council on Learning's Métis Holistic Lifelong Learning Model and the work undertaken by the Métis Centre of the National Aboriginal Health Organization, help to outline guiding ethical principles for Métis-specific research.[31] Of note, the publication *In the Words of Our Ancestors: Métis Health and Healing* attests to a shared worldview among diverse Métis life stories. This now defunct arm of the National Aboriginal Health Organization notes: "During early analyses, the diverse group of Elders, from every part of the Métis homeland, had very distinct and divergent views ... [However] a great deal of the information shared between the Elders and the Métis Centre was based on a series of similar Métis principles."[32] Some of the shared values identified across diverse origins are respect, collectivism, collaboration, and spirituality. In moving towards the goal of self-determination in education, we hold steadfast to these values as guiding principles.

Images can be a powerful means of conveying the complex nature of interconnectedness. A decade ago, the Canadian Council on Learning identified the four primary sources of knowledge (and knowing) as clusters within the symbolic form of a living tree in its "Métis Holistic Lifelong Learning Model": (1) self; (2) people; (3) land; and (4) languages and traditions (see Figure 11.1).[33] This national initiative, meant to effect meaningful change within Indigenous education, used the following to explain how the Métis are positioned:

Yvonne Poitras Pratt and Solange Lalonde

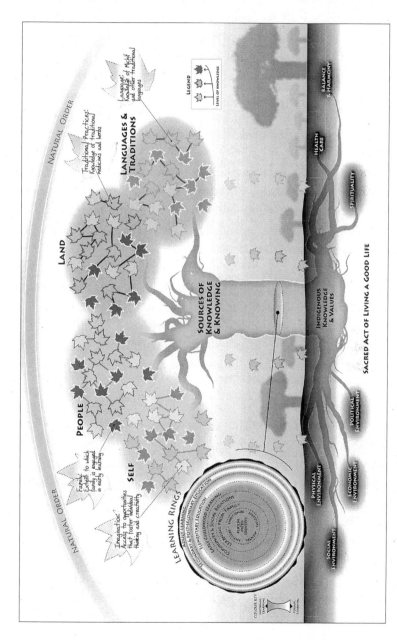

Figure II.I The Canadian Council of Learning's Métis holistic life-long learning model. | Courtesy of the Gabriel Dumont Institute.

The integration of Western and Métis learning approaches is understood, and reflects the Métis history of union between two cultures, European and Aboriginal. The iconic image of the red Métis sash ... conveys this understanding of worlds co-joined. As an integral part of Métis cultural celebrations, the sash represents connectedness. It symbolizes how Métis identity, language, culture, history and tradition are one and that the Métis vision for education is woven in.[34]

The manifestations inherent in the shared "space of engagement" represent the interconnectedness of our work with that of provincial leaders.[35] In conceptualizing what this space looks like, Sandy Grande asks us to reinvent ourselves not only according to who we are, but also in view of the "materiality of social life and power relations."[36] Aligned with the Māori vision of self-determination as set out by Bishop, the concept of interconnectedness is requisite as we acknowledge that the majority of Métis students are enrolled in provincially run schools across Alberta. The Alberta education system currently ranks among the top five education systems around the world.[37] Given the strengths of our provincial education system, collaborating with educational leaders across our province will further improve the systemic capacity of educators to provide Métis education for all students.

White-Water Rafting within Métis Education

In mapping out a journey towards self-determination, we understand that the uncharted nature of the work can be perceived as risky or even dangerous. In this shared work, the ability to acknowledge that we are all learners, even while in leadership roles, is essential to moving forward. As Blackfoot Elder Casey Eaglespeaker reminded audience members at a large-scale education gathering in Calgary in 2014, "You don't know what you don't know."[38] His message echoes that of educational reform expert Santiago Rincón-Gallardo, who recently counselled system leaders to be *wisely aware* that learning is everyone's work and to make learning a visible practice.[39] By its very

Yvonne Poitras Pratt and Solange Lalonde

nature, educational reform creates turbulence, yet these are not un-familiar waters to us as we reflect on the policies and programming we have traversed and consider those areas that have brought a measure of challenge along the way.

Previously, in the realm of Indigenous education, the goal has been to close the achievement gap between self-identified First Nations, Métis, and Inuit students and all other students in the province. The discourse around the notion of a gap includes alarming statistics around low Indigenous student graduation rates and high dropout rates. For decades, measuring the gap has not achieved the objective of closing the gap. We argue, along with a growing group of educational leaders, that to make meaningful and lasting change, practising teachers and leaders must acknowledge their own gaps in knowledge when it comes to Indigenous peoples and perspectives.[40] The Alberta Education 2017–20 business plan, in which the focus has shifted from the education gap to systemic capacity and accountability, is seen as a promising move in this direction.[41]

Over the years, the Métis have faced numerous challenges that prevent meaningful participation in education, including vagueness surrounding jurisdictional responsibility by either federal or provincial authorities, structural constraints within Métis political organizations, and a lack of mainstream understanding, misunderstandings, or conflation with other Indigenous groups. Across the Métis homeland, which extends from Ontario westward to British Columbia, a 2014 inquiry into education, employment, and training programs revealed that "political jurisdictional realities continue to reproduce an unfair playing field for Métis in comparison to First Nations ... Provincial policies with respect to the Métis remain sectorial, piece-meal and usually pan-Aboriginal. In this context, policies tend to favour First Nations issues and agendas."[42]

Complicating matters even further, this same study found that previous governments, and policy holders in ministries outside of education, were often "more focused on treating the Métis, particularly the off-Settlement Métis, like any other Albertan."[43] The eight

Métis settlements situated in the northern regions of Alberta are a unique phenomenon in that they represent the only legislated, dedicated lands set aside for Métis across Canada.[44] In spite of this important distinction, the settlements are home to only a small percentage of the Métis population.[45] Brenda Macdougall and Nicole St-Onge's culturally driven and innovative concept of a kinscape is useful for explaining why this situation is untenable.[46] In many cases, our Métis family connections stem from, and extend to, the settlements, thereby making the tendency of policy actors to treat our communities differentially, and at cross-purposes with one another, a grievous practice. Through Rupertsland Institute's relationship with the Ministry of Education, the narrative is shifting to include more dialogue on how continued engagement with the collective Métis voice can enhance the design and implementation of future educational policy.

Wayfinding and Pathmaking: Portaging Forward

Along any learning journey, moving forward comes from a desire to make meaning from our experiences and in seeking understanding through reflection. In this process of way finding, there is a real opportunity to collect learning along the way. Pathmaking becomes a process of sharing this learning, leaving pebbles of information along the way as markers to help others find their way towards their own understanding.[47] The narrative account that follows offers insights gained along our journey.

In considering how to support educators and learners, we need to ensure that all oars are in the water, meaning that our efforts have to support educator training programs in postsecondary institutions as well as practising educators in our province. There needs to be a wholistic approach composed of professional supports for educators from diverse fields, including teachers, principals, superintendents, social workers, educational assistants, school psychologists, and postsecondary faculty, and within this approach, the Métis story must be told from a Métis perspective.[48] Rupertsland Institute, in keeping with its education mandate, is operating at the confluence of provincial ministries of education and advanced education to provide professional learning opportunities through research-informed practices. The intent behind the instructional design and delivery of these programs is to purposefully create opportunities for rich dialogue, deep learning, and decolonizing pedagogies.

Recognizing the moment as both timely and appropriate, Rupertsland Institute's decision in 2016 to organize and form the Alberta Métis Education Council was an indication that Indigenous groups are forging paths to self-determination within education. The following is an excerpt from the Rupertsland Institute website:

> As a volunteer advisory body to Rupertsland Institute, the Alberta Métis Education Council is a standing committee of Rupertsland Institute. AMEC focuses on key strategies, policies and actions that will enhance Métis education in the K-12 system while promoting the knowledge of Métis culture, language and history to Alberta education in its pursuit of reconciliation with Indigenous peoples.[49]

As new professional practice standards are advanced and debated, these policy directions have implications for educators across Alberta. The Métis people seek not only to have their voices heard in this dialogue but to also assert a position of self-determination, as articulated in our mission statement: "To implement transformational education through Métis research, collaboration, and expertise." Guiding our work are the following four strategic objectives that were developed using the Relational Model for Teaching and Learning:[50]

1 *Métis research-informed practice:* To design educational initiatives that reflect the collective Métis voice and perspectives through research-informed practice.
2 *Building capacity:* To build capacity to preserve, protect, and promote the interests of Métis people to achieve a quality education that reflects community values.

3 *Curriculum development:* To create educational resources and supports to evaluate and change educational program delivery and services.

4 *Collaboration:* To develop strategic partnerships leading to collaborative educational initiatives where the Métis community is actively engaged in educational programming.

In honouring our collective orientation, Rupertsland Institute and the Alberta Métis Education Council believe that a province-wide community engagement process is essential to the work of establishing and defining foundational knowledge of the Métis in Alberta. However, we also realize that our current capacity is extremely limited to undertake the scope of this work. With a large proportion of Métis learners currently enrolled in provincial schools, we acknowledge the need for meaningful engagement with the Government of Alberta on issues related to education. It is an opportune time for policymakers and system leaders to acknowledge and support this collective work, thereby aligning their practices with the principles of UNDRIP and the Truth and Reconciliation Commission.

A Collective Journey in Self-Determination

Given that Alberta is home to one of the largest provincial populations of Métis people across Canada, the Alberta Métis Education Council seeks to assert our rightful place in spaces of decision making around Métis interests.[51] The historical narrative of the Métis represents one of the darker chapters in Canada's history.[52] This history has affected how the Métis have experienced schooling and explains why the Métis are insistent in reclaiming their right to tell their stories. As we see it, the dominant version of the colonial past has robbed us of learning about our own histories and contributions from our own voice and fellow community members.

Looking back, community stories of Métis schooling reveal a diverse array of experiences ranging across the public, separate, and residential school systems.[53] This diversity is reflective of Métis stories in general, yet the mainstream tendency is to trap us in a single story.[54] Not only does this practice flatten our stories and who we are as a people, it also hides our truths. The final report of the Truth and Reconciliation Commission of Canada reveals that many Métis families faced limited choices for the schooling of their children because provincial or territorial governments made scant, if any, concessions for the education of their children. The report maintains that provincial and territorial governments "did not ensure that there were schools in Métis communities, or work to see that Métis children were admitted and welcomed into the general public school system. In some cases, Métis parents who wished to see their children educated in schools had no option but to try to have them accepted into a residential school."[55] In other cases, communities demonstrated strong initiative by building schools in their own communities.[56] For instance, in the mid-1940s, community members from Fishing Lake travelled miles to the colony's townsite to help cut trees, make lumber, and build their own school. These stories of Métis remembrance are increasingly being revealed through the work of Métis scholars working alongside community members. In telling our own stories from our own perspectives, these lived experiences reveal a broader perspective around the impact of education in Métis lives.[57]

As a largely unknown chapter in Canadian history, the Métis experience in residential schools reflects the original intent of the federal government to recruit Indigenous children of Status, non-Status, "half-breed," or Métis ancestry into church-run boarding schools.[58] In the minds of federal government bureaucrats, the Métis represented "members of the 'dangerous classes' whom the residential schools were intended to civilize and assimilate."[59] As such, Métis children were intermittently included in government policies on residential schooling.[60] At the same time, the federal government was concerned that deliberate recruitment practices would eventually translate into jurisdictional responsibility for the Métis, and in light of this eventuality, the "federal government position on the matter was constantly shifting."[61] Complicating this shifting policy terrain was a belief held by some government officials that the Métis were "already regarded as 'civilized' enough."[62] This highly subjective and individualized perception of acculturation by policy-makers, based on factors of appearance, kinship ties, and community recognition, played out in both policy arenas and on the school grounds. Stories of residential schooling reveal that Métis children were treated differently than other children, either worse or better, based on assumptions held by those in charge.[63] This differential treatment translated into their peers seeing them as "different," which had its own repercussions. Expanding outwards, the commission explains that, "despite their perceived constitutional responsibility, provincial and territorial governments were reluctant to provide services to Métis people."[64] Métis children were both recruited into and excluded from residential schooling on an irregular and erratic basis.

Looking back, the legacy of the forgotten Métis is that the collective voice of the Métis has traditionally been excluded, ignored, or not heard by policy-makers. The Knowledge Synthesis study *Painting a Picture of the Métis Homeland,* funded by the Social Sciences and Humanities Research Council of Canada, found that there is often only one staff person dedicated to the provincial Métis education portfolio, as compared to hundreds of First Nation members in similar roles.[65] As a result, power holders often bring in someone who self-identifies as Métis to represent the collective Métis voice within the important work of curriculum development. While the practice may be based in good intentions, those in positions of power have to understand the danger of bypassing a collective perspective for the sake of expediency and efficiency. We see a new way for future generations to experience their education by intentionally involving the collective Métis voice.

Through innovative and engaging professional learning opportunities, and through regional community engagement sessions, we can educate ourselves and also create resources that will support educating others within the educational community. In keeping with the

Yvonne Poitras Pratt and Solange Lalonde

Figure 11.2 The Alberta Métis Education Council's logo represents the Métis Nation's past, present, and future vision for education. | Original artwork commissioned from Métis visual artist Stephen Gladue by the Rupertsland Institute in 2017.

spirit of reconciliation, now is the time to take these ideas and innovations, combined with appropriate funding, to breathe life into policies that allow ideas to become actions. In this way, we can continue to build a strong collective Métis Nation and a foundation for future generations.

We need to learn together – with and from one another – so we can take a leadership role as a collective group and establish ourselves as the authority on our own culture. We have the agency and the determination to establish our own resources, and we have the right to have these resources used in educational programming for the benefit of all students and educators. It is no longer acceptable to have government officials or outside "experts" writing our stories in the curriculum and the textbooks. We have the expertise within the Alberta Métis Education Council, as well as within senior management at the Rupertsland Institute, to guide the work and to take the lead.

The Alberta Métis Education Council's logo exemplifies our past, present, and future vision for education (see Figure 11.2). We signify this part of our journey with a quote from Willie Ermine that is appropriate for the days ahead: "The new partnership model of the ethical space, in a cooperative spirit between Indigenous peoples and Western institutions, will create new currents of thought that flow in different directions of legal discourse and overrun the archaic ways of interaction."[66] The Métis voyage of self-determination continues in good faith.

Notes

The views expressed in this chapter are those of the authors and are not necessarily the views of Rupertsland Institute or its officials.

1 The naming conventions used here reflect the current practice of using the term *Indigenous peoples* to refer to the original occupants of lands around the world. The use of the term *Aboriginal* aligns with the recognition of First Nations, Métis, and Inuit peoples in the Constitution Act, 1982. For a national definition of *Métis*, see the Métis National Council's website. We also recognize the right of specific nations, and peoples, to be named according to their own conventions and acknowledge that diverse life experiences may mean that one term is preferred to another by individuals. In this, we honour the right of First Peoples to self-identify as they wish.

2 "Mission Statement," Métis Nation of Alberta, http://albertametis.com/about/mission-statement/.

3 *Daniels v Canada (Indian Affairs and Northern Development)*, 2016 SCC 12, [2016] 1 SCR 99 [*Daniels*]; and United Nations, *United Nations Declaration on the Rights of Indigenous Peoples*, March 2008, http://www.un.org/esa/socdev/unpfii/documents/DRIPS_en.pdf.

4 United Nations, *Declaration on the Rights of Indigenous Peoples*, 7.

5 Truth and Reconciliation Commission of Canada (TRC), *Final Report of the Truth and Reconciliation Commission of Canada*, vol. 1, *Summary: Honouring the Truth, Reconciling for the Future* (Toronto: Lorimer, 2015), 21.

6 Dwayne Donald, "Forts, Curriculum, and Indigenous Métissage: Imagining Decolonization of Aboriginal-Canadian Relations in Educational Contexts," *First Nations Perspectives* 2, 1 (2009): 1–24.

7 Russell Bishop, "Te Kotahitanga: Kaupapa Māori in Mainstream Classrooms," in *Handbook of Critical and Indigenous Methodologies*, ed. Norman K. Denzin, Yvonna S. Lincoln, and Linda Tuhiwai Smith (Thousand Oaks, CA: SAGE, 2008), 440, emphasis added.

8 Donald, "Forts, Curriculum, and Indigenous Métissage."

9 Alberta Education, "Ministers on Task to Implement the Objectives of UN Declaration on Indigenous Rights," press release, July 9, 2015, https://www.

alberta.ca/release.cfm?xID=3829383ECC178-FCCA-F36A-8D2EC714192
D76A2.

10 Emma LaRoque, *Defeathering the Indian* (Agincourt, ON: Book Society of Canada, 1975), and *When the Other Is Me: Native Resistance Discourse, 1850–1990* (Winnipeg: University of Manitoba Press, 2010).

11 TRC, *Truth and Reconciliation Commission of Canada: Calls to Action,* 2012, http://nctr.ca/assets/reports/Calls_to_Action_English2.pdf.

12 Jonathan Anuik, "'In from the Margins': Government of Saskatchewan Policies to Support Métis Learning, 1969–1979," *Journal of Native Education* 32 (2010): 83–99; Jonathan Anuik and Laura-Lee Bellehumeur-Kearns, "Métis Student Self-Identification in Ontario's K–12 Schools: Education Policy and Parents, Families, and Communities," *Canadian Journal of Educational Administration and Policy* 153 (2014), https://journalhosting. ucalgary.ca/index.php/cjeap/article/view/42860/30717; Larry Chartrand, Tricia Logan, and Judy Daniels, *Métis History and Experience and Residential Schools in Canada* (Ottawa: Aboriginal Healing Foundation, 2006); and Kristine J. Friesen, "An Exploration of the Perceived Impact of Selected Factors Related to Successful Métis Education: The Voices of Métis Graduates of a Rural Manitoba High School" (master's thesis, University of Manitoba, 2012).

13 Adam Gaudry and Robert L.A. Hancock, "Decolonizing Métis Pedagogies in Post-Secondary Settings," *Canadian Journal of Native Education* 35, 1 (2012): 7–22; and John Dorion and Kwan R. Yang, "Métis Post-Secondary Education: A Case Study of the Gabriel Dumont Institute," in *Aboriginal Education: Fulfilling the Promise,* ed. Marlene Brant Castellano, Lynne Davis, and Louise Lahache (Vancouver: UBC Press, 2000), 176–89.

14 *Daniels,* paras. 4 and 5.

15 Thomas Isaac, *A Matter of National and Constitutional Import: Report of the Minister's Special Representative on Reconciliation with Métis: Section 35, Métis Rights and the Manitoba Métis Federation Decision* (Ottawa: Minister of Indigenous and Northern Affairs, 2016), 3.

16 Ibid., 24.

17 Ibid., 25.

18 Isaac, *A Matter of National and Constitutional Import*; and John Weinstein, *Quiet Revolution West: The Rebirth of Métis Nationalism* (Calgary: Fifth House, 2007).

19 Indigenous and Northern Affairs Canada, "Frequently Asked Questions," 6, https://www.aadnc-aandc.gc.ca/eng/1334340118426/1334340187423.

20 Chartrand, Logan, and Daniels, *Métis History and Experience*; Isaac, *A Matter of National and Constitutional Import*; and Joe Sawchuk, *The Dynamics of Native Politics: The Alberta Métis Experience* (Saskatoon: Purich, 1998).

21 Donald, "Forts, Curriculum, and Indigenous Métissage," 9.

22 Willie Ermine, "The Ethical Space of Engagement," *Indigenous Law Journal* 6, 1 (2007): 193–203, http://www.sfu.ca/iirp/documents/Ermine 2007.pdf.

23 Paulo Freire, *Pedagogy of the Oppressed* (New York: Seabury Press, 1970); Budd Hall, "Introduction," in *Voices of Change: Participatory Research in the United States and Canada,* ed. Peter Park, Mary Brydon-Miller, Budd Hall, and Ted Jackson (Toronto: OISE Press, 1993), xiii–xxii; Stephen Kemmis and Robin McTaggart, "Participatory Action Research," in *Handbook of Qualitative Research,* 2nd ed., ed. Norman K. Denzin and Yvonna S. Lincoln (Thousand Oaks, CA: SAGE, 2000), 567–605; and Peter Park, "What Is Participatory Research? A Theoretical and Methodological Perspective," in Park et al., *Voices of Change,* 1–20.

24 Geraldine Dickson and Kathryn L. Green, "Participatory Action Research: Lessons Learned with Aboriginal Grandmothers," *Health Care for Women International* 22 (2001): 471–82; Karim-Aly Kassam, *Biocultural Diversity and Indigenous Ways of Knowing: Human Ecology in the Arctic,* Northern Lights Series 12 (Calgary: University of Calgary Press, 2009); and Natasha Lyons, "Creating Space for Negotiating the Nature and Outcomes of Collaborative Research Projects with Aboriginal Communities," *Érudit* 35, 1–2 (2011): 83–105.

25 Margaret Kovach, *Indigenous Methodologies: Characteristics, Conversations, and Contexts* (Toronto: University of Toronto Press, 2010); and Linda Tuhiwai Smith, *Decolonizing Methodologies: Research and Indigenous Peoples,* 2nd ed. (New York: Zed Books, 2012).

26 Marie Battiste, *Decolonizing Education: Nourishing the Learning Spirit* (Saskatoon: Purich, 2013); Jeff Corntassel, "Re-envisioning Resurgence: Indigenous Pathways to Decolonization and Sustainable Self-Determination," *Decolonization: Indigeneity, Education, and Society* 1, 1 (2012): 86–101, http://decolonization.org/index.php/des/article/view/18627/15550; Eric Ritskes, "What Is Decolonization and Why Does It Matter?," *Intercontinental Cry: A Publication of the Center for Indigenous Studies,* September 21, 2012, https://intercontinentalcry.org/what-is-decolonization-and-why-does-it-matter; Leanne Simpson, "Aboriginal Peoples and Knowledge: Decolonizing Our Processes," *Canadian Journal of Native Studies* 21, 1 (2001): 137–48; and Smith, *Decolonizing Methodologies.*

27 Ritskes, "What Is Decolonization," 9.

28 Joe Lyons Kincheloe and Shirley R. Steinberg. "Indigenous Knowledge in Education: Complexities, Dangers, and Profound Benefits," in Denzin, Lincoln, and Tuhiwai Smith, *Handbook of Critical and Indigenous Methodologies,* 135.

29 Ritskes, "What Is Decolonization," 9, emphasis added.

30 Anne Anderson, *The First Métis: A New Nation* (Edmonton: Uvisco Press, 1985); Marlene Brant Castellano, "Ethics of Aboriginal Research," *Journal*

of *Aboriginal Health* 1, 1 (2004): 91–114; Leah Dorion, Darren R. Prefontaine, and Lawrence J. Barkwell, "Deconstructing Métis Historiography: Giving Voice to the Métis People," in *Resources for Métis Researchers*, ed. Lawrence J. Barkwell, Leah Dorion, and Darren R. Prefontaine (Winnipeg/Regina: Louis Riel Institute of the Manitoba Métis Federation/Gabriel Dumont Institute of Native Studies and Applied Research, 1999), 3–30; Métis Centre of National Aboriginal Health Organization website, http://www.naho.ca/metis; and Margaret Jaffray with Mike Evans and Lisa Krebs, "Prince George Métis Elders Society," in *What It Is to Be a Métis: The Stories and Recollections of the Elders of the Prince George Métis Elders Society*, ed. Mike Evans, Marcelle Gareau, Lisa Krebs, Leona Neilson, and Heidi Standeven (Prince George, BC: UNBC Press, 1999), viii–ix.

31 The Canadian Council on Learning was started in 2004 as a nonpartisan education initiative with a wide-ranging scope of learning environments in its mandate, including First Nations, Métis, and Inuit education. Federal funding for this program was cut in 2009. For further details, see "Canadian Council on Learning," voices-voix, http://voices-voix.ca/en/facts/profile/canadian-council-learning; and Canadian Council on Learning, "Métis Holistic Lifelong Learning Model," in *Redefining How Success Is Measured in First Nations, Inuit, and Métis Learning* (Ottawa: Canadian Council on Learning, 2007). See also Métis Centre of National Aboriginal Health Organization website, http://www.naho.ca/metis/.

32 National Aboriginal Health Organization, *In the Words of Our Ancestors: Métis Health and Healing* (Ottawa: NAHO, 2008), 107.

33 Canadian Council on Learning, "Métis Holistic Lifelong Learning Model," 23.

34 Ibid., 22.

35 Sandy Grande, "Red Pedagogy: Native American Social and Political Thought," in Denzin, Lincoln, and Tuhiwai Smith, *Handbook of Critical and Indigenous Methodologies*, 234.

36 Ibid.

37 Conference Board of Canada, "How Canada Performs: Provincial and Territorial Ranking," 2014, http://www.conferenceboard.ca/hcp/provincial/education.aspx.

38 Casey Eaglespeaker, opening address, "Kindling Conversations" series, Werklund School of Education, University of Calgary, February 28, 2014.

39 Santiago Rincón-Gallardo, "Implementing Professional Quality Standards: The Australian Experience" (paper presented at the College of Alberta School Superintendents 2017 conference, Edmonton, Alberta, March 10, 2017).

40 Association of Canadian Deans of Education, *Accord on Indigenous Education*, 2010, https://csse-scee.ca/acde/2017/08/19/events-2-2/; Canadian Council on Learning, *Redefining How Success Is Measured*; and Allan Luke, Courtney

Cazden, and Rhonda Coopes, *A Summative Evaluation of the Stronger Smarter Learning Communities Project*, vol. 1 and vol. 2 (Brisbane: Queensland University of Technology, 2013), https://eprints.qut.edu.au/59535/.

41 Government of Alberta, *Ministry Business Plans Budget 2017* (Edmonton: President of Treasury Board and Minister of Finance), 52, http://www.finance.alberta.ca/publications/budget/budget2017/business-plans-complete.pdf.

42 Yvonne Poitras Pratt, Chris Andersen, Guido Contreras, and Kelsey Dokis-Jansen, *Painting a Picture of the Métis Homeland: Synthesizing Knowledge about Métis Education, Employment, and Training*, SSHRC Knowledge Synthesis–Funded study (Ottawa: Social Sciences and Humanities Research Council of Canada, 2014), i, https://www.rupertsland.org/wp-content/uploads/2017/11/Painting_a_Picture_of_the_Metis_Homeland.pdf.

43 Ibid., 12.

44 Métis Settlements General Council, "History," https://metissettlements.com/history/.

45 Statistics Canada in 2011 estimated the settlement population to be 5 percent of the total Métis population across Alberta, although it is also the case that these numbers are approximations only and can fluctuate from year to year.

46 Brenda Macdougall and Nicole St-Onge, "Métis in the Borderlands of the Northern Plains in the Nineteenth Century," in *Sources and Methods in Indigenous Studies*, ed. Jean M. O'Brien and Chris Andersen (New York: Routledge, 2017), 257–65.

47 Solange Lalonde, "The Relational Model for Teaching and Learning" (master's thesis, University of Calgary, 2017).

48 This particular spelling of *wholistic* is adopted in accordance with the wishes of Elders from across Alberta, Saskatchewan, Manitoba, Nunavut, Northwest Territories, and Yukon, who endorse this spelling over that of *holistic*.

49 Rupertsland Institute website, http://www.rupertsland.org/about/alberta-metis-education-council/.

50 Lalonde, "The Relational Model for Teaching and Learning."

51 Statistics Canada, "National Household Survey, Aboriginal Population Profile, 2011," http://www12.statcan.gc.ca/nhs-enm/2011/dp-pd/aprof/index.cfm?Lang=E; Drawing data from the 2011 National Household Survey, Statistics Canada reports that 451,795 people self-identified as Métis across Canada. This number represents 32.3 percent of the total Indigenous population across Canada. The largest Métis population resides in Alberta, which has 96,865 Métis residents who collectively represent 21.4 percent of all Métis in Canada.

52 Lawrence J. Barkwell, Leah Dorion, Darren R. Prefontaine, Gabriel Dumont Institute of Native Studies and Applied Research, and Louis Riel Institute, *Métis Legacy: A Métis Historiography and Annotated Bibliography* (Winnipeg: Pemmican, 2001).

53 Anderson, *The First Métis;* Métis Nation of Alberta, *Métis Memories of Residential Schools: A Testament to the Strength of the Métis* (Edmonton: Métis Nation of Alberta, 2004).

54 Chimamanda Adichie, "The Danger of a Single Story," TEDGlobal, July 2009, https://www.ted.com/talks/chimamanda_adichie_the_danger_of_a_single_story.

55 TRC, *Final Report*, 66.

56 Anderson, *The First Métis*, 390.

57 Maria Campbell, *Half-Breed* (Halifax: Goodread Biographies, 1973); Heather Devine, "Being and Becoming Métis: A Personal Reflection," in *Gathering Places: Aboriginal and Fur Trade Histories*, ed. Carolyn Podruchny and Laura Peers (Vancouver: UBC Press, 2010), 181–210; and Judy Iseke-Barnes, "Grandmothers of the Métis Nation," *Native Studies Review* 18, 2 (2009), http://ourelderstories.com/wp-content/uploads/pdf/Grandmothers oftheMetisNation_2009.pdf; Yvonne Poitras Pratt, "Meaningful Media: An Ethnography of a Digital Strategy within a Métis Community" (PhD diss., University of Calgary, 2011); and Yvonne Poitras Pratt and Lyn Daniels, "Métis Remembrances of Education: Bridging History with Memory," in *Proceedings of the IDEAS: Rising to the Challenge Conference 2014*, 179–87 (University of Calgary, Institutional Repository DSpace, 2014).

58 TRC, *Final Report*, 65.

59 Ibid.

60 Ibid., 66.

61 Ibid., 65.

62 Chartrand, Logan, and Daniels, *Métis History and Experience*, 19.

63 Legacy of Hope, *Forgotten: The Métis Residential School Experience*, exhibition, Canadian Museum for Human Rights, Winnipeg, November 2015, http://forgottenmetis.ca/en/.

64 TRC, *Final Report*, 65.

65 Poitras Pratt et al., *Painting a Picture*, 9.

66 Ermine, "The Ethical Space of Engagement," 194.

CONTRIBUTORS

Jonathan Anuik is an associate professor in the Department of Educational Policy Studies at the University of Alberta. His research interests are nourishing the learning spirit, Archie comic books as educational texts, and the pedagogy of the history of education in Canadian teacher education.

Sheila Carr-Stewart is a professor emerita at the College of Education at the University Saskatchewan and teaches in the Faculty of Education at the University of Alberta. A former teacher, she has worked extensively in the area of First Nations education, particularly on issues related to jurisdiction, administration, funding, and local control of community schools. In 2013, she received the University of Saskatchewan Provost's Award for Teaching and Research Excellence in Aboriginal Education.

Michael Cottrell is an associate professor and Graduate Chair in the Department of Educational Administration, College of Education, University of Saskatchewan. His teaching and research interests include Indigenous education, comparative and international education, and educational globalization. His applied research has supported various First Nation communities and organizations to develop educational capacity with a focus on retention of Indigenous language and culture.

Karlee D. Fellner is Cree/Métis from central Alberta, and is an associate professor in Indigenous education counselling psychology at the University of Calgary. Dr. Fellner has been working with diverse clients in counselling and assessment since 2007. Her clinical practice specializes with Indigenous populations, and she works with various communities, institutions, and organizations to bring traditional approaches to wellness into praxis. Dr. Fellner's areas of interest include transforming systems to better serve Indigenous people, community-based program development, Indigenous research, Indigenous curriculum and pedagogy, culturally appropriate counselling, trauma work, and holistic and traditional approaches to wellness.

Rosalind Hardie is a retired Saskatchewan teacher and school administrator. In 2011 she completed a doctorate in educational administration in the area of sustainable leadership for elementary schools focused on improving student learning. Her research and teaching interests include principal leadership, school improvement, student engagement, and succession planning. Rosalind can be contacted at Rosalind.Hardie@usask.ca.

Darryl Hunter is an associate professor in the Department of Educational Policy Studies at the University of Alberta. Prior to entering the academy, he held a variety of managerial roles relating to assessment and evaluation for the Saskatchewan, Ontario, and British Columbia ministries of education, and he was a senior policy adviser in a cabinet planning unit. He has also served on several provincial curriculum writing and advisory committees. He was a high school and middle years teacher of French and English language arts, social studies, and law in Saskatchewan for over a decade.

Harry Lafond is the executive director of the Office of the Treaty Commissioner in Saskatoon. He has been a chairperson for the Board of Trustees of the First Nations Trust since 2003. He served his nation as Chief between 1990 and 2000. Harry has worked extensively in the area of education as the director of education and, earlier, as principal of kihiw waciston School at Muskeg Lake. He served on the senate of the University of Saskatchewan (1995–2002) and was also appointed to the federal task force on education (2003).

Solange Lalonde (Métis) is the senior project manager, curriculum and learning, at Moodle Pty Ltd.; she is the former associate director of education at Rupertsland Institute, Métis Centre of Excellence, and was the lead project developer and facilitator for the First Nations, Métis, and Inuit Professional Learning Project. Solange introduced and conceptualized the Relational Model for Teaching and Learning in her master's thesis in educational research, curriculum, and learning. Her model is informed by Indigenous methodologies and inspired by the UNESCO pillars of education, and she has implemented the model in a variety of education settings and research publications.

Brooke Madden is an assistant professor within the Aboriginal Teacher Education Program and the Department of Educational Policy Studies at the University of Alberta. Brooke's research focuses on the relationship between teacher identity and teacher education on the topics of Indigenous education and truth and reconciliation education. Brooke has also published on whiteness and decolonizing processes, school-based Indigenous education reform, and Indigenous and decolonizing research methodologies. She works to acknowledge both her Indigenous and settler ancestries in complex ways that acknowledge privilege and resist appropriation.

Yvonne Poitras Pratt (Métis) is an associate professor and the director, Indigenous education, at the Werklund School of Education, University of Calgary. She teaches at the graduate and undergraduate levels and is the recipient of two teaching awards. Yvonne has published in the realms of social justice, Métis studies, reconciliatory pedagogy, service-learning, and the integration of arts in education, and is looking forward to the release of *Digital Storytelling in Indigenous Education:*

A Decolonizing Journey for a Metis Community in 2020. Yvonne was the recipient of the 2018 Confederation of Alberta Faculty Associations Distinguished Academic Early Career Award.

Jane P. Preston is an adjunct professor at the University of Prince Edward Island. In addition to conducting research on Indigenous issues, her research topics include educational leadership, rural education, parent involvement in school, higher education for international students, and technology and student learning. She can be reached at jpreston@upei.ca.

Larry Prochner is a professor of early childhood education and the chair of the Department of Educational Policy Studies at the University of Alberta. His research examines the historical, comparative, and international dimensions of curriculum and pedagogy. He has published thirteen books, including *A History of Early Childhood Education in Canada, Australia, and New Zealand*. Dr. Prochner is vice-president of the International Froebel Society, which promotes child-centred kindergarten and early education worldwide.

Noella Steinhauer is Plains Cree from Saddle Lake Cree Nation, Alberta. She is an assistant professor in the Department of Educational Policy Studies at the University of Alberta. Noella has spent more than thirty years in education, including ten years as a secondary classroom teacher, eventually becoming a principal in both First Nation and public school systems. Her research topics include First Nations education, leadership, and Cree ways of knowing.

INDEX

Note: (f) after a page number indicates a figure.

BC Ministry of Education, 242, 245, 246, 258, 262*n*12, 263*n*27
Bennett, Carolyn, 224
Berryman, Mere, 221, 226, 229, 232
Bishop, Russell, 233, 267
Bivens, Donna, 128–29
Blackfoot Confederacy, 85–87
Blood Tribe. *See* Kainai (Blood) First Nation
Blue Quills school, 186
boarding schools: manual education, 56; previous day schools, 60; staff salaries, 50*n*54; terminology, 77*n*4. *See also* church-run schools; day schools; industrial schools; residential schools
Bond Head, Lieutenant-Governor Francis, 55
Bouvier, Rita, 226, 232
Brendtro, Larry, 209
British North America Act (BNA), 9, 25, 37, 88
Britzman, Deborah, 261
Brokenleg, Martin, 209
Brougham, Henry, 54, 66, 67, 68–69, 70
Buller, Solomon (teacher), 39
Byron, Lady, 67, 71, 82*n*73

Cajete, Gregory, 46
Canadian Council on Learning, 272–73(f), 274, 285*n*31
Cardinal, Harold, 3
Carlisle Indian Industrial School, 73
Carter, Sarah, 73
children and poverty, 61–63, 66, 229–31
Chisholm, W. J., 34
Christie, William J., 26–28, 35
Church Missionary Society (CMS). *See* Anglican Church of Canada
church-run schools: building and funding schools, 8, 10–11, 12, 47,

91–100; church-state partnership, 47, 87–88, 89, 101; day schools, 91–97; demolition, 44; denominational competition, 26, 40–46; government policy conflict, 96–97; missionary efforts, 90–91; teacher salaries, 31–33; Western perspective vs Indigenous practices, 25–26. *See also* boarding schools; day schools; industrial schools; residential schools
circle model, 197–98
Citizens Plus (Red Paper), 4
colonialism. *See* settler colonialism
community engagement, 199–200, 227–28, 230, 250(f), 257, 278
community schools (on-reserve): attitudes to, 120, 135–36, 188; opt out of Indian Act, 18–19; vs provincial schools (off-reserve), 120, 135–36, 188; resources and standards, 101, 128–29, 135–36; student self-esteem, 126, 129, 136. *See also* Indigenous education
Constitution Act (1982), 19*n*2, 269
Cornell, Stephen, 220–21
Cosentino, Gina, 224
Cottrell, Michael, 17, 225
Couchin, Father, 40–44
Council of Ministers of Education, 190
Cree: Chiefs' role, 26–29; curriculum development, 194–96; education system, 5, 197–98; hunting and hunger, 35–36; language, 188–89; leadership, 26–29, 194–95; reserve lands, 34–36; spirituality and democracy, 178–79, 193–96; traditional knowledge, 121, 206; traditional territory, 26–28, 34–36; treaty making, 193–94; treaty rights, 26–28. *See also* Indigenous peoples
Cresswell, Tim, 61

cultural genocide, 3, 13
Cummins, Jim, 227, 232–33
curriculum development. *See* Indigenous curriculum development

Daniels v Canada (2016) decision, 266, 269
Davies, Brent, 235
Davin, Nicholas Flood, 11, 73–74, 76, 88
day schools: attendance, 34; become boarding schools, 12, 56, 60; church-run, 90–97; closing, 46, 95–96, 97; curriculum, 38–39; demolition, 44; enrollment statistics, 38–39, 45–46, 52n122; expenditures, 33–34, 50n54; failure, 11; inspections, 33–34; missionary efforts, 90–91; opening, 37; opposition to, 40–46; teaching staff, 38–39, 41, 43, 50n54; treaty rights, 26. *See also* boarding schools; church-run schools; industrial schools; residential schools
decolonization, 15–16, 157, 271–72
denominational schools. *See* church-run schools
Department of Indian Affairs. *See* Indian Affairs
Desmarais, C.T. (teacher), 39
Dewdney, Edgar, 31–32, 36
Diocese of Calgary. *See* Anglican Church of Canada
documentation function, 247–48
Donald, Dwayne, 267, 270
Dorion, John, 268
drug addictions, 132–33
DuFour, Richard, 227
Duran, Eduardo, 154

Eaglespeaker, Casey, 274
Ealing Industrial School, 71

early-learning programs, 174, 190–91, 230
education. *See* Indigenous education; settler education
education debt, 221–25, 237n11
Edwards, M.B. (teacher), 39
Eisenstadt, Schmuel, 206
Elders, 244–45, 250(f), 255–56, 257
England (schools), 62, 71
Ermine, Willie, 14, 138, 214–15, 225, 281–82
ethical spaces (worldview exchange), 16, 138, 214–15, 225–29, 267, 270
European worldview. *See* Western worldview

farming, 27, 73, 87, 184
federal government: assimilation policy, 4, 11, 13, 29, 55, 73, 88; church conflict with, 87–88, 96–97; church-state partnership, 47, 87–88, 89, 101, 112; education policy, 9–11, 56, 73, 88–89, 108, 275–76, 279–80; legislation, 108, 113, 174; relationship with Indigenous, 6–7, 13–14, 270; treaty obligations, 36–37, 54, 73, 87, 89. *See also* Indian Act (1876); Indian Affairs; settler colonialism
federal government funding (education): call to action, 6; church-run schools, 10–11, 12, 31–32, 50n54; early-learning programs, 230; jurisdictional responsibility, 37, 101, 275–76; language learning, 174, 189; per capita system, 74–75; recommendations, 31–32; teacher salaries, 31–33, 50n54; violations, 5, 74–75, 87–97
Fellenberg, Philipp Emanuel von, 11, 54, 57–58, 65, 69, 71, 78n8
Fellenberg, William von, 65
Fellner, Karlee, 15, 151–52

Printed and bound in Canada by Friesens.
Set in Calibri and Sabon by Artegraphica Design Co. Ltd.
Editor: Lesley Erickson
Proofreader: Caitlin Gordon-Walker
Indexer: Margaret de Boer